"Picture Books *for* Looking and Learning"

Awakening Visual Perceptions through the Art *of* Children's Books

by Sylvia Marantz

Oryx Press
1992

The rare Arabian Oryx is believed to have inspired the myth of the unicorn. This desert antelope became virtually extinct in the early 1960s. At that time several groups of international conservationists arranged to have 9 animals sent to the Phoenix Zoo to be the nucleus of a captive breeding herd. Today the Oryx population is over 400, and nearly 800 have been returned to reserves in the Middle East.

For all the children who looked and listened,
especially Daniel Charles, Jonathan Francis, Stefan Josef,
and Rebecca Julia,
and, of course, thanks to Ken.
May, 1992

Copyright © 1992 by The Oryx Press
4041 North Central at Indian School Road
Phoenix, Arizona 85012-3397

Published simultaneously in Canada

Printed and Bound in the United States of America

∞ The paper used in this publication meets the minimum requirements of American National Standard for Information Science—Permanence of Paper for Printed Library Materials, ANSI Z39.48,1984.

Library of Congress Cataloging-in-Publication Data

Marantz, Sylvia S.
    Picture books for looking and learning : awakening visual
perceptions through the art of children's books / by Sylvia S.
Marantz.
    p. cm.
    Includes bibliographical references and index.
    ISBN 0-89774-716-X
    1. Visual perception. 2. Art appreciation. 3. Illustrated books,
Children's. I. Title.
N7430.5.M28 1992   92-14953
701é.1–dc20   CIP

Contents

Introduction

We have this immense responsibility because we are working for a generation of children who have been, in a sense, visually overstimulated in a way that is unique to this century. They see vast amounts; their visual circuits are heated up from a very early age. To slow them down, to get them to look at a still picture, is terribly important . . . Learning to look at a picture and your own visual exploration is crucial.   *Shirley Hughes*

Children need experience to learn. Unfortunately most of their experience comes to them through a barrage of photographed images from a television screen. The children have no opportunity to examine what they see, to question its form or validity, to compare or contrast it critically with the other pictures their eyes are receiving or with those their imaginations might provide if given the chance.

Artists have always drawn from their visual and emotional experiences for their creative output. Research has shown that many, if not most, important scientific and technological breakthroughs have occurred as much from intuitive leaps of creative thinking as from the methodical steps of experiments. Developing high-order thinking skills requires, in addition to inductive, deductive, and analogical practice, some intellectual playfulness and risk-taking. If we can help children see alternative ways of visualizing the world around them, we can help them build into their imaginations the resources needed for productive years ahead.

Children, of course, ought to see and learn about the masterpieces of the world of art as part of their general education as well as for their store of visual images. But few such works are readily available to the teacher except in reproductions, many of which fail to do justice to the originals. Every school and public library, however, is a treasure house of small works of art—picture books. The texts of some of these books are brief gems of polished prose worthy of study as a form of literature in their own right. But more important for the purposes we are considering, each good picture book displays a set of well-reproduced works of art, carefully designed for the space provided. Each set is combined by the artist into a flow of images across pages and from page to page as the reader turns them. A child can hold this bound creation in both hands, study it closely, and make observations, comparisons, and connections. A teacher can share the experience of the book with a group—guiding, informing, probing, and questioning. For a small amount of money each child can even own a copy, for more and more picture books are being printed in paperback editions with the same care as the hardbound.

Combining the wealth of art available in picture books with references to both art "masterpieces" and the folk and popular art of the world around them, students can begin to learn the language of art. They can start to look at their world with more educated eyes. They can accumulate a variety of images and the tools with which to examine, analyze, and compare these images with those they will encounter in the future. Visual learners, of course, flourish in this environment. But all students can find an increased awareness and an ability to perceive visually if these skills are developed.

But haven't teachers and librarians already been using picture books to build this area of student awareness? Most have not; most reviews say little about the visual aspects of what is the major portion of such books, because most reviewers do not have the vocabulary or the confidence to discuss art technique, media, or style, nor do teachers and librarians. They all lack confidence in their own aesthetic judgment, so they are uncomfortable discussing the visual aspects of any pictures—on the wall or in books—with their students.

HOW TO USE THIS BOOK

This book has been written to help teachers and librarians gain some of the information and confidence they need to share visual experiences with their students. Some of the best picture books available will be used as springboards for analyses of style and technique.

The analyses begin with the books for younger children, with subsequent chapters covering selections for older and more sophisticated picture book readers. Although the books are suggested for grade levels ranging from preschool through fourth grade, you may find that older students also benefit from discussing the artistic merits of these picture books. Appendix B, "Picture Books for Experienced Evaluators," describes picture books for evaluating by students above the fourth-grade level. Since you can choose among the books in each chapter in any order, the titles are arranged simply in alphabetical order, by illustrator. The art of each book is then analyzed page by page or by two-page spread. **The symbol ✳ indicates that you should turn the page.**

At first it seemed that this book about illustrations would be absurd without any. But there are two reasons for their absence. The first is cost. Color reproductions would be prohibitively expensive; black-and-white illustrations would omit the essential element of color. But more important, the page-by-page analyses offered here really require the actual book. You must look at the entire art object as a whole, rather than simply at some of the pieces.

Finally, from the thousands of picture books that are published each year, why have I chosen the 43 I have? As in any such selection, hard choices had to be made. Everyone is sure to miss a favorite.

I have not discussed artists who have been extensively analyzed elsewhere, such as Maurice Sendak or Ezra Jack Keats. Aside from these, first consideration was given to books that have generally been well reviewed and are by artists considered to be of high caliber. The books needed to be generally available in libraries and bookstores for obvious reasons.

But in the end, of course, the choice has been personal. All the books discussed evoked a pleasurable response when read and have continually delighted children as well. All will certainly not be equally enjoyable to everyone. But the aim is to practice looking and learning to appreciate what each picture book artist has created; the skills gained while judging books on these pages can then be applied to other books as well.

One thing to keep in mind in reading the descriptions is that many of these books have slight differences from edition to edition and many publishers print special library editions. Therefore, some of the descriptions, especially of the covers and end papers, may not exactly match the books you are reading. You might think about whether the changes affect the design in any way.

Chapter 1
The Anatomy of a Book

INTRODUCTION

Every field has its own special vocabulary, including the book publishing world. So we need to introduce and define certain terms that will be used throughout our discussions. Acquainting students with these terms will help them better discuss picture books as well. As children become familiar with the structure of the picture book and its components, they can compare and contrast. How much they have absorbed becomes apparent when they make their own books. Their cover design, careful choice of type face, placement of their copyrights and ISBN numbers, and illustrations matched precisely across pages, all contrast with books made by students who may have learned how to write a good story but have not studied the art of the book with equal care.

WHAT MAKES A BOOK A PICTURE BOOK?

Picture books can be read and appreciated without a precise definition of what a picture book is. There are many definitions and descriptions in the writings about children's literature, including such subdivisions as picture books versus picture story books, or illustrated story books. But these definitions do little to help with the appreciation of the art. Certainly, picture books are those books that have illustrations which can be examined and analyzed like any pictures. Generally we have called books "picture books" when they have a lot of pictures, or are predominantly pictures. Many picture book artists and critics have added the proviso that the pictures in a picture book should do more than simply reinforce the words of the story; they should also add to the story, give it new dimensions, even tell another additional story. Sometimes there are few words or no words at all, and the pictures "tell" the entire story. We will be examining the art of all of these kinds of picture books.

A picture book becomes a work of art as much for the care that goes into its overall design as for the individual pictures within it. Children can both appreciate and criticize this concept once they understand the components involved.

HOW IS A PICTURE BOOK PUT TOGETHER?

Understanding the physical elements of a book and how they are combined can enhance the appreciation of the components of its design. Decisions about each such component must be made which affect the total product. A book consists of a cover, with or without a dust jacket; end papers to hold the pages to the cover (if it is not a paperback); and pages inside, usually sewed or fastened together in one or more sections called **signatures.** A standard signature is 16 pages. In the printing of a book, each signature comes off the press on one large sheet printed on both sides. To see how this sheet is printed so it can be folded and gathered, then cut and bound into a book, fold a sheet of paper in half three times. Number the "pages" from front to back, 1 to 16, then open up the sheet to see where the numbers appear and which are right-side up. That is how each page is printed on these sheets. Sometimes publishers will make these "proof sheets" available for teaching purposes. The proof sheets may even have color corrections noted on them, to fix the colors before the final printing of the book is done.

The **dust jacket** is the paper jacket that is folded over the hard cover of some books, with flaps over the front and back covers. Generally this jacket has the important author, illustrator, title, and publisher information on the front cover and the spine, which is the back part of the book opposite the opening, i.e., the part that shows when the book is on the shelf of a library with other books. Frequently the dust jacket includes a summary of the story on the front flap, and information on the author and illustrator on the back flap. The jacket may be designed with a separate picture for the front, spine, and back, or as a single picture, sometimes including the flaps. The lettering may be as simple or as complex as the artist and designer desire. Even the bar code may be incorporated into the picture.

The **cover** design is sometimes the same as the dust jacket. When there is no dust jacket, the cover itself must convey all the necessary information. It also may be designed as a whole or in two or three pieces. Of course there are no flaps. If there is a dust jacket, the book may have a cloth binding, with lettering and perhaps a picture incised or pressed into the cloth like a reverse relief. The colors and design are chosen to harmonize with the rest of the book.

The **paper** used for the dust jacket, as well as that used for the end papers and the pages of the book itself, relates directly to the overall quality of the book. The weight, color, opacity or transparency, smoothness or roughness, and shine or dullness of the paper all make a difference in the appearance of the art in the book. Low-quality paper can be so transparent that the pictures and words on the reverse are visible. Poor paper can tear easily as soon as children start turning the pages. The choice of paper by the publisher is not an easy one, since good paper costs money. But in most cases good paper is worth the extra cost. If you handle many picture books, you will begin to feel the difference in paper as well as see it.

The **end papers**, encountered inside the front and back covers, are usually heavier than the paper inside the book. They are frequently colored, occasionally incorporate pictures or designs, and sometimes form part of the story. They sometimes change in later editions, as may be found in the books analyzed in the following chapters. They are used to attach the pages of the story to the cover, so they are not usually part of paperback editions, unfortunately. In considering the role of end papers in the overall design of the book, economics plays a large role. Even if the end papers are simply heavier paper, higher quality will cost more, and so will color. Because the size of picture books is generally predetermined by the number of pages in a signature (sixteen or multiples of sixteen) and by the cost per signature, if artists or designers want the end papers to be part of the sequence of pictures printed on the proof sheets, they may have to sacrifice pages from the book to be used for the end papers. Because the first page of the first signature has to be pasted onto the inside of the front cover, and the last page of the last signature on the reverse of the back cover, these two pages are lost.

The **half-title page** comes before the title page and can be elaborately designed and illustrated, or it can simply include words. The existence of a half-title page sometimes means less space for the story, so the author, artist, and/or designer must feel the need for this extra page to set the stage, or they would not use it. Sometimes, however, if the story can be told in 29 pages, the designer or artist may add the half-title page to fill out the 32 pages of the signature.

The **title page** can also just list the title, author, illustrator, and publisher. It can also include illustrations or part of the story. It can be one page or go across a two-page spread. Usually the copyright and other publishing information are on the back of the title page, but they can also be facing it or in the back of the book. The **dedication** and other acknowledgements usually follow the title page.

The overall quality of a picture book consists of many small things that add to or detract from the appearance of the book as a whole. The typography and color used for all the words on the front matter and the way they are placed on the pages, along with any illustrations, all add to the appearance of the book and must be considered in evaluation. After the front matter, as the story begins, the words and pictures are placed on individual pages; sometimes the words and pictures go across two pages in what we call a two-page spread. Careful binding makes this spread one large picture; carelessness, however, may cause an awkward break where the pages meet in what is called the **gutter**. The artist also may use one large picture on a page, or many small ones arranged in comic-strip-like sequences or randomly on the page. These arrangements should be part of the story and design, and should add to the enjoyment of the book. In a well-designed book, the text is incorporated as part of the design of the page; it looks as if it belongs there. Carelessly assembled books frequently look as if the text was stuck wherever it would fit. The gutter should even become part of the picture rather than an interruption. If the proof sheets have been printed with care, the colors of people and objects throughout the book will be consistent, and when colors have been printed on top of one another they will match precisely. Only by perusing a book from beginning to end can the reader appreciate these more subtle aspects of the overall design. A well-designed picture book has an overall rhythm and pacing that can be compared to that of a film. The story board of a short film actually resembles the story boards made by many illustrators, even to the use of "long shots" and "close-ups."

Finally, the pages of a book can be altered to make lift-ups, pop-ups, or other kinds of toy books by paper engineers working with the illustrator. The entire book, except for the spine, can be cut into the shape of an animal or object. Other materials, such as cloth, can be incorporated into the book for children to feel or manipulate. Assembling and binding these books create problems beyond the usual, but underneath they are still considered books, and need to be evaluated using similar criteria. Many artists, from Tony Ross to Jan Pienkowski, are making such books today.

Chapter 2
Media and Techniques

INTRODUCTION

"I'm not an artist. I don't know anything about art. I know what I like, but I can't tell you why. So I can't possibly discuss pictures with my students." This is, in essence, what hundreds of teachers and librarians have said over the past few years at conferences and meetings where picture books were the subject. Of course you can't. You may have spent hundreds of hours over the years reading, discussing, and analyzing the words in books with the help of teachers and professors and on your own. But most of you have barely spent minutes looking critically at pictures under comparable conditions. In addition there is, for whatever reason, a mystique surrounding art, a sense of the undefinable that seems beyond rational analysis. We seem to accept the fact that there may be some aspects of the humanities that defy precise analysis, but we still discuss great literature despite such limitations.

So, too, the aspiring picture book appreciator can acquire the descriptive vocabulary necessary to talk about the materials and techniques used by the artist to achieve that perhaps undefinable effect. Frequently students and teachers together can discover ways the artist has employed these tools to make the story meaningful for each of them.

If there is an artist or art teacher available as colleague or friend, perusal of picture books together can be the best learning experience of all. If not, spending some time examining the picture books discussed here, alone and with students, should begin to give you the confidence to deal with the art aspects of the books as well as you do with the literary aspects.

MEDIA USED BY ARTISTS

Within the limits set by the book format, artists today have myriad choices when they illustrate picture books. New technology available for reproduction makes it possible to print on the book pages something very close to the original work of the artist, whatever the media used. Meanwhile, the continuing evolution in the "fine" art world offers an ever-wider range of possibilities, as new materials and new ways of making art in two and three dimensions keep pushing the boundaries of the possible. Controversial and unconventional as some of contemporary art may be, its very existence on the front pages and in the TV news must have some influence on both artist and public. We have begun to accept, even in picture books, abstractions and other forms of representation of the world that we could not have accepted forty or fifty years ago. So picture book artists, having in mind what they wish to communicate to their readers, decide on an appropriate style and technique to produce a book that is as "old-fashioned" or "modern", or as simple or sophisticated as they wish.

Entire books are available describing the media and techniques used by artists, detailing how they do it and how to tell whether it has been done well. You will find here brief, simple explanations of some of the most common techniques used by picture book artists. A trip to the library for a book from the bibliography at the end of this book can offer much more for the curious. But the best aid to understanding, beyond looking at many examples, is a trip to a school art room or an art supply store. Trying the media yourself can yield the keenest insight into what each can and cannot do. It can also bring a deeper appreciation of the skill of the artist who uses each well.

Collages are collections and arrangements of objects. Collage pictures can be made of cut-out or torn shapes from paper, pieces of fabric or wallpaper, or even twigs, shells, or leaves. The choice and placement of these pieces can produce pictures that give a very different effect from other media, because of their unusual appearance, as well as the association some of the original objects may have for the viewer. Artists who use this technique include Ezra Jack Keats, Leo Lionni (p. 40), and Lois Ehlert (p. 30).

Pencil drawings are made with hard pencils, for a lighter line, or soft pencils, for a darker line. Fine lines can be made with only the sharpened point; a dull point or the side of the pencil point can produce wide lines and fill in spaces. Shading and cross-hatching can be done with any part of the pencil point. Colored pencils can do all of this plus produce color lines and areas of single or overlaid colors and shadings. Artists who use pencils skillfully produce pictures that not only have recognizable creatures in believable activities, but also have clean, unhesitating, rather than muddy or uncertain, lines. Ed Young (p. 179) and Stephen Gammell (p. 139) are among the artists who have used pencil drawings successfully.

Drawings can also be made by rubbing off or sanding the dust from a carbon or Conté pencil, then dipping the pencil in, like a brush, to apply the dust to the paper and blend it with the pencil line. Chris Van Allsburg has used this technique.

Crayon, charcoal, chalk, and pastel drawings, like pencil drawings, are made by abrasion, by rubbing the materials onto paper, but they usually require a rougher "toothed" or textured paper to rub the color off the medium onto the paper. These materials can be hard or soft, also like pencils, making lines of a texture determined by the roughness of the paper. The lines they make can easily be rubbed or blended with fingers or cloth, and get smudged if not stored carefully or sprayed with a fixative. Charcoal is, of course, black, while the others come in many colors. Carole Byard uses charcoal and chalk; Vera Williams (p. 98) uses crayons.

Paint is available in many forms and colors. It can be applied to wet or dry, shiny or rough surfaces with large or small brushes, cotton swabs, or even with a palette knife. All paint has the ability to appear more or less transparent, translucent, or opaque, and more or less intense or bright depending how it is diluted and applied.

Water color paint comes in semi-moist or liquid form, is diluted with water, dries quickly, and cannot be easily corrected or altered. Tempera paint has similar qualities, as do colored inks and dyes. Some artists feel that inks have a more intense color. Paper is the surface generally painted upon. James Stevenson and Margot Zemach's (p. 188) illustrations are water colors.

Oil paint tends to be more opaque. It can be applied directly from tubes with brush or palette knife, or thinned with turpentine and mixed with other colors on a palette or on the canvas, board, or paper surface of the picture. Gouache and acrylic paints have similar properties, but are water-soluble. Pictures made with these paints dry slowly and can be manipulated, or changed, or covered with varnish or gels. Paul Zelinsky's paintings (p. 183) illustrating fairy tales are done in oils or acrylics.

Scratchboard pictures are made by applying color pigment, usually gouache or India ink, to cover a clay-coated or other nonporous surface which is already the color of the desired outline. Then parts of the ink-covered or gouache-covered coating are scratched away or removed so the color of the underlying surface is revealed. The result looks like and can be confused with a wood cut or wood engraving, but only one copy is possible. Scratchboard pictures are usually designed to be reproduced for books and posters rather than for exhibit. Leonard Everett Fisher has done scratchboard illustrations in black and white. Brian Pinkney does color scratchboard illustrations.

Graphic Arts

Graphic arts enable the artist to make multiple copies of pictures from an image on a block of wood, piece of stone, or metal surface. A stencil or silk screen can also be used to make multiple copies. Each technique yields a different kind of picture with its own special quality.

A **wood cut** is made by cutting away areas on the surface of a block of wood, leaving the desired image. The image on the surface of the block is then covered with ink and paper is pressed down across the top. The ink on the image is thus transferred to the paper when it is lifted off the block. Because the wood may have a grain, wood cuts frequently show wood grain in addition to the image. For each additional print of the image, ink is added and another sheet of paper is pressed upon it. The lines made in a wood cut tend to be thick and heavy because of the difficulty of carving out the wood. If the picture is to have more than one color, a separate block must be made for each color, and the paper carefully placed in the same position for each color. Mary Azarian and Marcia Brown (p. 121) have done wood cut illustrations.

Wood engravings are also pictures made by cutting wood blocks, but they are cut from the end grain of the wood rather than with the grain. The desired line itself is what is cut into the wood, rather than what is left uncut as in a wood cut. The line you get is the color of the paper, since the surface is inked, and the paper pressed on it picks up the black or other color, leaving the line untouched. There will be no wood grain pattern from the end grain block. When lines are cut into linoleum or potatoes to make prints, they give similar pictures.

Etchings and **engravings** are called **intaglio processes.** This means the ink is rubbed into already cut or incised lines, then wiped off the surface, rather than rolled onto it as in wood cuts and wood engravings. When the paper is pressed onto the surface, what is printed is what has been cut in and had the ink pressed into it. The lines are there because they have been scratched through a treated metal surface. They are then etched by acid for etchings or more deeply scratched into the metal by special tools for engravings. The lines can be finer than in wood cuts, but must be deep enough to catch and hold the ink. Then heavy pressure like a press must be placed on the paper to enable the ink to be transferred onto the paper. Again, pictures of more than one color require separate plates and pressings for each color. An etched or engraved picture has a distinctive quality that comes from both the incised lines and the pressure of the printing, sometimes called the "bite" of the print. Aquatints and drypoints are other intaglio processes. Drypoint gives a softer, fuzzier line than an etching. Arthur Geisert's illustrations show the qualities of intaglio prints.

Lithographs are pictures made on special stones that have been polished. Then the desired image is drawn on the stones with a grease pencil that leaves a deposit on them. After treatment with a special chemical, an inked roller is passed over the wet stone. The ink adheres to the grease image but not to the rest of the stone. Then dampened paper is placed over the inked stone and it is put through a special press to transfer the image to the paper. Lithographs have a soft-edged image that can range in tones from delicate gray to deep black. Of course they can be in any color, but a separate stone and pressing is needed for each color used. The D'Aulaires have used lithography for their illustrations.

Stencils and **serigraphs** or silk screens are other processes that can yield multiple copies. Stencils can be as simple as the cut-out alphabets in plastic used to make the needed letters on signs and posters. Silk screens are stencils made from fabric stretched on frames. Glue or film covers what will be the blank areas of the picture, while colored pigment is forced through the untreated parts of the cloth to make the colored sections. A different stencil or screen is needed for each color. Silk screen pictures can have lines like those of a brush, pen, or crayon, or large areas of solid color, but no shadings within those areas. Such pictures can also include the texture of the fabric through which the color has been squeezed. When artists separate their colors for reproduction in books, they get color areas like those in a silk screen. Some of the books of Pat Hutchins (p. 64) and Ann Jonas (p. 37) have this quality.

Other Media

The **batik** process can make only single pictures rather than multiple copies, but the resulting art sometimes resembles silk-screened fabric. Wax is applied to both sides of fabric for the designs that are not wanted in the first color. Then the unwaxed part of the fabric is dyed. Those colored parts must then be covered with wax, while the wax is scraped off the areas that are to be dyed for each successive color. These too must be rewaxed after being dyed. Then another area is scraped clean, dyed, and rewaxed. Finally all the wax is removed with boiling water, and any undyed areas remain the color of the original fabric. This very complicated process yields pictures with areas of solid color and the texture of the fabric used. Such pictures are photographed like any other art for picture book pages. Patricia Mac-Carthy (p. 76) has used batik for her illustrations.

Some artists like to make **three-dimensional objects** as the original art for their illustrations. They may sculpt illustrations in relief (built up from a flat background) or in the round (as a free-standing object, able to be viewed from all sides) from folded or cut paper, clay, plasticine, or even wood or stone. They may also combine found objects or incorporate them into the sculpture as collage artists do in two dimensions. Although this kind of art is dependent on good photography to be adequately reproduced for picture book illustration, it has a texture and "feel" not available from any other techniques. Jeannie Baker uses this for her pictures. (See p. 112.) Embroidery and/or quilting can be used alone or incorporated into pictures begun in other media. Cynthia and William Birrer make embroidery pictures for their fairy tale retellings.

Photographs can seem the simplest and most direct representations; after all, they are direct reproductions of reality in black and white or color. But when we compare our snapshots with the illustrations of Tana Hoban or Bruce McMillan, we can begin to appreciate their skill. Photographs can also be manipulated, combined, hand-tinted, or painted. M. B. Goffstein has recently used photographs which she has taken depicting groups of actual figurines and objects. Ken Robbins hand tints or colors his photographs for an old-fashioned feeling of long ago, while Sarah Moon uses light, shadows, and odd juxtapositions to make her pictures look strange and surreal.

ELEMENTS OF DESIGN IN ART

Now that we have discussed the parts of a book and the media used by artists, we need to describe the elements of basic design considered by artists as they apply their chosen media to the pages destined to be bound into picture books.

Composition refers to how the picture and its parts are arranged on the surface of the page. This can be a balanced or symmetrical arrangement, which tends to make the viewer feel at peace and gives a pause to the rhythm of a book; however, it may be a bit boring if used too often. A clearly asymmetrical arrangement is usually more interesting for the viewer. An ambivalent arrangement, slightly off-center perhaps, can be unsettling to the viewer. It means the artist was uncertain of what effect was desired.

Shapes, solid or formed by lines, make up a picture. Pointed shapes generally are less restful than rounded ones, perhaps because of their associations with the menace of sharp objects. Rounded objects tend to seem more comforting—"a hug is round." Rectangular objects parallel to the bottom of a picture suggest solidity of objects with the ground. The shape of the lines in a picture can be diagonal, leading the eye upward or downward. Diagonal lines are less restful than those that parallel the bottom. Lines that go up and down parallel to the sides of a picture may appear to reach to the sky. Lines lead the eye to what the artist feels is important. The lines themselves can be clear or fuzzy, thick or thin, nervous and busy (as when they are made up of many tiny lines), or straight and calm. The type of line used by the artist forms a part of the style.

Size or scale of the shapes in a picture tells the viewer how these objects relate to each other. Large objects dominate small ones and appear, at least at first, to be more important, whatever the composition.

Perspective, or the lack of it, will affect the point of view. If the artist has accepted traditional Western perspective, things will appear larger if they are closer to the viewer, and conversely, larger shapes will seem closer. If there are large shapes in the background, they will still seem closer than if they were small, and they will tend to confuse the viewer because we expect the largest, closest objects to be in the foreground. If, however, the artist is working in another tradition, such as that of the Middle Ages, important objects may be large wherever they appear in the picture. In traditional Western perspective, roads appear to narrow as they go off into the distance, making diagonals, while roads in a different cultural tradition may stay the same width throughout the picture, making it static.

The point of view, that is, the point from which the artist has the viewer look at the scene, affects our feeling about the picture as well. If the scene appears to be one that we are looking up at from below, we may feel intimidated. On the other hand, if we are looking down from a height at the scene, we can feel either large and powerful, or so far above that we feel removed from involvement. We can look through a keyhole or a mouse hole as well as a window or skylight; each changes our feelings about the actions viewed.

As already mentioned, artists can draw from other cultures for their point of view. But then our understanding of such illustrations depends on our knowledge and acceptance of the artistic conventions of these cultures, just as our ability to understand what is happening in a traditional Renaissance painting by Leonardo relies on our background of Western tradition. For example, figures like those from Egyptian tomb paintings, with feet and faces in profile, and frontal bodies marching in lines around all four sides of a pond in a picture, give a different quality to an illustration than does an illustration with such figures growing larger marching toward us, or with tiny figures almost lost in a traditional Chinese landscape painting. How much our cultural background affects what we actually see when we look at pictures is still being researched. But it is a question that we should keep in mind as we try to expand the awareness of the children with whom we look at picture books.

Each **color** can be scientifically analyzed according to its place on the spectrum. Placing certain colors next to each other seems to make them change, according to their place on the traditional color wheel. Books on color theory are available to help deepen understanding of these phenomena. But simple tests of red next to yellow as opposed to red next to green can show this clearly. A large block of color will always seem more intense when placed next to a smaller one of the same color. Blending of colors always yields the same result—red and yellow always make orange—and diluting them will always make the color less intense. The effect of color on our emotions, however, is more subjective, since each of us has favorite colors with pleasant personal associations, and colors we dislike. But there are some conventional associations with colors, at least in our culture, that artists can use to communicate feelings. Colors like red and yellow, for example, relate to sunshine and are generally cheery. Blues are considered more restful. Clear, unmixed colors seem happier than murky ones. Black relates to night and darkness, and so to quiet or to fear. In our culture people wear dark colors to funerals, but brides wear white; in China white is the color for funerals.

When used realistically to simulate nature, color in a picture conveys the usual or the expected. Hence the artist can shock the viewer by using an unusual color in an otherwise natural setting. Conversely a picture with unnatural colors can immediately convey that something is wrong, or that we are "out of this world."

Type can be an inconspicuous part of the page of a picture book, but it remains an important element in its design. Typefaces have names, which are important only to the curious. But of interest to all are the use of capital letters only or of upper and lower case, the size of the type, the simplicity or complexity of the letters, and the use of italics or even hand-written text, like that in the books about Babar the elephant. Elaborate initial capital letters evoke medieval illuminated manuscripts, while printing that resembles old German brings different visual associations, as well as distinctive patterns, to the printed page. Comparisons of different typefaces from different books can show how some are easier to read than others, and how various typefaces give a different feeling to the books. Sometimes different typefaces are used in the same book for a particular effect.

What we call the artist's **technique** is simply the way the *elements of design* are combined with media to make pictures. We judge the skill of the artist by noting how competently the media are handled in this combination. A successful artist shows us a recognizable setting with people and animals whose anatomy is believable, and whose characters and behaviors resemble those described in the story. Walls meet floors and ceilings, cars have wheels that can carry them on the road, horses have legs that look like they can gallop. Although artists may choose to abstract or eliminate some details for a particular effect, the picture must still be recognizable and convince us that the object or scene is believably real.

Picture book artists use their technique in **styles** that can reflect those in the world of television and magazine advertising or of "fine art." They range from *naturalistic* or *realistic,* which can be very detailed, through all stages of *abstraction,* which means omission of details; they also range from *impressionism,* which tries to convey objects as they are affected by light, to completely *non-objective* art, which is concerned with the manipulation of media or shapes in space without necessarily referring to the natural world, and frequently without emotional content. Styles can be naturalistic but add exaggeration or caricature, like that of James Marshall. Or they may be so real they are surreal, depicting a world where very realistically drawn objects are in unreal situations or juxtapositions, as in the work of Anthony Browne.

Media, techniques, and even styles are merely tools. Picture book artists choose the tools they require to create the total book they have in mind. What distinguishes the work of one artist from that of another in their books is what we call the style of that particular artist. Some may be identified with a particular medium. Some may use a distinctive kind of outline, heavy and black or thin and irregular, or arrange solid blocks of color with no outline at all. Some work very realistically, with almost photographically real people and scenery. Others may give only an impression of the characters set in little or no background. Some may regularly use one or more non-Western conventions, so their work always has a foreign feeling. Some British illustrators have been said to have a distinctive "scatty" sort of line.

When all of the elements work well with each other, with the words, and with the overall design of the book, they can make us amused, excited, dreamy, sad, happy, or whatever the author and illustrator had in mind.

Examining how they work in some successful cases, we can begin to appreciate the art object called the picture book. We must continue to keep in mind, however, that the media used for the original art were chosen for the effect they would produce in reproduction in the book. The book we hold is the work of art we examine to see how well the author and illustrator have succeeded in their purpose.

Chapter 3
Preschool into Kindergarten

INTRODUCTION

At some time from three to five years of age, children become able to sit in groups and listen to whole stories in picture books for fifteen or twenty minutes, although reading with a parent or caregiver on a one-to-one basis is still important to the individual child. It is also still vital for children to have the opportunity to peruse books on their own, taking the time they need to examine each picture or to go back and forth within a sequence of pictures after having had the initial discussion with the adult and/or the group.

Some children will begin early to perceive the difference between the two symbol systems operating in most picture books, i.e., letters combined into words versus pictures. They may even demand, pointing to the letters, "What dat SAY?" But the vital role of the pictures in telling the story must never be slighted.

As part of the preparation for learning to read, many teachers have found wordless picture books a good introduction to narrative for children who might be intimidated by the mystery of letters and words they do not yet understand. Children are encouraged to "read" these stories aloud to themselves, a group, or a tape recorder.

While the preparation for the all-important skill of reading proceeds, children can continue to develop their visual perception. Parents of five-year-olds report that their children have become able to recognize the work of individual picture book artists and pick them from the works of others after having read and discussed these artists in class. The illustrators we have chosen to analyze in this chapter are popular and distinctive, and kids enjoy their books.

Happy Birthday Moon
by Frank Asch

The simplicity of both art and story in the books of Frank Asch belies their attraction for three- to five-year-olds. Although his books do not have the multiplicity of details that we expect children to require for rereading, they seem to contain enough to sustain enthusiasm and continued appreciation beyond the surface. Children feel an affection for the bear in Asch's stories; he becomes an old friend, and they eagerly anticipate his next adventure when they see him on a cover. To understand the story of *Happy Birthday Moon,* children need to be aware that although the moon changes its place in the sky, it seems to be moving with us when we walk or drive at night. They also need to know what an echo is.

✳ We meet the bear star of this and many other Asch stories on the cover, admiring his beloved moon. Asch has painted the bear with the minimum detail needed for us to recognize "bear." Bear almost looks as if he was cut out with a cookie cutter. He is always in profile. His arms and legs, if we may call his front and back paws that, move, his eyes and mouth open and shut, and that's about it. The moon is simply a flat circle, the stars an evenly placed pattern of dots, and the hills just rounded shapes. Asch paints his simple shapes with nonshiny opaque pigment, using no shading or modelling of the edges for a three-dimensional look. The figures are outlined with a contrasting color. An outlined square frame surrounds the cover picture evenly, its purple color repeated in the round frame around the picture on the back cover. This equally simple picture contrasts daylight with the night on the cover. The circular hat brim is part of another piece of the story inside. The perky tail of the bird breaks out of the circular frame completely, while blades of grass cut into the inside frame line, making the picture less static.

✳ The title page is framed in the same purple, with a darker purple outline repeated around the circle picture in the center. The yellow-filled letters of the title repeat the color of the moon. The semicircular shape of the title surrounds the circle picture. This picture is slightly different from the cover as well as being smaller. Having the hill the bear is standing on darker than on the cover, as well as cutting out the other hills, makes it seem closer. On the title page the bear appears to be far away, as if we are viewing it from a distance.

* On the two-page spread for publication information and dedication, a series of four small pictures shows the moon as it moves across the sky. This can lead to a class discussion on the moon's movement, or can simply be noted. Asch frequently uses these pages before the story for a short course on the relevant scientific facts.

* On the first page of the story, Asch has added the simplest of shores and water, indicated by a few strokes, with the ripples of the moon's reflections. The minimal tree does not even have twigs, much less leaves. In this and all succeeding pictures, the frame is surrounded by lots of white space and is rarely broken.

* On the next two-page spread, eight lines of text on the left are balanced by the picture on the right. A quick leafing through the subsequent pages shows how Asch has established a rhythm of pictures and text: two separate pictures, one line of text under each, then a two-page spread and three words, then lines of text on the left and picture on the right, etc. This rhythm works for the reading of the story, words along with pictures. The picture on the right-hand page has the tree break the frame as a counterbalance to the bear up in the tree. Whether the bear really appears to sit on a branch in that tree is not a question that seems to occur to young viewers. But it should be remembered when we compare Asch's pictures with those of other artists. It is also a good example of how children at a young age already accept as illustrations pictures that are very abstracted and lacking in realistic detail.

* In the next two-page spread with two separate pictures, we follow bear across minimal water and through more minimal trees, with the paddle and the boat pointing our way.

* The next illustration spreads the mountains across the gutter, with the small yellow moon standing out because of both color and placement on the page.

* The next picture is almost the same as the cover. The color may differ slightly because the paper is different. But the picture is slightly smaller, so Asch has moved the moon closer to the bear to have it the same distance from the border. The star pattern has also changed.

* As the echo pattern continues in the story, children get the idea immediately, and like to participate. As bear thinks "goody," the children seem to as well. The simple lifting of his foot in the picture on the right seems to convey the bear's pleasure.

✳ On the next two pages, the left-hand picture is a circle like the moon, inside which is another slightly different version of the cover. Asch's reasons for the small changes in this basic picture are interesting to speculate about. On the right, we are back in the square-shaped outline, broken only by a flower, as circular coins echo the curves of the moon and the bear's ears, tail, tummy, and eye, matched by that of the piggy bank.

✳ The next two square-framed pictures and almost unnecessary text are again very simple. Compare the downtown street with that of any more realistic artist, Shirley Hughes (p. 33), for example, to see how simple Asch's drawings are. "Fatz Hats" is an unusual joke in this book. Only the barest corner of the store is shown.

✳ The next sequence of four pictures is like a cartoon strip or movie story board, or like pages from some wordless books. Here the moving of the moon is the focus, and actually the only change in the first three pictures. Bear almost dances in the last picture. Although bear wears no clothes, he certainly indulges in human-like rather than bear-like behavior throughout.

✳ On the next two pages we have the basic minimal house and text on one side, with focus on bear and hat on the other.

✳ Here again is a simple picture of bear reaching, while two lines make the wind that whisks the hat away on the right-hand page.

✳ A circle frame on the left encloses a small bear on the bank with the hat breaking the frame as it gets away. On the right, we are back to the night and the bear paddling, where the words and picture are almost the same as the earlier trip.

✳ The hike through the forest is different on the next page, perhaps because it is on a new left-hand page instead of across from the paddling scene. On the right-hand page, bear talks to the moon again, in a slightly different picture.

✳ On the next two-page spread, type is again on the left. Bear is in the foreground on the right, with the moon. Note how much of bear's feelings Asch can convey with just the position of the head and the closing of an eye.

✳ The final circle frame, repeated on the back cover, again echoes the cover picture but in a sort of "happy ever after" circle, which "explains" what happened to the hat.

SUGGESTED ACTIVITY

Prepare cut-out shapes of the bear ahead of time. Children enjoy coloring these, pasting them onto a large sheet of paper, and drawing some part of his adventure there. If they have read more of the books, they can choose any adventure.

One class decided to have each child choose a different part of one of the stories to illustrate and made their own book of bear's adventures. You can provide cutouts of the moon, or the bird, or any other characters the children may have a problem drawing by themselves but want to add to their picture. To obtain a cutout, simply photocopy or trace the picture and cut it out.

ASCH BOOKS ABOUT THE BEAR

Bear Shadow. New York: Simon and Schuster, 1988.
Bear's Bargain. New York: Simon and Schuster, 1989.
Bread and Honey. New York: Parents, 1982, Crown paper, 1988.
Happy Birthday Moon. New York: Simon and Schuster, 1982.
Milk and Cookies. New York: Parents, 1982.
Mooncake. Englewood Cliffs: Prentice-Hall, 1983.
Popcorn. New York: Parents/Crown, 1979, Putnam paper, 1990.
Sand Cake. New York: Parents, 1979/Putnam paper, 1990.
Skyfire. New York: Simon and Schuster, 1988.

OTHER ASCH BOOKS

Baby in the Box. Holiday House, 1989, paper, 1990.
Goodbye House. New York: Simon and Schuster paper, 1989.
Goodnight Horsey. New York: Simon and Schuster, 1989.
The Last Puppy. New York: Simon and Schuster paper, 1989.
Oats and Wild Apples. New York: Holiday House paper, 1988.

The Snowman
by Raymond Briggs

Raymond Briggs's biting wit is only occasionally glimpsed in his books for young children, but it is wicked in works such as his treatment of the Falklands War, *The Tin-Pot Foreign General and the Old Iron Woman*, now out of print. His strong social conscience is also apparent in works for adults and young adults like *When the Wind Blows*, while he delights in tweaking convention in that wonderfully disgusting favorite of middle schoolers, *Fungus the Bogeyman*. He uses pencils, charcoal, or pen to outline his figures, and fills them in with paint, ink, or colored pencils. Frequently he tells his stories in the form of comic strips, or movie story boards, varying the number and size of the "frames" to produce the rhythm and effect he desires.

---

* In *The Snowman*, you can easily see the strokes Briggs has made with pale-tinted colored pencils or crayons on a heavily textured paper, and how he has allowed the white background to show through, using it to represent the snow as well. There are no hard edges; the forms are as soft as the snow. The snowman himself was recently turned into a cuddly stuffed toy. He almost seems a human in a snowman suit. He smiles at us on the cover, pictured with a minimum of detail, his white body blending into the background and the snow. The simple black letters of the title seem stamped on top. The blue of the sky, where the white paper showing through becomes the snowflakes, is repeated as background to the white-framed picture with rounded edges on the back of the cover, where the benevolent snowman walks with his arm around the boy into the impression of a landscape.

* The blue color is used again for the end papers, which are made of specially textured paper. On the jacket flap, the boy and snowman shake hands.

* The snowman on the title page is similar to the one on the cover, this time with more white and a blue frame with rounded corners, and the same black lettering for the title.

* The white page serves as background to the copyright information as well as to all the other scenes throughout. On the right, we watch the boy wake up to the excitement of snow in a series of pictures almost like those in a flip book. He's in such a hurry he loses his hat as he runs out. The boy and his mother are not drawn in great detail, but they are convincingly real. Just enough of the background is shown to make the setting believable: the walls and floor are shown, but no rug or pictures; the door and wall of the house and the ground are drawn, but no bushes or trees.

* The snowman is built and finished in the series of pictures on the next two-page spread. The boy's actions are clear; no words are needed. Note how carefully Briggs has positioned him in each picture, for variety as the eye goes from one picture to another, across, down, and over the page. The boy stands out clearly against the background. Briggs emphasizes the

importance of the snowman by having his head break through the frame on the right-hand page, top left and lower right.

✳ Another series of action frames cover the next two pages; in one the snowman is observed from the window, back to the boy; in the other, the boy has opened the door and the snowman has turned and is tipping his hat. The adventure begins.

✳ Children particularly enjoy telling the story of the snowman's adventures inside the house. He has acquired legs to better enjoy himself. Briggs uses the warm reds for the light and fire, and to differentiate the inside from the outside. It is interesting to speculate why he uses three panels across only once in this spread, and in general why he chooses one, two, or three for his purposes.

✳ Again on the next two pages he varies the panels, using four in one case, each for a separate event.

✳ On the next two pages Briggs really varies the sizes of the panels. Dressed in pants, tie, and hat, the snowman really looks human. Note how Briggs tucks the last frame into the lower left corner.

✳ More fun and action adventures occur in a never-boring arrangement of panels. The position of the boy and snowman in the lower right really portrays exuberance.

✳ As they move into the bluer area outside near the car, we still get the yellow from the light. Briggs also repeats the glow the snowman got earlier from the refrigerator now emanating from the freezer, causing him bliss.

✳ Back in the warmth of the house, another arrangement of different-sized panels ends with the long one on the lower right, bodies inclined toward the door and the outside.

✳ Three long panels accelerate the action toward the full page on the right, where the two are flying off, leaving the now tiny red house behind. Note the wedge-shaped snow area pointing, but level with the house, and how Briggs has put in the impression of branches, and even two birds, to make a solid corner below the flying figures. The placement of every line and shape here works for the picture.

✳ After all those small panels, what a visual change! It is not a shock, because it was gradually led up to by the previous two pages, but it is still a real change of visual rhythm. In little more than a suggestion of snowy landscape, town, and moon, our two characters are almost lost as they fly. Briggs has drawn the lines of the countryside and the sky not so flat as to be dull, but level and peaceful.

✳ Over the exotic domes and steeples, which could be the Brighton Pavilion, they fly, the ground flat and the fliers almost horizontal.

✳ The next spread has a panel across the two pages, echoing and extending the postion and mood of the last pages. What fun the landing seems! Children love spotting the touch of red on the right-hand page and realizing what it means. The pier could also be in Briggs's home town of Brighton. Back in the other direction they fly.

✳ Compare the upper return picture on the next two pages with the full-page take-off picture. Again the reds show the warmth of going inside, along with the light of the coming dawn.

✳ The pace of the sleeping and waking sequence builds to the rush past mom and dad to the daylight outside.

✳ After all the crowded small panels and visually shocking large ones, the one small rectangle on all that white space really draws attention. The boy's body attitude shows his dejection. Try to picture this illustration filling the page to imagine the different impact it would have.

✳ All is not sad, however, for on the flap of the dust jacket, boy and snowman run happily together again, if only in memory. And of course, on the back cover is the cozy picture discussed earlier, a happier ending to the story also.

ART ACTIVITY

Have children practice making pictures, with or without snowmen, that leave areas of the page white to represent the snow, as Briggs does. Have them try to get a snowy texture in their pictures by swirling and layering paint, chalk, or crayon; by tearing rather than cutting paper; and by using tiny strokes of colored pencils.

BOOKS BY BRIGGS

Father Christmas. New York: Putnam, 1973, Penguin, 1977.
Father Christmas Goes on Holiday. New York: Penguin paper, 1977.
Fungus the Bogeyman. New York: Penguin paper, 1990.
Jim and the Beanstalk. New York: Putnam paper, 1989.
The Snowman. New York: Random House, 1978.
When the Wind Blows: The Story of the Bloggs and the Bomb. New York: Penguin paper, 1988.

COMPARISONS

Compare Briggs's snowman to the snowmen in these books:

Bauer, Caroline Fellers *The Midnight Snowman* illustrated by Catherine Stock. New York: Atheneum, 1987.

Miller, Edna. *Mousekin's Frosty Friend.* New York: Simon and Schuster, 1990.

Have You Seen My Cat?
by Eric Carle

The bright colors, unusual design, and innovative use of materials have made Eric Carle's books perennial favorites with young children. He seems never to have forgotten his early love of animals and nature, or his happy experience with the paper and paints of the kindergarten. All the creatures who inhabit his books seem friendly and lovable to his young fans. Surprises such as pop-up pages, cut-out holes, and even sound add to their appeal.

The recent reissuing of *Have You Seen My Cat?* attests to its continuing popularity. This deceptively simple story with few words and lots of repetitions the children love is enlarged enormously not only by what is happening in the pictures, but by what the adult can add to supplement the story: photographs of the other kinds of "cats" Carle introduces, or of people and landscapes of the other cultures portrayed.

✳ Carle's typical style is clear from the cover. From front to back across the spine stretches one large cat, with several smaller kittens around it. All are unmistakably from the cat family, although they are certainly not photographically real. Carle has captured the essence of cat structure, stance, and look. He begins his pictures by preparing sheets of paper in the colors and patterns he wants to use, even marbelized if appropriate. From these he cuts out the shapes he desires, combines them, and pastes them down, and then he supplements lines and textures by drawing or painting on any additional details he wants to add, for example, whiskers and claws. He has designed the cover so that it works just on the front and on the unfolded jacket or cover as well. The lettering used for both the title and author information has a hand-lettered feeling, an informality that goes with the loose lack of detail of the art.

✳ The end papers, the same front and back, picture and name all the cats in the story for those interested in the exact names. They can be studied before and/or after reading.

✳ The title page lettering is similar to that on the cover. The dedication and the publisher are lettered in the same loose print. The cat on the title page is almost hissing right at us, teeth and claws bared, tail rigid, back arched. This look contrasts with the stance of most of the cats in the book. It may be a reminder to children that cats can be like this. Or it may belong to the dedication; is it one of "the cats in my life"? Children do not seem frightened of this cat at all, despite its ferocious appearance.

✳ On the first page of the story, the young boy asks the title question; his question is printed in the same lettering. The figures of the boy and man are isolated against the plain white background without even a ground line. Is a ground line necessary? Carle uses just a few simple shapes to bring these people alive. The boy's hands reach toward the man, whose finger points us to turn the page.

✳ Two very different pictures are on this two-page spread. Here we have a ground or floor line which, although it runs across the gutter giving a connection between the pages, clearly shows us that they are different scenes by the change in color. On the left, with the second of the repeated refrains, the boy's response is to the king of beasts. Carle has used relatively few crayon or pastel lines on top of the cut paper shapes to show the tangle of mane and tail. The cage is minimal. On the right-hand page, under a typical Carle sun, our boy asks his question of a cowboy. The horse, although little more than a silhouette, is obviously an anatomically believable horse, thanks to Carle's skill.

✳ The next two-page spread shows that the patterns will repeat as well as words: the simplified "cat" on the left, the ground line tying the two pages together, and the boy and his new informant on the right-hand page pointing our way to the new "cat" to come. With just a few spiky green cut-out shapes, Carle conveys the essentials of the maguey plant of the Mexican desert, while a few circular forms in the basket on the donkey are enough to indicate he is carrying something like fruit. The green grass the "cat" is standing on is carried over from the previous page. The desert or rocky ground on the right will lead, along with the pointing arms and fingers, to the next page.

✳ The same ground becomes a hill, breaking the straight ground line before it becomes monotonous. On the right, we have no ground shown. The reason for this will be apparent when the next page is revealed. On the right-hand page we have the boy again, this time asking his question of a Native American sitting in front of a nonspecific shelter. Perhaps the parrot is enough to make this the jungle where jaguars live. Or perhaps the enormous leaves behind the shelter suggest it. The leafless trees certainly do not have a jungle feeling, although they do make the composition more interesting and are shown again on the next page. The horizontal angle of the pole or spear held by the native almost gives us a ground line, while it echoes the line of the pointed finger. Try to picture the scene without it. Also continue to note the lines Carle adds to his cut-out shapes.

* On the next page we see that our "cat" is up in the air, needing no apparent ground line but on a branch of one of the trees from the previous page. The break here in the gutter between the two pages is abrupt. On the right-hand page we pick up a new kind of ground again for the new location. The hut and the costumes place the scene in Africa with the simplest of outlines and few details.

* The panther on the next page stands on the same ground, turning his head to snarl and show his teeth, perhaps the fiercest of all the "cats" in this book. On the right, the ground changes to what could easily be sand. Again with the simplest of forms, so small here, Carle conveys the characters, camel, tent, and palm trees.

* On the next two-page spread, for the first time, the ground and the cat jump across the gutter, a real visual change. But still, Carle has not broken the pattern completely. He has balanced the leaping of the cheetah at the left with the small picture on the right; he has tucked the whole scene in behind the cat's tail. The "wagon" is only two thin rectangles, a square, and a small and larger open circle, but it makes a wagon. And again Carle has put in the ground for the next page.

* Another large cat sprawls across the two-page spread, with another small picture to balance it in the upper right. It's a repeated pattern, perhaps for a rest in the rhythm.

* A carpet makes the background rather than the base on which the next cat stands. This change of perspective is disturbing, but then perhaps Carle wants to use the carpet as a frame. Or he may be influenced by the perspective of the art sometimes used in the Middle East or India, which would place the rug just like that. The boy on the right is not standing on anything. He has finally changed his words. Carle makes his impatience apparent from his stance and expression.

* The boy has the next page to himself as he repeats his question. On the right-hand page sits a couple with squirrel, birds, and carriage, bringing us back home again. A careful look will reveal how much Carle conveys with the minimum of detail. A few lines make a bench, a few shapes a

carriage and the perky, lively creatures. There is no ground here, leading naturally to the grand finale.

✳ "This is my cat" says the delighted boy to the cat and kittens of the cover, spread across the two pages for us to enjoy again and compare with the cover.

✳ The plain white pages with the publication information give the eyes a rest before the end papers.

COMPARISONS

Comparisons can be made with the collage work of two other artists discussed later, Leo Lionni (p. 40) and Lois Ehlert (p. 30), as well as the old favorite, Ezra Jack Keats.

You might want to have children join you in the library to find books with pictures or photographs of all kinds of cats, wild and domesticated, to compare with Carle's. The pets will be classified in the 636's, while the others will be in the 590's.

BOOKS BY CARLE

Eric Carle's Animals Animals. New York: Putnam, 1989.
The Grouchy Ladybug. New York: Harper paper, 1986.
Have You Seen My Cat? Natick, MA: Picture Book Studio, 1987.
A House for Hermit Crab. Natick, MA: Picture Book Studio, 1987.
The Mixed-up Chameleon. New York: Harper Trophy paper, 1988.
Pancakes, Pancakes! Natick, MA: Picture Book Studio, 1990.
The Very Busy Spider. New York: Putnam, 1987.
The Very Hungry Caterpillar. New York: Putnam, 1989.
The Very Quiet Cricket. New York: Putnam, 1990.

Parade
by Donald Crews

Donald Crews's books not only share his sense of design and color, developed over years as a graphic artist in advertising, but also use very few words, with the "story" clearly conveyed by the pictures. This makes his books particularly useful for encouraging children to tell the story or read it into a casette recorder as they prepare to read actual words. The books are perennial favorites, for their simple, satisfying stories, but also perhaps because children relate immediately to the subject matter: trucks, trains, school buses, carousels, and bicycles.

✳ *Parade* is a typical example. As always in Crews's books, the type of the lettering is clear and easy to read. The spine has a blue segment half-way down to mark the title off from the band marching on the front cover, but the waiting crowd on the back cover is looking toward the band; when open, the covers make a single picture without the spine. Crews uses bright colors for the band, the more important subject, but more subdued colors for the crowd. He applies his colors opaquely, and with no shading to make the figures appear three-dimensional. The faces are drawn with simple dots for eyes and a line for the bottom of the noses and for the mouths. The minimum detail needed beyond color and shape is used for the uniforms and instruments. The waiting crowd does not even have features on their faces at all. Yet we feel these are actual people waiting and watching.

✳ The end-paper color carries over from the top part of the cover, but the top portion of the title page, on a line with that on the cover, switches to the blue of the uniforms for contrast. The letters of the title use the same type as the cover, but the author's name, in the same letters as on the cover, is now white instead of black, perhaps for better contrast against the blue. A simple, flat fire hydrant is the only thing pictured on the title page. It is interesting to see where else it appears in the book. The publication and dedication information are in gray, as is all the text. This was Crews's choice. Do you think it is readable enough?

✳ The book begins in the dark, with the sanitation truck's lights shining across the gutter of the two-page spread. If your copy is not carefully bound, there will be a break in the top of the light beams across the gutter. This shows how an imperfect match by the printer or binder can spoil a spread, no matter how careful the designer. The light beams and the angle of the street on the left lead the eye to the important part of these pages, the notice that there is a parade today.

✳ The vendors prepare for the parade. On the plain white background there is not even a ground line, although one is implied. But we accept the scene as realistic, as we do the people. That they are real is clear from their posture and dress as well as their equipment. No words are really necessary.

✳ As the people begin to gather, Crews places some at the bottom of the pages. Even without any background they seem closer to us because of their size and position. Note how many different individuals he portrays with so few details.

✳ The crowd assembles on what appears to be two sides of the street. Most are looking to the right; we sense from their posture that they are waiting. Children can find children like themselves and people like their parents in this crowd.

✳ The arrival of the parade is signaled by the banner with the letters that match the title. Note how large Crews has made the marchers, the important figures here.

✳ The flags make a vivid splash of color in contrast to the beige and brown uniforms; interested readers may want to research what country each flag represents.

✳ The drum major and the first part of the band march across the next two pages. The picture differs slightly from that on the cover, partly because it is printed on different paper.

✳ The next two pages are all of the band, different rows playing different instruments. Only a few balloons represent the watching crowd behind them; yet the reader never doubts that the people are still there. As the band passes, the words tell the curious reader the names of the instruments, but that is not necessary for the action.

✳ As the last of the band goes by, the watching crowd is revealed again. The pictures of the band are almost a continuous scroll, as if this were all done as one long picture and cut into segments; they flow into each other without a break. It might be fun to try copying the pages and pasting them together to see if this works. Also, despite their lack of features, the crowd of spectators has certain recognizable characters that children like to follow from picture to picture, for example, on the first pages the child in the stroller, or the lady in gray with the blue purse. It's good eye training. After the band passes, we seem to get different people. But people at parades do move around.

✳ The float gives Crews a chance to put people into costumes that give curious children an opportunity to research their nationality. We see here his first full-face people, still done simply, but looking different from all those marching profiles. No angle here; the float goes straight across the two pages.

✳ The baton twirlers break the straight line with the angles of their legs, arms, and batons. Although they are multiracial, they are all women, which is a bit sexist. Fortunately, all the band members are depicted ambiguously enough to be either men or women.

⁕ The old-fashioned bicycles and cars come next, the red caps on the bicyclists picking up the red of the car. Crews has balanced the curves of the bicycle wheels on the left with the curved arm of the man and the child waving on the right.

⁕ The cruise ship gives Crews another chance at full-face characters, so simply drawn, yet each having quite a different face. The confetti starts to flow here.

⁕ Every kid loves a fire engine. Crews's has minimal detail, but everything needed to make it look real is there, along with more confetti.

⁕ As the crowd starts home, the confetti gives us a ground line for the first time since the sanitation truck page, along with our old friend the fire plug, and a lone balloon. Most of the crowd is looking toward the end of the parade, with just a few people and gestures in the other direction toward the hydrant.

⁕ On the last page we return to the clean-up that began the book. The truck has swept a swath on the right. There are still balloons, a motif that can be traced through the book. Astute readers will note that this is a different number truck. Why is an interesting question only Crews can answer.

COMPARISONS

Compare Crews's book with other books on parades, especially the marchers and musical instruments as well as the art style (paint versus collage), for example:

Baer, Gene. *Thump, Thump, Rat-A-Tat-Tat.* Illustrated by Lois Ehlert. New York: Harper, 1989.

SUGGESTED ACTIVITY

Trace or copy and cut out shapes of marchers, hats, flags, and instruments from both parade books for children to combine and paste down in their own parade. They can see how simple these shapes are, especially Ehlert's, and perhaps try some of their own. For those curious about the instruments, any library should have drawings or photographs of the actual instruments on the shelves with the 780's or in encyclopedias.

BOOKS BY CREWS

Bicycle Race. New York: Greenwillow, 1985.
Carousel. New York: Greenwillow, 1982.
Flying. New York: Greenwillow, 1986, paper, 1989.
Freight Train. New York: Greenwillow, 1978, paper, 1985.
Harbor. New York: Greenwillow, 1982, Morrow Mulberry paper, 1987.
Parade. New York: Greenwillow, 1983, Morrow Mulberry paper, 1986.
School Bus. New York: Greenwillow, 1984, Puffin paper, 1985.
Truck. New York: Greenwillow, 1980, Puffin paper, 1985.

Fish Eyes: A Book You Can Count On
by Lois Ehlert

Art teaching and free-lance designing were part of Lois Ehlert's background, along with illustrating. But it is only in the last few years that she has begun illustrating books with her special kind of collage. Along with fabric and objects, she uses cut paper that she has purchased for its special characteristics. She also may paint plain white or textured paper with water color paint in colors and/or designs to produce exactly what she wants to cut and place in a particular part of a picture. Many of her books show her interest and careful research in nature—growing plants and flowers, and birds and animals. Her background in graphic design is immediately apparent in all her books.

✳ *Fish Eyes* uses several of the techniques just mentioned. The background color on the cover is blue, like the water fish swim in, but it is a much deeper, darker blue than most of the water we usually see. Across this water swims what is obviously a fish, but not a photographically realistic one. Having photographs of actual fish available while reading this book can show clearly how Ehlert has used fish as models but has stripped away detail to leave the essentials only. She has made her fish from shapes with the sharp edges that show they were cut from already colored paper. The colors used are intense, what artists call "saturated," meaning not tints or shades with whites, grays, or other colors added, but pure color. She has also juxtaposed certain colors next to and/or on top of others. In some cases they contrast more strongly than others, for example, the red tail against the blue background versus the pale purple or fuschia on the red. She has also used the effect of contrasting colors, primary to secondary, such as red on green.

The red mouth almost seems to come forward from the green head, while the tail seems flat against the blue. The white letters of the title are easier to read than the red of the subtitle and author, as much for their color as for their size. The green of the back cover picks up the color of the head and fins. If the blue background carried around to the back of the book, the words would barely be readable. Ehlert has put basic fish shapes in lighter green on the bottom. You might miss them at first but those eyes won't let you.

✳ These same fish shapes swim and carry us across the end papers, which are the same deep blue as the front cover. But there is more here. The careful reader will notice what is almost lost against that dark blue background: a black fish with an eye that does not call attention to him, saying "hurry up!" This begins a story within a story that adds another dimension to this carefully crafted book.

✳ On the title spread, if you look for the black fish, he has his own message. The title information is printed to match the cover. Ehlert has added different-shaped fish, however, making the spread more interesting than it would be with the other fish only. One large fish swims left to balance the design, but the rest lead us into the book.

✳ On the next two pages, we have a different-shaped fish on the same blue background. His tail, on which our little black friend comments, neatly contains the dedication and copyright information. Ehlert has put a "secret word" in the suit of scales for the reader to find. (Note that color blind children will not see this.) Check the pale purple dots at an angle. The large, easy-to-read words in white contrast with the black fish's messages. These little asides are common in Ehlert's work and add to the fun.

✳ Back and forth swim other interesting fish shapes, some similar, others different, across the two pages. Don't lose track of our little black friend. In order not to miss the swing of the rhyme, this book really needs to be read fairly quickly the first time, then reread several times for the details.

✳ The fish shapes and colors become even more exotic. Ehlert has said that she sometimes moves and rearranges the shapes on her pages for days, until they "feel right." But the small black fish and the green one are still with us.

  ✳ The beginning curves on the previous pages turn into a circle of fish here, while the rest lead you to the counting heart of the book. Note how pointed the large fish is.

  ✳ One green fish is simple enough, but our black friend begins adding.

  ✳ The two fish offer us contrasts in shape and design, going in different directions. At this point, if they haven't noticed yet, children can be alerted to the cut-out eye holes. These offer a tactile experience to add to the verbal and visual. They also made a challenging problem for Ehlert, which perhaps only older children can understand. She had to place her colors on each page in such a way that the holes would reveal the color she wanted seen through them, whichever way the page turned, forward or back. Try moving the pages around under the holes to see how different they could look.

  ✳ The three smiling fish make the viewer smile. The more holes Ehlert adds, the more complicated her planning had to be.

  ✳ Through five, six, seven, eight, nine, and ten fish and their two-page spreads, Ehlert continues to invent new shapes for her fish, places them so the colors through the eye holes work, and gives the reader similarities and differences to hold attention. Meanwhile, the black fish does his own addition and then flees the ten fish to the following two-page spread.

  ✳ There we find our friends from the cover, front and back, leading us to the last spread.

  ✳ There all the fish are black on blue, not just our small friend, but their shapes all relate to the fish seen earlier. Their eyes really jump out at the reader.

  ✳ On the end papers we return to the fish that led us into the book from the front end papers. Here, however, our black fish says goodbye.

Have several books with photographs of fish available for children to look at after they have heard this story, especially some with pictures of those fish mentioned on the back flap. Colorful tropical fish are the most fun to look at and may be inspirational for the art activity to follow the book.

ART ACTIVITY

Students are usually inspired by Ehlert's books to try to cut and paste their own collages. Most children at this age will be happy using ordinary colored paper, but a few may want to paint their own colors. Their work will look more like Ehlert's if you can find shiny, brightly colored paper in an art supply store or even on a gift-wrap counter. With help, children should be able to cut out their own fish, or whatever else Ehlert may inspire them to want to cut and paste. If some would like to play with holes for other colors to show through, use a large hole punch. They can even make counting books.

One teacher had some children do fish pictures in cut paper, while other children painted fish like those they saw in Leo Lionni's *Swimmy* (see p. 43), or in the books of fish photographs.

BOOKS WRITTEN AND/OR ILLUSTRATED BY EHLERT

Baer, Gene. *Thump, Thump, Rat-A-Tat-Tat.* Illustrated by Lois Ehlert. New York: Harper, 1989.
Circus! New York: Harper, 1992.
Color Farm. New York: Lippincott, 1990.
Color Zoo. New York: Harper, 1989.
Eating the Alphabet: Fruits and Vegetables from A to Z. San Diego: Harcourt, Brace, 1989.
Feathers for Lunch. San Diego: Harcourt, Brace, 1990.
Fish Eyes: A Book You Can Count On. San Diego: Harcourt, Brace, 1990.
Growing Vegetable Soup. San Diego: Harcourt, Brace, 1990.
Martin, Bill, and John Archambault. *Chicka Chicka Boom Boom.* New York: Simon and Schuster, 1989.
Planting a Rainbow. San Diego: Harcourt, Brace, 1990.
Red Leaf, Yellow Leaf. San Diego: Harcourt, Brace, 1991.

Alfie Gets in First

by Shirley Hughes

Shirley Hughes has been writing and illustrating books about and for children for as many years as it has taken her own children to grow up and present her with grandchildren. Throughout this time she has been drawing and painting active, realistic children who seem to play in England the same kinds of games our children do here. Lately her illustrations have included children of many races and backgrounds, as Great Britain becomes as multicultural as the United States.

✳ Alfie really needs no introduction. He appears on the cover of *Alfie Gets in First,* the first book in the series about him, and we seem to know him at once. Hughes's skill at portraying real people in action is obvious. Every part of Alfie is anatomically realistic, and he's all in motion. Even his hair is going this way or that. His feet are really not even on the ground. Hughes gives us, in only a few lines, a sort of ground and a shadow to anchor Alfie down. Cover the bottom of the picture and see how important these lines are. On the back cover sits Annie Rose, more passive but no less real than Alfie, patiently sucking her thumb, with her "idiot mittens" on strings echoing her hands. Her shadow ties her solidly down and connects her to the shopping basket with the all-important key on top. Hughes applies paint sometimes transparently but frequently opaquely, not brush stroke by brush stroke, not by filling in heavy outlines, but freely, without ever seeming careless.

✳ The end papers pick up the yellow of Alfie's jacket.

✳ The story itself begins on the half-title page. Children can absorb a lot of information from this picture, aside from more about the main characters. Note the placement of the figures, and the man and woman in the back. Try blocking them out to see what they add. Shopping is clearly taking place. Here is one of the few places where Alfie is not in motion.

✳ On the title page is a circle vignette, with Alfie moving again, and mother breaking through the top of the circle. Again children can see that they are moving. This is an introduction to the actual start of the story, when we find that they are going home.

✳ On the left-hand page, only a few leaves break out of the rectangular picture. The street is portrayed very realistically, including the cat. Hughes uses traditional perspective, with the narrowing sidewalk going up to the right. Alfie doesn't wait for his mother; he runs across the right-hand page over the top of the text, with only the brush of a shadow holding him down.

✳ On the next two-page spread, he's resting on the steps on the right, while mother and Annie Rose are coming along on the left. Although they are moving to the left here, mother is looking over at Alfie, making him part of the picture even though he is outside the rectangle on the left. The text is minimal, almost unnecessary, since we can see what is happening, even how Annie Rose's eyes are closing. In fact, Hughes's pictures throughout make this a book children can read from the pictures alone. Hughes has made the street even more alive with various animals and people.

✳ On the next two pages, Alfie runs in, as on the cover, barely touching the ground. But the other characters are also there in action, mother with the key, in a red case, perhaps to call our attention to it, and Annie Rose watching. Here the door makes a frame for them within the larger rectangle, with Alfie center stage. The vignette on the right is another action scene, with the door again framing the characters. In both pictures the items behind the door balance the shopping basket.

＊ The next two pages need no text. The slam of the door is obvious from Alfie's action and from the lines that come from the door like the wind from the slam, even breaking the frame on the top of the picture. On the right-hand page, Hughes begins a series of pictures which use the white space and the gutter. Note that on the right, Alfie contemplates what is actually only a heavy brown line with a doorknob attached. But it is clearly meant to be the door. The text fits into this picture, as throughout the book, without intruding into the picture, but without getting lost in it either.

＊ The door is clearly there between mother and Annie Rose on the left and Alfie on the right. Mother's hand reaches through the frame, but not through the door. Meanwhile, behind her, life on the street goes on. We can almost feel Alfie straining to reach the door catch. The vital key sits center stage, useless.

＊ On the next two-page spread another character, Mrs. MacNally, crosses over to join the action, while the cat jumps away in the other direction, paws out of the frame. Tears flow on both sides of the door.

＊ More tears continue on the next two pages. Mrs. MacNally is leaning through the frame. Another character is arriving for alert viewers to notice.

＊ Even more tears flow, as Mrs. MacNally turns to direct our attention to the next character, her daughter Maureen, crossing the street. We know Annie Rose is really upset because her hat has fallen off.

＊ On successive pages, action takes place on both sides of the door. On the left, more characters arrive and join the concerned bunch in a typical cumulative story. But on the right Alfie is up to his own actions.

＊ As the milkman peers in, and Maureen looks across the street to spot the man with the ladder, Alfie is marching off to the right. Nothing in the text tells us this; we must notice it ourselves.

＊ While Maureen goes to get the window cleaner with his ladder, and Annie Rose continues to cry and push Mrs. MacNally away within the group at the door, here comes Alfie with his chair from the right. Again no words are telling this, but some children are already seeing and understanding what Alfie is up to.

＊ While the ladder and the window cleaner lean over to the house and all eyes are on him, even two watchers across the street, Alfie is climbing onto the chair and the text is asking the reader to guess what is about to happen. Note how Hughes balances the diagonal of the ladder on the left with the different diagonal of the basket and the shape of Alfie as he climbs the chair toward the latch on the door. She has continued to wash a simple wide line of paint for the floor and another to indicate the wall.

✳ In the next two-page spread, on the left and framed by the doorway, the other bodies, and Annie Rose's outstretched hand, is Alfie. On the right he stands proudly, letting everyone in.

✳ The next picture spreads across the pages, with the two men on the left leaning toward our hero, resting at last, eating his cookie. Mrs. Mac-Nally's rounded body on the right, around chubby Annie Rose, balances the picture on that side. Hughes has made each character here a real, believable person.

✳ On the last page mother, Annie Rose, and Alfie are framed in that same doorway, but within a cozy oval, waving goodbye to their company and to the reader.

RELATED ACTIVITIES

Alfie stories lend themselves to dramatizing very well. Of course, everyone wants to be Alfie, as he finally opens the door, or shares at the party (*Alfie Gives a Hand*), or mixes up his boots (*Alfie's Feet*) when they perform small plays of his adventures. Children also enjoy using Alfie's figure, copied and cut out for them, to paste on a page and put into a situation from one of the books, or one they invent themselves. It's always full of action.

BOOKS ABOUT ALFIE

Alfie Gets In First. New York: Lothrop, 1982.
Alfie Gives a Hand. New York: Lothrop, 1984, Morrow/Mulberry paper, 1986.
Alfie's Feet. New York: Lothrop, 1983, Morrow/Mulberry paper, 1988.
The Big Alfie and Annie Rose Story Book. New York: Lothrop, 1989.
An Evening at Alfie's. New York: Lothrop, 1985.

HUGHES'S TALES OF TROTTER STREET

Angel Mae. New York: Lothrop, 1989.
The Big Concrete Lorry. New York: Lothrop, 1990.
The Snow Lady. New York: Lothrop, 1990.
Wheels. New York: Lothrop, 1991.

The Quilt

by Ann Jonas

Although many of her books are for very young children, Ann Jonas's art techniques are far from simple. Her attempts to create pictures that work when a story is read through, and work again when the book is turned upside-down as the story continues back to the beginning, are of particular interest to curious older children. She has done this in black and white in *Round Trip*, and in color in *Reflections*, although it is not done in *The Quilt*. Her background as a graphic designer is apparent on every page of her books. *The Quilt* is not only a favorite with children, but it is also a good introduction to her work as well as a bridge to other related materials.

✳ The heroine and narrator of the story smiles out at us from under the title quilt, snugly snapped into her pink feet-pajamas, her blue stuffed dog at her side. The quilt is a wonderful riot of color, with certain key squares that will take important parts in the story. But for now, it is enough to enjoy the variety of patterns that flow across to the back cover, real enough to cast shadows. The flower design on the back of the quilt also forms its border, which Jonas has used to frame the top and part of the sides of the front and back cover. Jonas has painted large areas of mostly flat, bright color on the quilt with acrylics or gouache that contrast with the paler pastel pink of the pajamas and blue of the dog. The title, in a red that is repeated in the quilt, and the author's name, are printed in an easy-to-read type face favored by Jonas.

✳ Looking at the end papers is like seeing the back of the quilt hung up for our pleasure.

✳ The title and author, in the same type and color as the cover, are joined by the publisher and copyright information on the right-hand page. An old-fashioned sewing machine sits with its base only indicated by a line. But it is obviously the creator of the wonderful quilt, again spread across two pages for us to admire.

✳ Our narrator begins her story as she comes out from under her new quilt, dog in hand. Her appearance and stance are that of a real child, even to the unsnapped snap. If you care to check, the quilt squares stay the same throughout the book, showing Jonas's attention to detail. There is no background to distract us here.

＊ Off they go to the new bed. The leaning body of the girl and the pointing of the dog, plus the horizontal spread of the quilt all lead us, with the girl's eagerness, to the bed.

＊ Jonas gives us a room from just lines and squares to indicate window and baseboard, and a picture on the wall. The attention is focused on the bed and, of course, the quilt, as the girl tells us where some of the squares come from. Jonas has used the white of the paper for the wall, floor, and even for the turned-down top sheet. The dust-ruffle picks up the pink of the pajamas.

＊ As the girl continues to examine the pieces, the scene is the same, but the light subtly changed. Almost all that was white is now a soft gray, with a streak of light on the picture. The blue outside the window darkens. Children love to find the piece of cloth in the quilt that matches Sally.

＊ Now all the gray is darker, it is obviously night outside, and our heroine is beneath the covers, with only her hand reaching out to Sally. Yet no reader doubts that Sally is there. The perceptive will note without a reminder that things are already happening to some squares of the quilt.

＊ For the next two-page spread, no words are needed. Children know immediately what is happening. In the dark, the details of the room and bedstead disappear. The reflection on the picture, left white, becomes a full moon, as stars drift from the black squares that are all that is left of the window. The squares of the quilt are really becoming three-dimensional.

＊ Now the background is black for night. The print of the text becomes gray to be read against the black. The elephants were not on the quilt, but some readers will remember the picture on the wall. Children can go back to find where the balloons, tents, clowns, etc., first appeared.

＊ Jonas combines circles, ellipses, and active bodies against the black background in this dramatic two-page spread. A crowd of people is indicated by just touches of paint in the different colors of reflected light.

＊ The bright colors of animals and cages contrast here with the dark shadows and bodies of the elephants. The small tiger looks as worried as the girl searching for her Sally.

＊ As she continues the quest through the houses and patterns seen earlier on the quilt, we see the "moon" reappear over hills in the still-black "sky," with shadows all around. The pink "cliffs" appear first here, but few realize what they represent.

＊ Jonas takes the opportunity here to let the flowers from the quilt really bloom. Black shapes still surround almost all the picture. Instead of a plain fence, she gives us one with a diamond pattern and round knobs on top as part of the black frame on the bottom of the picture. But it also appears with white circles at the upper right, echoing the moon and circle on top of the gazebo, which also has the diamond shapes. The pink cliffs appear again at the top right.

* Arches form the scary tunnel, all framed in the black of the night, with dark shadows. The hanging branches at the top are like hands with clutching fingers. Children who have heard echoes in tunnels will appreciate the three echoing "Sally"s printed in the darker gray, barely visible against the black. All lines lead the eye toward the tiny light at the end of the tunnel.

* Jonas brings us back to the moon and a more peaceful scene, still framed in black, but with many horizontals along with diagonals of the sails, kites, and hills. The boats, ducks, and kites can all be found on the quilt. The reds and yellows cheer the scene as well.

* The black frame and trees, the purples and shadows, all make this scene somber despite the boat glimpsed on the upper left. But this is the darkest hour before the dawn.

* From the black shadows on the left, we come out to the brightness of the sun, the pink cliffs, and the lost Sally.

* Quilt, girl, and dog are now all on the floor, coming from the left where all the action was. Again, only lines and now yellow squares of light define the window. Much of the two-page spread is left white, as the girl and dog form a circle of love and comfort, enveloped by the quilt. Is there too much white here? Children will now recognize the pink cliffs of the dust ruffle. Most now enjoy going back to trace all the elements of the story in the quilt.

This story is, of course, only one of many which involve dreams. Some are listed in the section on Nancy Tafuri's *Junglewalk* (p. 48). If the children want to pursue other books about dreams, this is a beginning.

There are also many books about quilts, some of which will be covered later, for older children who can make actual quilts.

ART ACTIVITY

Although they cannot make real quilts at this age, children can build paper squares of cut-out patterned or colored paper. Old wallpaper pattern books are good sources. Then the squares can be combined for a large class paper quilt. They can also each make a square picture of themselves, or of a favorite activity, for the class quilt. One class had the children draw pictures with crayons on plain white cotton squares, which willing and able parents ironed, sewed together with other colored squares, and quilted into a wonderful hanging for the classroom.

BOOKS BY JONAS

Aardvarks Disembark. New York: Greenwillow, 1990.
Color Dance. New York: Greenwillow, 1989.
Holes and Peeks. New York: Greenwillow, 1984.
Now We Can Go. New York: Greenwillow, 1986.
The Quilt. New York: Greenwillow, 1984.
Reflections. New York: Greenwillow, 1987.
Round Trip. New York: Greenwillow, 1983, paper, 1990.
The Trek. New York: Greenwillow, 1985, Morrow/Mulberry paper, 1989.
Where Can It Be? New York: Greenwillow, 1986.

OTHER QUILT BOOKS

Chorao, Kate. *Kate's Quilt.* New York: Dutton, 1982.
Coerr, Eleanor. *The Josefina Story Quilt* illustrated by Bruce Degen. New York: Harper, 1986.
Johnston, Tony. *The Quilt Story* illustrated by Tomie dePaola. New York: Putnam, 1985.
Polacco, Patricia, *The Keeping Quilt.* New York: Simon and Schuster, 1988.
Vincent, Gabrielle. *Ernest and Celestine's Patchwork Quilt.* New York: Greenwillow, 1982.

Frederick
by Leo Lionni

Leo Lionni is a designer and graphic artist as well as a writer and illustrator of many popular picture books. *Frederick* was the first of many of his books ostensibly about mice and other animals but really about people. Although the child reader may not completely understand the "lessons" of Lionni's stories, his books are favorites year after year, which must indicate that the stories mean something to the children beyond the obvious appeal of the deceptively simple illustrations. Lionni frequently uses cut and torn paper, but he also paints undersea scenes in transparent water color paint and draws and shades with a pencil.

✳ The hero appears facing us on the front cover, with eyes demurely lidded over the shy smile. The back cover is an exact reverse, as if we had walked behind Frederick. Lionni has painted the paper before cutting or tearing it to get exactly the color and texture he wanted. The rough, torn edges give a furry look to the bodies of the mice. The grays and blacks make the red of the flower stand out. A pattern of curves is repeated in the rocks, the mouse, and the flower and stem. Lionni uses a bare minimum of detail, but his simple forms are so convincingly arranged that it is easy to forget how simple they are. There is no background. Do you feel one is needed? The author's and publisher's names are printed in simple black type, upper and lower case, but the title is written in script. These are deliberate design choices. The curves of the writing seem to match the curves of the picture. Try putting a printed title, in all upper case or in upper- and lower-case letters, in place of the written one to see how different the cover would look.

✳ The end papers have the title written over and over again. This gives the paper an interesting texture and reinforces the importance of the title character.

✳ The half-title repeats the title once.

✳ The title page repeats the writing and printing of the cover, but the accompanying picture is the same as that on the back cover. We can only speculate on why. Is Frederick looking ahead into the book? The rocks on the page facing the title page are carefully placed to balance those on the title page.

✳ Again the written title leads us into the story, balancing the copyright information on the left.

✳ On the first two-page spread, the flat-painted rocks of the wall contrast with the three-dimensional texture of the meadow. The little circular shapes of red and white stand out as flowers. The vertical tree shape is carefully set against the horizontals of wall and field, with the shape of the branches adding directions and curves. The meadow slopes slightly from left to right, balancing the tree. There is ample room for the text on the side opposite the branches.

✳ On the next two pages we meet the "chatty family of field mice." They are not distinct individuals; they are simply the mice. Lionni has the rocks of the wall here with nothing to hold them together. Yet somehow we do not feel that they will fall. Certain touches relieve the gray of mice and rocks here, notably the scattering of green and gold "leaves," the brilliant red of the berries that two mice hold, the butterfly, and the procession of ants. The pointed "leaves" contrast with all the other circular shapes. Circular leaves would really have looked boring.

✳ On the next two-page spread, the mice march across the pages, the leader carrying the stalks of grain at an angle. Try to picture those stalks tilted further in either direction to see how carefully Lionni has placed them. Why is the mouse on the far left not marching with the rest? The curve of his tail makes up part of the design.

✳ We find that it is Frederick who will not work with the others. He faces in the other direction, eyes closed in concentration, gathering the rays from the bright yellow sun. It is certainly no coincidence that the other mice are carrying bright yellow corn rather than some other food. Lionni balances the brown of the tree trunk with the section of ground on which Frederick is sitting, which in turn separates him further from the mice moving onto the green.

✳ Frederick has turned his back on us. The rocks are as gray as he tells us the winter is. But the colors he gathers are scattered across the bottom of the two-page spread.

✳ Again on the next page, Frederick is looking in the opposite direction from the other mice. The interesting shapes of the green plants contrast with the line of marching mice; one of whom has disappeared off the page, carrying something long and straight. The words of text are carefully placed among the plants.

✳ Lionni uses the white of the page as well as the bits of white paper for snow. Note where his background painting begins and ends.

✳ The circular shapes on the next two pages give a cozy feeling, while the yellows and browns add warmth.

✳ On the next two-page spread, the circles are still there, but broken pieces suggest that all is not well. Also, with just the placement of eyelids and eyes, Lionni suggests an unease in the mice.

✳ The broken pieces remain, but the mice are looking up to Frederick now, with hope. Again the placement of the eyelids conveys a lot of emotion.

✳ Frederick sends the yellow glow, or its memory, out to the mice, who have their eyes shut. The reader can decide whether it is "real" or not.

✳ Next he reminds them of the colors he has saved for them. There is one color they seem to see that he does not name. It is interesting to see whether any children notice this. They can go back and see the lavender in the flowers even if he does not mention it.

✳ When Frederick comes to the words, Lionni needs more space for them, so he clears a rock-shape for them, and they fit right in. He has the mice turned as if they are looking at the words.

✳ Frederick concludes by facing us and blushing on a quiet, balanced page.

✳ The back end papers again tell us who is important in this book.

ART ACTIVITIES

Have students make pictures and/or books using cut paper shapes like Lionni's cut by the teacher or the students, with water color paint or crayon added. Lionni's stories seem to inspire children to make pictures.

LIONNI BOOKS WITH MICE

Alexander and the Wind-up Mouse. New York: Pantheon, 1970, paper, 1987.
Frederick. New York: Knopf paper, 1987, reissue, 1990.
Frederick's Fables: A Leo Lionni Treasury of Favorite Stories. New York: Pantheon, 1985.
Geraldine the Musical Mouse. New York: Pantheon, 1979.
Matthew's Dream. New York: Knopf, 1991.
Nicolas, Where Have You Been? New York: Knopf, 1987.
Tillie and the Wall. Knopf, 1989.

For other mice stories of all sorts see *Booklinks* February 15, 1991.

OTHER LIONNI FAVORITES

Cornelius. New York: Pantheon, 1983.
It's Mine. New York: Knopf, 1986.
Little Blue and Little Yellow. Astor-Honor, 1959, recently reissued.
A torn-paper masterpiece of simplicity in art and complexity of meaning.
Six Crows. New York: Knopf, 1988.
Swimmy. New York: Knopf paper, 1987.

We're Going on a Bear Hunt

retold by Michael Rosen, illustrated by Helen Oxenbury

The babies and children in Helen Oxenbury's pictures are the ones you see passing you in the supermarket carts, or drowsing in their strollers at the zoo, or shyly peering at you in the dentist's office. They are the children of your friends, or the friends of your grandchildren, doing all the adorable and exasperating things that real children do. With dark outline drawing and more or less transparent water color paint, Oxenbury illustrates people, particularly parents and children, acting in realistic situations. Without drawing every detail, she depicts familiar-looking people acting in groups, with gestures and expressions that show their feelings and relationships. Her board books and simple early picture books have become favorites for these reasons.

✳ Using the rhythmic measures and expressive language of Michael Rosen's poem as her base, Oxenbury has soared above it, adding meaning and substance to the adventure of the bear hunt. The letters for the title, author, and illustrator on the jacket are printed in italic-like letters that seem to lean forward like the characters. The letters are dark gray, like the shading of the outlines of the figures, which are done in charcoal or Conté pencil. Through a few scratched-in blades of grass, father and the children walk and skip off on the hunt. The boy runs ahead with a stick, as boys do, pointing up and back, while the girl's arms are at the same angle as the stick as she skips or jumps, hair flying. Baby's head separates the author's name from the illustrator's name. On the back of the jacket, the parade continues, with the older girl striding along, hair blowing behind, while the dog sniffs the trail, tail held high. All the characters are in animated action. The cloth cover is a textured dark red, a color used inside the book as well.

✳ The front end papers are different from the back ones, which belong at the end of the story just as these belong at the beginning. Oxenbury allows the white paper and its texture to become a large part of this peaceful seaside scene. Birds fly on the right and land on the sand on the lower left; waves are rolling in, but essentially this is a placid scene. A few sails and rocks point up toward the sky, but most of the lines are restfully horizontal.

✳ The title page resembles the open book jacket. The animation of the characters contrasts with the peaceful scene on the end papers.

✳ The first double-page spread has no color, only the blacks and grays of the rubbed charcoal or pencil and the print. The large, clear, widely spaced print makes its own pattern on the page, with its repeated refrains. Oxenbury has spread the tall grass and flowers across the two pages, all blown by the wind, with just a sketch of clouds and birds for the sky. Amid the grass, the boy runs ahead and away, stick held high. Father and the dog watch the girls as the baby leans and reaches toward the boy. The younger girl playfully pulls the older; all are in action.

✳ The refrain, in its bright yellow frame, gets larger and louder, and the rest of the double-page spread erupts into color. Oxenbury makes the grassy, flower-dotted hill fill most of the pages in an even arc, with trees and landscape on the right, along with the characters, to balance the text on the left. The dog leads the way into the corner, dad and baby right behind, as the other three children make different patterns with their gestures and positions. Oxenbury makes each face real with minimum detail. The landscape is also more impression than realism.

✳ We see the family from the back as they confront the next obstacle, again with no color but with the lines and patterns deliberately placed. The horizontals now are a barrier that temporarily has halted the family. The hands on hips and thigh show the contemplation of the problem. Note that the leaning boy and baby on the left match the angle of the dog's body and tail, and that the angle of the stick on the right matches with the two taller bodies vertical at the center, arms bent.

✳ The family wades happily toward us in close-up on the right-hand side of the two-page spread, now back in color. The repeated refrain on the left is framed in blue-green from the water. Tree trunks and the grassy bank make a frame across the top as the water washes the rest of the pages. The brighter colors are in the children's shirt and dress. Oxenbury has them all reaching in or toward each other in family unity.

✳ Color is gone again as the family contemplates the next obstacle. Only dad's position shows concern. Baby is already happily trampling the mud, and the boy is throwing it, while the younger girl seems glad enough to get her shoes off again. The strength of Oxenbury's line is easier to see when the color is absent; follow the lines of body positions that are set against the horizontal boards and vertical posts.

✳ In the color landscape across the two pages, the refrain is again on the left, framed now in green. Ominous darkness appears in the sky as the family picks its way from right to left and away on the right-hand page. Dad carries the shoes, big sister carries baby, and they are all in realistic action. Oxenbury has used a lot of the white on the page here, again effectively.

✳ A different point of view is given us as we watch the family examine the forest obstacle. Not only have we gone again from color back to black and white, but the whole pattern of the pages is different. Instead of the mainly horizontal lined two-page spread she has been using, Oxenbury gives us the wavy pattern of the hill and the arrangement of heads from left to right. Father and younger daughter sit on the hill on the left-hand page, baby holding dad, while older daughter and dog point to the forest. Brother is already marching down there, stick in hand. Surely all the children listening have joined in the refrain by now.

✳ Oxenbury puts us in the forest of tree trunks and green leaves, grass, and shadows. The dog is already marching purposefully off to the left, beyond the green-framed refrain. Brother seems to drag baby along; older sister has tripped and is falling. Younger sister holds the tree and leans in the other direction, while father seems to look it all over from the fallen tree, hands on hips. The trees really dominate here. No one looks very happy, as the mood is changing.

✳ The dark sky really menaces the landscape and people here. Children listening to the story shiver along with the huddled family as they repeat the refrain.

✳ The snow swirls through the air and covers the ground. The touches of color are almost all we see of the family struggling against the wind and snow on the right, with just shadowed hill and the blue-framed refrain on the left.

✳ The family frames the dark hole of the central mound surrounding the cave as they peer in or lean out. The dog slinks slightly back on the left, while baby tries to pull younger sister away on the right. The rocks do not add any warmth to the feeling of menace in this picture.

✳ Although it is in color, this spread is predominantly the dark brown of the cave. The brown-framed refrain has moved to the right here and added the large, black, startling question, "What's that?" The dark brown arch on the right is matched on the left by the arched tunnel through which the family is coming. Far off on the left, we see the sun and sparkling water. The sun lights the cave entrance enough for us to see the apprehensive group and their shadows. They are still connected by position and gesture.

✳ Still in color is the shock of the confrontation, as the brown bear emerges from the dark on the right into the brown of the cave. Some light still shows on the left, where the gray frame includes the shocking information about the bear. Under the frame, the dog pulls back, tail between legs, as he looks up at the bear. Note the touches of white to highlight the eyes, nose, and claws of the bear.

✳ The format changes completely as the verse and the adventure go into reverse. Three horizontal rectangles on each page give us freeze frames of the trip back through the obstacles, with the bear chasing behind. A comparison with the pictures of the family going through with those coming out is interesting, but not at first reading; the pace is too rapid, as seen by the body positions of the family, and we want to see what happens next.

✳ Now we have two vertical rectangles per page, with text underneath. The up-and-then-down-again scenes on the left-hand page are frantic but funny. Action is clear from the bodies. On the right-hand page, the bear menaces through the glass, as four members of the family lean and push. Then it's under the comforting-looking pink coverlet.

✳ The puffy pink spreads across the two pages, covering and protecting them all. As they peer out apprehensively, only the baby seems completely at ease, happily tossing his teddy bear. Maybe he thought it was just a big teddy and wasn't afraid at all.

✳ Perhaps he was a friendly bear, some of my listeners have suggested. Across the same beach we saw in the front end papers, the moon shines peacefully as the bear walks back. He does look a bit dejected; maybe he just wanted to make friends, or at least some of the children think so.

BOOKS BY OXENBURY

Oxenbury has not published any other books for this age recently, but some children may want to go back and reminisce with some of her board books, her books about Tom and Pippo (New York: Macmillan, 1988-1989), or her stories of family life like *The Birthday Party, The Car Trip, Eating Out,* etc. (New York: Dial, 1982-1984) now out of print, but still at libraries and favorites in home collections.

We're Going on a Bear Hunt retold by Michael Rosen illustrated by Helen Oxenbury. New York: Margaret K. McElderry. Macmillan, 1989.

Compare words and pictures with other collections of rollicking rhymes by Jack Prelutsky and Shel Silverstein, and with Michael Rosen's other books, like *Smelly Jelly Smelly Fish* illustrated by Quentin Blake (New York: Prentice-Hall, 1986).

Junglewalk
by Nancy Tafuri

Using dark outlines and more or less transparent water color paint, Nancy Tafuri fills her pages with large, simple, clearly defined shapes that appeal immediately to young children. Her stories, or those by others that she illustrates, frequently include animals as well as children. She does not include fussy details or model with shadows, but is concerned with a larger pattern of shapes and colors on the page. Despite the lack of detail, children recognize and identify with her characters. Tafuri lives out in the country, where she can observe some of her models directly from her windows.

---

* On the cover of *Junglewalk* Tafuri emphasizes the exotic, in the flowers through which the tiger stares straight at us from the exotic jungle itself. The very large, bold letters of the title and author are printed within heavy black frames, through which parts of the leaves and flowers and the ears of the tiger are breaking out in selected places. The blue of a sky is carried up past the frame behind the title, while a sort of green grass is behind the author's name. On the back cover, stepping out of a small square of that same grass-green background is a related character, the cat, looking at us just as the tiger does. Even his color and stripes are like a pale reflection.

* A jungle vine of the same green and tiger-brown as the cover grows across a splash of blue sky at the top of the end papers, leading us into the book.

* Against the white of the two-page spread, the same black letters as the cover stand out even more sharply on the title page. The publisher information and what's in the toucan's beak ("a bean," insisted one of my listeners) repeat the green from the cover. From the toucan, and the tiger and cat on the cover, we can see how Tafuri has painted for this book. Her figures are large and naturalistic, and somewhat simplified, i.e., not every feather on the bird or hair of the cat is shown. They are outlined, then filled in with intense colors. The fruit in the bird's beak is modelled, or shaded to round its contour, as are the bird's beak and eye.

※ A lined-off area on the left, in the same warm yellow as the lamplight, includes the dedication, copyright information, and a note on what Tafuri used for her full-color illustrations. The rest of the wide, two-page spread is the beginning of our story. The only words the reader needs to know are the titles of the book itself and, in the same type style, that of the book the boy is reading. The curves of the cat in repose are echoed in the curves of the lamp and its light, the bedposts, and the curtains, giving a restful feeling, while the angle of the curtain on the right sweeps us toward the next page.

※ The same curtains frame the night scene and the shadowy rabbit on the right of the two-page spread, as the boy turns in similar curves to put out the lamp. Notice how the point of view has changed. The alert cat attends to the rabbit across the page. The green of the boy's book is echoed by a darker green across the page and outside. Note the restful horizontals on the left, diagonals on the right.

※ On the left, all still seems restful. On the right, however, the transformation has begun, with the vine we first saw on the end papers now creeping through the window, across the gutter, and around the bedposts, as the cat's tail also curls. The cool, restful night blues on the left continue around to the right, but from the window come the contrasting bright yellows and orange-reds of wakeful day, painting a rectangle of light on the bed.

※ When asked what is happening on the left, most children five and older readily reply that the boy is walking in his dream. Some say it is his shadow. Red from the window is now touching the blue of the covers. The children also notice immediately that the tail on the right no longer belongs to the cat.

※ Even knowing of the transformation, the enormous tiger overflowing the next two pages brings a gasp. It takes a minute or so for children to spot the boy peering through the leaves. Tafuri uses black pencil strokes to give texture to the tiger's fur. Note the touches of yellow on the upper right and left. The yellow appears on several pages as a sort of motif, sometimes as the moon, finally as the sun.

※ The next six two-page spreads introduce a variety of creatures in jungle settings. All are simplified but readily identifiable amid the crowded scenes. And in each, the reader must spot the boy still pursuing the tiger. The toucans are active and moving;

* so are the gibbons;

* while the crocodile lies so still across the bottom of the page that he is almost missed in all the green of the page.

* The hippos seem quiet as the tiger rests.

* The gorilla holds a banana of that brilliant yellow we saw in earlier pictures. On the right, the vine from the end papers winds by the parrot.

* The elephants march left, but the tiger keeps us moving right.

* The zebras are so brilliant in their black-and-white contrast that they divert us briefly from the boy, who is closing in on the tiger on the right. It also takes a moment to notice the pride of lions at the upper left.

* On this spread, the jungle-related grass on the left gives way to the grassy lawn, tree, and house on the right, in daylight.

* Back through the window comes the cat, as the boy awakens. The green outside matches the cover of the boy's book exactly now.

* The warmth of the hug is unmistakable. Outside the window, Tafuri has simplified the landscape, with a bird and that bright yellow sun.

* The bird leads us into the final picture, a small one against the white that continues across the page and onto the end papers with the vine. The boy and the cat set off on a real adventure together into a landscape that pales next to the exciting jungle.

BOOKS BY TAFURI

The Ball Bounced. New York: Greenwillow, 1989.
Do Not Disturb. New York: Greenwillow, 1987.
Early Morning in the Barn. New York: Greenwillow, 1983, paper, 1986.
Follow Me! New York: Greenwillow, 1990.
Ginsburg, Mirra. *Asleep, Asleep* New York: Greenwillow, 1992.
Have You Seen My Duckling? New York: Greenwillow, 1984, paper, 1986.
Junglewalk. New York: Greenwillow, 1988.
Pomerantz, Charlotte. *Flap Your Wings and Try.* New York: Greenwillow, 1989.

COMPARISONS

Compare this dream adventure with those by Briggs (p. 19) and Peter Collington (*The Angel and the Soldier Boy* New York: Knopf, 1987) and, for a real stretch, with:
Van Allsburg, Chris. *Ben's Dream.* Boston: Houghton Mifflin, 1982.
Van Allsburg, Chris. *Just a Dream.* Boston: Houghton Mifflin, 1990.
Weisner, David. *Free Fall.* New York: Lothrop, 1988.

Chapter 4
From Kindergarten through Second Grade

INTRODUCTION

The task of mastering the skills of reading occupies so much of the students' time and energy during these years that it is easy to ignore picture books entirely. But there is still so much for children to learn and enjoy about the art and artists that these books should not be forgotten. Choosing from among the many fine, easy-to-read books illustrated by some of the artists we are examining should ensure good looking along with good reading.

Another important method of sustaining interest in the art of the picture book is to use authors and illustrators who not only are fine writers and artists, but who also display a sense of fun that tickles the children who are struggling with beginning reading and writing. The art style and technique can be appreciated along with the humor. All the books discussed in this chapter are not only high-quality picture books but also winners in the popularity polls as well.

Strega Nona

by Tomie dePaola

Tomie dePaola is one of the most popular illustrators with children. He brings his inimitable personal style to the illumination of stories by other writers and to old myths and legends as well as to his own original fiction and nonfiction tales. Frequently, he seasons them with the flavor of his Italian heritage. He fills in his heavy dark outline drawings with transparent and opaque color. *Strega Nona* is typical of his work in many ways. She also has remained one of his most popular character creations over the years, and many books with her in them can be found in the reading list following this discussion. By this time, having drawn her curved nose and matching chin so many times, dePaola could probably do it in his sleep. But simple as she appears, Strega Nona has her true essence only when he draws her.

✳ On the cover, she smiles at a stylized, simplified bird of paradise sitting on a kind of peasant-embroidery tree. The whole front cover is a sort of stage-set frame, with Strega Nona stepping out onto the stage, pasta pot in hand. DePaola has been a designer of stage sets, which appear frequently in his illustrations. The bird, rabbit, and greenery are all very simplified and stylized, as is the house, which barely looks large enough to have Strega Nona fit inside. Everything is outlined with heavy, dark lines, while shading makes the tree, bird, pot, etc., rounded and sculptural rather than flat. The outline color is also used in the title lettering. The subtitle, center stage, forms a second arch. The colors used are not pure but seem mixed, like pinkish purple and blue-green, and stained rather than opaque. Perhaps they are meant to remind us of the colors of the stucco houses of Italy. The tiles on the houses and the arches depicted on the back cover certainly have the flavor of Mediterranean towns. The pastel crayon or charcoal shading on the textured paper also recalls the roughness of stucco.

✳ An arched and columned arcade and village, with doves on the cobblestones at the bottom and a dePaola-style moon and stars in the sky, lead us across the end papers into the story.

✳ The lettering from the cover is repeated on the title page, but there is no arch. Instead there is a rougher, brown-outlined frame, broken by balanced leaves on either side of the flowering band across the bottom, and by the tails of the bird on one side and the bunny on the other. A simple band forms the ground line. Between that line and the flower band is a band of color matching the pot, which encloses the publication information. All is peacefully in balance: the curves of the pot, the bunny, Strega Nona's arms, the house, and the tree or plant. More dePaola stars and the moon here seem to float in the void, each surrounded by just a touch of sky, perhaps to help the title stand out.

✳ The same stylized stars and moon float on the dedication and copyright page. The first illustration shows a scene that could come from a medieval painting without perspective; the costumes and buildings are from a far-off place and time. A sun floats in an uncolored sky, all framed by a line broken by two trees on top. Here and throughout the book, the characters have the simplest of features and costumes, but in every case they are clear and distinct characters. The strong horizontals and verticals make the design of the page peaceful without being boring, as we focus on Strega Nona's diagonal arm.

✳ Next on the left-hand page, dePaola gives us three sets of wordless comic-strip-like pictures of Strega Nona in action. We see here that her magic works. On the right-hand page, the village square is again a stage set, with products marking off the bottom, the arcade forming the top, and the actors in costume.

✳ We meet the co-star, Big Anthony. DePaola draws us the tile floors, stucco walls, fireplace, and drying herbs of an Italian cottage. The bunny and bird reappear, and we meet the goat. On the other side, we see Anthony in action in four framed pictures. The house or shed is down one side of each picture, as Anthony acts in the rest of the space. A touch of blue wash indicates the sky in the top two pictures, while the stars and moon mean night in the bottom two.

✳ On the left-hand page, the text for the magic song makes its own shape on the page, set against the horizontals of the pictures. Note the simplicity of the figures and furnishings. On the right are four squares of the vital three kisses, framed with the same heavy line. Each square is again like a stage set upon which Strega Nona is performing, breaking the frame slightly with her action.

✳ Two pages of balanced text and pictures include another town square set with costumed folk, and, on the right, the farewell and the warning. Even without all the words, children can tell what is going to happen, as they follow the warning finger to the pot, led by the lines of both the roof and the twisting vine.

✳ On the left-hand page, the song text fills the space between the house scene and the two of Big Anthony. The house scene looks so empty because, as the children will tell you, "Big Anthony's inside." On the right, the tile roof divides the two pictures of the announcement and of the arrival of the townspeople with knives and forks. Even the bunny is looking toward the pasta.

✳ Across the two-page spread we can see inside the house to where Anthony is giving out the pasta, as various folk eat on the left or wait near the door. Again all the faces are simplified, and the costumes lack details, but still the stage is full of distinctive characters. Cut-off, stylized flowers form a border on the ground by the house.

✳ The same ground and border underline the two pictures on the next two pages. On the left are the peaceful bird and bunny, as Anthony stretches out his arms to stop the pot. Although there is a break between the two pictures, and Anthony and the bird appear in both, the roof runs across the page, as does the ground, almost making it one picture. The horizontal flying bird matches the arms of Anthony on the left and the nun on the right, along with the reaching pasta.

✳ The next four pictures are dominated more and more by the undulating pasta as it takes over the room. The four are designed to work together with the balanced placement of the windows and herbs, but each picture is planned to stand by itself as well, with the pasta starting to break through the outline.

✳ On the next two-page spread, the bunny watches from the roof as the pasta flows on a diagonal from the house, carrying Anthony with it. There is a break between the two pictures, but dePaola has designed the two pages so the pasta continues to flow into the right-hand picture and the town.

✳ This time, the picture goes across the two pages without a break. The raised arms and angles show the distress as the pasta pours down from the upper right. The tile-roofed arcade stabilizes the upper left, while two horizontal solids, a table and a railing, anchor the lower right.

✳ On the next two-page spread, the pasta seems to flow in from the left, over most of where the frame would be, and out the bottom, across the gutter. Anthony's arms try to stem it, in vain. But tucked neatly into the bottom right-hand corner, entering the stage from a doorway, is Strega Nona, a balance and a match for all that pasta. Her stick firmly on the ground, she appears ready to counter the pasta. Around the central circled figures are the fleeing birds and cat, with some folks dressed in blue at the top right; blue-veiled nuns kneel in prayer facing the oncoming waves.

* In three of the four pictures on the left-hand page, Strega Nona performs her magic on the stage, with expressive gestures. In the last picture, the pasta has the stage to itself, as it pauses, coming out of the frame. On the top right, all hands reach in friendly thanks to Strega Nona. On the bottom, the anger of the men shows clearly in their gestures, as Anthony seems to slink backward out of the scene.

* The almost full-page double-page spread has real impact on the eye. Strega Nona reaches the fork out toward the dismayed Anthony contemplating the small mountain of pasta coming into the picture lower right. The arcade frames the top and back across the two pages.

* On these two pages, dePaola is again using the white page for his background. The frame is also the horizon line. City houses on the left balance Strega Nona's house on the right, where the tree still grows, the bunny still sits, and the moon and stars have just a tiny bit of the blue sky in the white of the page. Unflappable Strega Nona watches, smiling, as a sick-looking, bulging-stomached Anthony rolls more spaghetti on his fork.

* The story ends without a word. Now the bird watches; Strega Nona sleeps; and overstuffed Anthony lets the fork drop through the frame with the last strand of pasta. Note the bird's tail over his head, and Strega Nona's smile, echoed by the rabbit.

Children will "see" more in this and other dePaola books if they have available pictures of Italian towns. These can be found in the library in the 915's or 945's. One example of a book with photographs is *Italy* from the Children of the World series, edited by Rhoda Irene Sherwood (Gareth Stevens, 1986). Books with peasant patterns can help children see how dePaola has incorporated these into his pictures. Costume books can be found in the 391's in the regular and reference sections.

Teachers have spent months with the books of Tomie dePaola, which lend themselves to all types of extensions, from comparing Bible and Christmas stories; to learning about the commedia dell'arte with *Sing, Pierrot, Sing;* to making pasta and bread dolls. Below are just a few general areas for further study.

BOOKS ABOUT STREGA NONA

Big Anthony and the Magic Ring. San Diego: Harcourt Brace, 1979.
Merry Christmas, Strega Nona. San Diego: Harcourt Brace, 1986.
Strega Nona. Englewood Cliffs, NJ: Prentice Hall, 1975.
Strega Nona's Magic Lessons. San Diego: Harcourt Brace, 1982, paper, 1984.

BOOKS ABOUT DEPAOLA'S LIFE

The Art Lesson. New York: Putnam, 1989.
Nana Upstairs and Nana Downstairs. New York: Putnam, 1973, Penguin, 1978.
Watch Out for the Chicken Feet in Your Soup. New York: Simon and Schuster, 1974.

WORDLESS BOOKS

The Hunter and the Animals: A Wordless Picture Book. New York: Holiday House, 1981.
Sing, Pierrot, Sing. San Diego: Harcourt Brace, 1983, paper, 1987.

LEGENDS RETOLD

The Legend of the Bluebonnet: An Old Tale of Texas. New York: Putnam, 1983.
The Legend of the Indian Paintbrush. New York: Putnam, 1988.
The Mysterious Giant of Barletta. San Diego: Harcourt Brace, 1978.

Simon's Book
by Henrik Drescher

Danish-born Henrik Drescher brings a different, foreign look to his picture book illustrations that children recognize, remember, and like to read and reread. Adults may find themselves recalling some of Paul Klee's work, or the lines of George Grosz and the German Expressionists. Children just think the pictures are funny.

---

* The monster with sharp teeth that comes from the back of the dust jacket/cover across the spine to the front to chase the fearful boy is frightening, but not too much so for children of school age. Drescher uses an agitated, broken rather than smooth, pen and ink outline, and transparent to opaque water color paints, even colored pencils, in all shades and colors for his pictures. There is action in the beast, with all his feet off the green grass, leaping at the boy, and certainly in the running boy. Both are going so fast that sweat seems to be flying off their heads. The monster is coming into the cover frame, which is made up of odd, assorted sticks of color. The title is drawn freehand and filled with colors in a child-like fashion. The author's name is seemingly scratched in by the pointed head of the serpent-like pen coiled around the frame. Another such pen rears its head up against the monster. The curves of the pens contrast with the lines of the frame. Despite the shadowed rounding of the boy's figure, he and the beast have a flat, cartoon-like appearance that makes them less than real, and thus, perhaps, less frightening. Above the monster, on the back cover, shines a peaceful moon, while behind him trail objects of many strange shapes and colors. The "sky" color ranges from dark behind the moon to bright lavender around the boy. The snake-pen sputters more inky lines on the flap of the dust jacket.

 ✳ Drescher has hand-drawn, painted, and spattered the end papers, which are the same for front and back. They seem to represent the doodles and splashes of the artist.

 ✳ On the first two-page spread, a yellow semicircle arches across against a dark blue background. Framed in multicolored and patterned sections, the apprehensive boy, sitting on the front of a pen, pulls a rope toward the upper right, while the beast swings happily on the back of the diagonal pen. Small marks are scattered on the yellow background; the pen scribbles more curves, and probably dated the book; two strange eyes watch from the inkwell.

 ✳ Loops and curves abound on the title page, as one pen lands on the board, catapulting the inkwell off. The whirls of the spilling ink form the background for the same author and title letters as on the cover. Another pen coils in balance on the lower right. The green grass or ground drawn straight across the bottom of the two pages is like that on the cover, but here there is sky-like blue above, with the publisher's name written by the left-hand pen. Fine pen lines indicate the vibration of the board that seems to have just shot the inkwell into the air. What a lot of action Drescher has given us before the story even begins!

 ✳ Small ink blots continue onto the next page, which has the copyright information. The mottled yellow background goes across both pages. On the right, the seated beast is chewing up a white ribbon or roll of paper on which the dedication is printed. Three empty pairs of shoes lie ominously below him. Children may not recognize that one pair is of traditional Japanese clogs, or that another is evidently odorous. We can guess that the shoes relate to the names Drescher has sketched in below and are part of a private joke.

＊ Drescher has colored this two-page spread a soft pink. On the left, inside another of those complicated multicolored and multipatterned borders, the young author/artist sits in the dark, his lamp making a triangle of yellowish light on the yellow tablecloth, whose hanging corners make more triangles. The inkwell and pen now look familiar, as do the boy and the monster he draws, which are barely visible. The articles scattered on the floor could be from any boy's room, but Drescher has had some fun with the titles of the books. He has cleared a space for the text on the right-hand page, highlighting the written first word and adding some blots for emphasis. The bird on the left-hand page has an unknown role.

＊ Now the picture spreads across the two pages, with a frame around the dark background; the boy is peacefully asleep on the left toward the back of the page, and the chair and bird are in the foreground. We are close to the table on the right now, close enough to see the sketched beast and boy, and the pens coming alive. The horizontal bed contrasts with the diagonals of the table and sketch pad.

＊ As the action begins, the border disappears, and the background becomes bright yellow. The sketch pad is close enough that we can see the doodles on it, while the eyes from the inkwell and the liveliness of the pens are clearly visible. Even the hairs of the paintbrushes seem to be stirring. Some children may have seen on television the very old black-and-white cartoons in which characters come out of an inkwell just like this.

＊ The typical frame reappears on the right-hand page, around a scene of Simon and the pens. The "tail" of one pen trails behind and past the frame and the page. The other "tail" curls for Simon to shake, as he raises his arm up in a curve. On the right-hand page, a series of events are shown in unframed but colored vignettes.

＊ Drescher puts separate frames around the left-hand and the right-hand page pictures, with scribbles on the white paper outside. But the beast leaps over the frame from the left, and the curled tail of the pen runs across the gutter, tying the two pictures together. The beast emerges from darkness on the left. Simon climbs through the hole to yellow light on the right, providing an obvious contrast.

＊ Now the beast leaps from the dark hole across the two-page spread. One pen twists back to confront him, while the other is already off the page with Simon in hot pursuit. Drescher has scratched in just a shadow-like ground line. He has used colored pencil or chalk under the text for emphasis, otherwise the words might be missed.

＊ The frame around this two-page spread has become simple red and white, but it is jagged like the rocky hill. Around it, the paper is multicolored.

Drescher balances the text in the upper left with that of the lower right and places the hill just past the gutter, so it is almost centered but not broken by the gutter.

✳ No frame here, as beast and hill come down on the left-hand page, with the rolling Simon and pens. The ink spills to the upper right echo the same angle of the hill on the left-hand page. Contrasting with this unreality, we find green grass and a blue night sky, moon, and stars.

✳ Touches of white are all we need to see the beast. He emerges in the ink splashed on the left over the unframed purplish pink background that goes across to the right-hand page. There, below the text, in a Drescher frame, the pens twine around Simon, the upside-down inkwell, and the frame, on a dark green background.

✳ Now the background is dreary black, with text printed in white in the upper left and lower right again for balance. On the left-hand page, the heavy beast weighs down the frame on the upper left, as the other characters stare back from the lower right. On the right-hand page, the open-jawed monster, inside the frame now, comes toward Simon diagonally from the upper left as Simon recoils diagonally lower right.

✳ The background is still black, but it is spattered with other colors. The frame is irregular and multicolored as well. Although he has knocked Simon's shoes off, the beast is now coming horizontally across the gutter to kiss the still-apprehensive boy.

✳ The now friendly monster walks straight across the left-hand page, with the other characters comfortably resting on his back. His snout leads us across the gutter and into the frame on the right-hand page. There, within a smaller frame with text below, the beast and Simon can lie down together horizontally on the bed, with cover being drawn by the twining pens. The background is a soft, nonthreatening, shaded blue.

✳ Drescher moves the picture of the sleeping characters in bed onto the sketch pad, which he angles in from the left-hand page across the gutter. The background of the two pages is pale pink now, perhaps indicating dawn. The eyes of the ink bottle are now perfectly in keeping with its comparison to a hermit crab. The pens wriggle to the right and into the coffee can. The positions are a complete reversal of the yellow-background pages that are the third spread of the actual story.

✳ On the left-hand page is an echo of the first page of the story. The picture has no frame now and is almost all in the bright light of morning. Children will enjoy finding what Drescher has chosen to change, like the color of the bird, or the book titles, and will speculate why. On the right-hand page is Simon's book, the cover almost but not completely like the one on the book we are reading. Again we can speculate on the changes.

Children will certainly make comparisons between the monster in this book and those in Quentin Blake's and Pat Hutchins's (p. 64) books among others. Some will find Drescher's art more like the child-like pictures in Blake's. Comparisons with their own monster pictures, and some work by Paul Klee, may help children see the difference of skill involved.

BOOKS BY DRESCHER

Look-Alikes. New York: Lothrop, 1985.
Looking for Santa Claus. New York: Lothrop, 1984.
The Poems of A. Nonny Mouse selected by Jack Prelutsky, illustrated by Henrik Drescher. New York: Knopf, 1989.
Simon's Book. New York: Lothrop, 1983, Scholastic paper, 1987.
Whose Furry Nose? Australian Animals You'd Like to Meet. New York: Lippincott, 1987.
Whose Scaly Tail? African Animals You'd Like to Meet. New York: Lippincott, 1987.
The Yellow Umbrella. New York: Bradbury, 1987.

Hey, Al
by Arthur Yorinks,
illustrated by Richard Egielski

The characters and settings depicted by Richard Egielski are quite realistic. The outlined water color paintings give three-dimensional solidity, even to hair and eyebrows. But the situations are frequently a bit strange or fantastic. *Hey, Al,* like other texts on which he has collaborated with Arthur Yorinks, has a strange sense of unreality despite the realistic pictures and possibly real situations. One questions what children understand from them, but something seems to come through. Egielski's pictures certainly can be "read" without text because of his ability to make the characters appear alive and real, whatever the absurd situation.

✳ On the jacket cover, a natural-enough looking janitor mops a check-erboard floor toward a bucket on the lower right. The wainscoting behind him is marbelized; the wood of the decorative door frame has a real grain. But there is a sort of astonishment in his eyes, as there is in the face of his dog, who is looking back toward the left where a large assortment of bird-like creatures contemplates the worker. The birds flying overhead could be real but not the rest of the crew. Opening the dust jacket reveals that there are bigger and more incredible creatures spilling from the elevator on the back of the jacket onto the tile floor. The cover, taken as a whole, is one large picture framed in lines and a thin white border on a warm beige or tan background. Egielski has the bucket and some birds break the frame on the front. The colors of the hall, man, and dog are in drab contrast to the vivid colors of the birds, a juxtaposition that sets up the opposites of the story. The title is printed in bright red upper-case letters, edged in black, to be easily seen amid the action. The author and illustrator names are also apparent in black in the lower border. With all the figures in the scene, the strong verticals of doors and horizontals of walls and floor lend stability. Although most of the birds are looking at Al, a small group at the lower left on the back balance the others and, of course, Al when the jacket is opened out. Al and the bucket lead us into the book. The cloth cover under the dust jacket is the same rich blue as the bird close to Al.

✳ The pale tan of the front end papers assumes meaning as part of the opening of the story, especially in contrast with the back end papers.

✳ The half-title page is just the pail with mop and scrub brush; the mop handle points us into the story.

✳ On the left-hand page, Al marches in, whistling and looking straight ahead, mop handle still pointing in. Only a touch of shadow puts the figures on the ground; there is no setting. The dog looks up and back at the three blue birds that seem to follow the oblivious Al. On the right, the upper-case letters of the title now stand out in bright yellow, outlined in black and underlined, with all the other information in plain black below.

✳ Two more plain white pages with plain black letters seem really dull. Perhaps this is to reinforce the drabness of the early story, which is in such contrast to later events.

✳ The story begins on the white right-hand page with black printing, with only the letters "Al" echoing the title page color. On the left, the room is pictured in a sort of box placed on the white page. The box emphasizes the tiny, cramped space that Al and his dog Eddie share. Egielski does open the door out of the box on the left to allow Al to walk in. Kids note with amusement and interest details like the containers from a Chinese restaurant, the cracked ceiling, the missing parts and tilting frame of the bed. But mainly they need to see the drabness, the lack of color. Only the yellow of Al's jacket and the reds of Eddie's bowl and the hanging bathrobe add any brightness at all.

✳ Text again appears on a plain white page, while on the left, the box-like room really confines the confronting figures of Al and Eddie, both expressing feelings through body language. Only the doorknob on one side and the newspaper outside the other door relieve the lines of the box they are in.

✳ Into another realistic, drab, square box (the bathroom), intrudes a beautifully colored bird. Al is obviously astonished. Eddie listens outside the door. The robe hangs outside now, tying this scene to the bedroom we saw before. The realism of everything else, even the reflection in the mirror, makes the bird that much more unbelievable.

✳ Before we get tired of seeing the picture on the left and the words on the right, Egielski switches places. But the words are still confined on one side and the characters in the box on the other. Al now has the door open, suitcase half in and half out. The blue feather contrasts with the colorless bathroom, as Al's contemplative position contrasts with Eddie's eager searching.

✳ Out of the little boxes they go, into a much larger picture, spreading across two pages but still within a line frame and on the white background. The island breaks through the frame on the top, but the scene is still very pale and dream-like in contrast to the realism of Al, Eddie, and the falling suitcase, as well as the vivid colors of the bird carrying them.

✳ Another framed two-page spread brings them to a fanciful tropical paradise. Birds and wings and leaves break the frame here. Al's position is awkward and his expression is not happy, but Eddie seems glad. Other colors become more intense here.

✳ No words are needed on this two-page spread, as the vividly colorful, fanciful birds we first saw on the cover come into the frame to welcome the amazed Al and Eddie. The little stepladder for the penguin is a funny extra.

✳ A tree branch arches across the gutter so the large bird can sit across the center to talk to the blissful Al, who even has a drink in a coconut shell. The gentle curves of the rocks and waterfalls add to the peace of the scene. All the birds' attention is focused on Al. Even Eddie's leaps at the butterflies are in Al's direction.

✳ But suddenly, amid the still-vivid colors, the leaves seem too large and the fruit too ripe; the curves of the leaves seem menacing. All the birds have now turned their backs on the changing Al and Eddie. Despite the bizarre action, Egielski has included minute details like hair on Al's legs.

    ✳ Al, now with wings, flies up through the frame on the left, watched by some of the birds. The extent of the transformation of Al and Eddie is interesting and raises difficult questions of choice for children this age. Surprisingly, most children accept the fact that Al would rather mop floors and not be a bird, although some like to consider the possibility of his staying on to become a bird.

    ✳ This wonderful scene of city, ocean, flying feathers, and falling dog gains meaning if children know the story of Daedalus and Icarus, and/or have seen reproductions of the painting "The Fall of Icarus" by Pieter Bruegel. Eddie certainly looks like a goner here, plunging through the bottom of the frame as Al breaks through the upper right.

    ✳ Al crawls back into the drab box on the right-hand page, while the text returns to the left. Only the newspapers are on the outside left, showing that time has passed.

    ✳ A touchingly happy reunion scene takes place in the center of the box on the right, with the door, at least, opening out. Compare this with the earlier confrontation scene in the bedroom, to see how much emotion Egielski puts into the two figures in the same grim room.

    ✳ Sometimes people change and can change their lives. Eddie and Al look happily at each other. The shelves are clear, the newspapers have been put to good use, and the door remains open as Al, dressed in a shirt that recalls the dream island, begins to brighten the drab room with a bright yellow that is matched by the end papers, which contrast with those we saw at the beginning of the book.

Many people who admired the art of this book seriously questioned its appeal for children. Certainly youngsters cannot "get" the dry humor of the New York City vernacular or understand some of the deeper questions the book raises about the quality of life. But they are immediately involved with the characters and the story. As mentioned earlier, serious discussions about life on "bird island" versus life as a person emerged. Some children insisted that the journey was only a dream, despite the pile of newspapers. Others recalled the change from black and white to color in the film of *The Wizard of Oz* when Dorothy left Kansas, and said it was the same when Al and Eddie were on the island. So children can gain more from all of this book than I, for one, ever thought possible.

ART ACTIVITIES

Hey, Al, is a good stimulus to inspire pictures of jungles and exotic birds, using whatever media the children prefer. Other books discussed here that would also be useful include *Junglewalk* (p. 48) and *17 Kings and 42 Elephants* (p. 76) and those listed in their bibliographies. Some children might want to go to the library to find books with photographs of actual tropical birds and jungles.

BOOKS BY YORINKS AND EGIELSKI

Bravo, Minski. New York: Farrar, Straus, 1988.
Hey, Al. New York: Farrar, Straus, 1986.
It Happened in Pinsk. New York: Farrar, Straus, 1980.
Louis the Fish. New York: Farrar, 1989 (reissue).
Oh, Brother. New York: Farrar, Straus, 1989.
Ugh! New York: Farrar, Straus, 1990.

PICTURE BOOKS ILLUSTRATED BY EGIELSKI, WRITTEN BY OTHERS

Burgess, Gelett. *The Little Father.* New York: Farrar, Straus, 1985.
Conrad, Pam. *The Tub People.* New York: Harper, 1989.

The Very Worst Monster
by Pat Hutchins

Pat Hutchins is a storyteller as well as an artist. Her longer books tell complicated stories with many words as competently as her picture books with no words at all. Although she has worked in different styles, she tends to use clearly defined, bright areas of color and pattern for her mostly happy stories. Through all her work runs a strain of humor that is particularly evident in the two books about Hazel, *The Very Worst Monster* and *Where's the Baby?* Children always love to read about monsters, and Hazel and her family fulfill this desire in a satisfying, nonthreatening way.

✳ The cover sets the stage with a black frame where actual curtains are drawn to the sides. The black is repeated in the letters of the title, printed in heavy, elaborate serif type to balance the activity in the picture. With the sweep of the curtain from the left, the main characters swing to center stage. On the lower right, a group of suitably ugly monster characters are all made individuals. All look to the center. From the lower left, mother and father also look and point toward the central characters. The scene appears even more crowded because of Hutchins's use of patterns, which make it border on chaos. There are flowers, dots, and squares in a multitude of bright colors, painted in more or less opaque water colors, within outlines. On the back cover, framed in black on a plain white background, Hazel and her brother confront each other in a scene that will be repeated on the half-title page. Diagonals add to the tension.

✳ If your book has a dust jacket, Hazel looks in from the lower left of the flap.

✳ The red end papers pick up the red in her dress.

✳ The half-title page repeats the scene on the back cover. Here there is no frame, so the bottom of the page is the only ground line. Note how in the heavy type of the title, like that on the cover, the bone has pushed the *s* out of line.

✳ On the two pages of the title spread, the typical baby-walking scene is different because the characters are monsters. Hutchins has added trees, leaves, rocks, and ground for a setting, but their colors are muted, so as not to distract from the important characters. The right-hand page focuses on the baby in the carriage, but father does look toward the left-hand page, so we don't pass it by. There on the left grandma and grandpa are leading Hazel, whose feet are pointing in the opposite direction.

✳ On the cataloging information page sits the apprehensive little brother, squeezing down a line of the type, apple on head. On the facing page by the dedication stands Hazel, with bow and arrows in hand and impish look on face. The reader doesn't have to know the William Tell story to appreciate these pages, but it helps.

✳ The actual story finally begins with the birth of Billy. Note how Hutchins has filled the left-hand page, spilling onto the right, with a multiplicity of colors, patterns, and details. We may have a cave-like ceiling, but we also have an ordinary hairbrush, slippers, and even a rose in the window. We also have monsters, but they are humanoid and not frightening, dressed in suits and pinafores. Hutchins makes the baby the focus of attention on the left, setting Hazel by herself on the right. The rocky wall and floor, and the curving bannister, frame off the words.

＊ Again the baby is the focus on the left, with Hazel even further away on the right. The curtain on the right makes even more of a frame for both the words and Hazel's action.

＊ The group on the left spreads out a bit, while Hazel glares on the right. The words here, as on the other pages, can be seen as planned for and carefully placed as part of the design of the two pages.

＊ Now all eyes and gestures are turned on the swinging baby, and none on Hazel. From the far left enters a new character, toward whom the baby swings.

＊ Now Hutchins switches the scene, and the placement of the words, before we tire of it. The focus now is on the treed postman. By her position, Hazel gets our attention on the right, if not that of the characters. Hutchins has a chance here to have fun inventing the architecture of a monster's house as well as some unique plants.

＊ A parade of benignly ugly monsters marches across the pages to another interesting building. Hazel seems as solid on the left as the rocks on the right. Obviously from her stance, she does not wish to join the others.

＊ The next two pages are grounded across the bottom by the crowd of creatures, colors, and details. Hazel anchors the left again, finger pointed up. Above the judging platform, Hutchins has left out background to bring into focus the action of the struggling judge and the two belligerent babies.

＊ On the left, the babies and judge make a shape reminiscent of the winners in the Olympics, while the crowd, glum Hazel above them, is clumped across the bottom on the right, with a pointed umbrella and father's raised arms breaking out.

＊ Off goes Hazel on the left, as she did on the flap of the dust jacket, while all attention is on the baby on the right.

＊ Hutchins frames the picture on the left with her imaginary vegetation, all leading to Billy at the center, while Hazel walks right out of the picture. On the right, the expressions of both Hazel and Billy clearly depict their feelings.

＊ Two more pages give us pseudo-monsters and Hazel in action, but in a composition different from that of the previous two pages.

＊ Now we are back in the house, with the photo and prize cup from the contest on display. This time Hazel is on the carpet, finally the center of the stage. Sharp eyes will have already spotted Billy now moved to the right-hand page.

＊ All eyes and bodies turn toward Billy in delight.

＊ The last page is almost exactly like the scene on the cover, with the absence of the audience, and set inside the house. The slight differences, such as the position of the children's eyes, are interesting to think about. Hutchins deliberately did two different pictures for two different places and purposes.

RELATED ACTIVITIES

Monster books abound in the library, fulfilling children's interest. Just check the subject file. After looking at some other artists' ideas, children can draw their own monster. They should also try to imagine what kind of a house their monster might live in.

BOOKS BY HUTCHINS

The Doorbell Rang. New York: Greenwillow, 1985, Morrow/Mulberry paper, 1988.
Tidy Titch. New York: Greenwillow, 1991.
Titch. New York: Macmillan, 1971.
The Very Worst Monster. New York: Greenwillow, 1985, Morrow/Mulberry paper, 1988.
Where's the Baby? (sequel), New York: Greenwillow, 1988.
You'll Soon Grow into Them, Titch. New York: Greenwillow, 1983, Penguin paper, 1985.

BOOKS WITH NEW BABIES AND SIBLINGS

Cole, Joanna. *The New Baby at Your House* photographs by Hella Hamid. New York: Morrow, 1985.
Henkes, Kevin. *Sheila Rae, the Brave.* New York: Greenwillow, 1987.
McCully, Emily. *The New Baby.* New York: Harper, 1988.
Szekeres, Cyndy. *The New Baby.* New York: Golden/Western, 1989.

The Day the Goose Got Loose

by Reeve Lindbergh,
illustrated by Steven Kellogg

The lighthearted joy of Steven Kellogg's art has delighted children for well over a decade. Whether he illustrates other people's words or tells the story himself, Kellogg uses the tale only as a minimal frame on which to build so much more with his pen or pencil and paint for the reader to enjoy. There is always humor in the exaggerated gestures and expressions of his characters, human or animal, and in the wild, crazy, and unexpected events that keep happening to them. Above all, Kellogg's work is characterized by its detail and complexity; the overwhelming volume of things to look at in the foreground and background as well as the center; and the vigorous strength of his line, and his bright colors, which match the humor and cheer of his stories. Children really love rereading his books, becoming friends with his characters like Pinkerton and Jimmy's boa.

✴ Reeve Lindbergh's verse is fun for children to listen to, and to chime in with the chorus of "The day the goose got loose." It can be read aloud the first time through while the children form their own mental pictures of the events. Then it's time to let them see what Kellogg has done with it.

The title and author have their own black-outlined gold frame, with the title, in the red of the sun on the jacket, in lower-case letters like part of the refrain. The author and illustrator information is printed in the gold of the frame and of the sunlight. The girl protagonist peers anxiously over the top of the frame, sun arching behind her, as she watches the action spilling over in front of and below the frame. A powerful-looking, angry bull confronts the happy-looking goose, who is flying toward him. The bull's tail curls up, end also flying, as a cow and a calf look out from behind the title frame. Two equally active chickens are on the other side of the bull. A stable, horizontal fence with vertical posts gives stability to the foreground, with a matching fence along the top behind the frame. The colors of these characters are all quite realistic. The blue fence and the greenery are all touched with the orange glow of the sun. The back of the jacket uses solid orange for background. A frame similar to that around the title surrounds the goose, in a quieter but still happy mood, contemplating a goose-portrait in a much more elaborate frame. The black of the wall background matches the black in the title frame. This cover is about as full of action as it could be.

 ✳ Dark blue end papers take us back into night from the light on the jacket.

 ✳ The title page repeats the frame from the cover, with publisher information added in white. An additional frame of black and gold surrounds the upper and lower pictures on a white background or frame. In the upper frame, the fading moon has taken the place of the sun from the cover. Through the starlit but paling night sky, geese are flying right out of the frame. In the lower picture, the goose of the title is confined in a cage, touched by the glow of the rising sun and not at all happy.

 ✳ The full panorama of the farm setting spreads across the two pages, with space for copyright and dedication. The geese continue to fly through the horizontal, fading night sky across the top. The horizon crosses at the center, all diffused with gold and orange. A fence meanders across the spread, while a road curves up from the active goose in the cage on the lower left toward the house and barn on the right. Trees on the left balance the buildings, while horses gallop in between. Across from the goose, the girl pauses from her bird-watching to look back at the probably squawking goose. This is a peaceful scene for Kellogg, with less activity than usual, to start the day and the story. The sunrise color touches everything; it is even reflected in the pond.

 ✳ A small, square picture on white on the left-hand page begins the story proper with the goose letting itself out. Kellogg breaks the frame as usual, with the wings, the sleeping bird, even the branch the red bird is sitting on. Action really starts in the larger frame with text on the right-hand side. Still in the sunrise glow, the goose bursts through the door as both birds fly out of the frame, the girl's binoculars fall out, and the frog who was sleeping in the previous picture leaps out of the lower left.

 ✳ Kellogg will vary his page format throughout the book to achieve the pacing and effect he wants. Here and for the next few spreads, he puts two broken-frame horizontal scenes on one side and a single large frame on the other, with events portrayed in time sequence. The color range stays the same here as feathers fly, chicks and other things break the frames, and action continues. We can tell how the chicks and hens feel from the way Kellogg portrays them, for example, the tears and despair of the chicks on the right.

* Chickens contemplate the first scenes from the outside. The two pictures on the left-hand side are quieter—an arc across the top scene, horizontal fences in both, sheep evenly spread across the bottom with the goose centered, wings raised. On the right-hand page, the happy goose meets the uncertain ram head-on, with the sunlit house in the background, setting up the action to come.

* The pace quickens with the diagonals in the pictures and the increased activity of the goose, building to the typical Kellogg chaos on the right-hand page, with everything spilling or breaking out all over. Children love studying the details of this picture as they enjoy the fun.

* Again the swirling and diagonal shapes increase the pace. Tails and hooves break out of the frame on the left-hand page, while the action on the right leads to the destruction of the bathroom in the lower picture.

* Another confrontation, with tension rather than action, is watched from outside the frame by a group of chickens on the left-hand page. Children will note, if they are close enough, the ram still chasing somebody, while the girl is still watching the story unfold. On the right, diagonal boards flying along with chickens and feathers give us another chaotic Kellogg happening.

* The goose seems delighted amid the tipping statue, flying trash, and startled policemen. So as the golden dawn breaks on the right-hand side, the fence leads us to the returning herd, watched by the animals. Make sure everyone sees the horse kick father right out of the bathroom. Meanwhile, the goose runs across the barn floor.

* Now it's the goose, coming into the frame of the boards of the barn, who watches the crowd scene, angry father, watching horse, and birds flying. On the right-hand page, the point of view changes, as we get a close-up of father, police, and others, with the goose watching top left; the birds now fly toward us.

* The sun is up; the cats, chickens, and bull watch the goose go off under the sun by the fence, as all the others focus on mother and her picture, the same one the goose was admiring on the back of the jacket. The porch pillar and boards of the barn are strong verticals around the central figure of mother. The bull's tail even arches and points to her. On the right-hand page, the goose hides in the left foreground, behind rocks but still pointed at by the fence and posts, while the girl in the center watches mother search and call. It's full daylight now, so we can see that the leaves are turning to autumn colors.

* In the series of three pictures on this spread, the colors go from daytime to approaching sunset. In the top left-hand picture, the autumn leaves and the wild geese are both flying. In the bottom left-hand picture, as the shadows lengthen, the fence posts rise up the hill, and the boy runs toward the goose on top. The geese fly far above the tiny house and barn. On the right-hand page, the geese fly in a V from the sun right out of the frame, as boy and goose extend arms and wings in matching V's of salute.

* As night and its shadows move in on these next pages, Kellogg still touches the pictures with golden luminescence from setting sun and fire-light. The boy brings the goose back home in the top left picture. We go inside for a cozy, quiet storytime with grandmother in the lower picture, as the cats aim for the stairs. On the right-hand page, although the girl and grandmother are hugging, the dog is asleep, and the clock and wall give us stable verticals, Kellogg still has one cat and the boy race up the stairs for some action.

* On the left-hand page, the goose leaning in the window seems to evolve and dissolve into the dream goose curled around the cozily tucked-in girl and teddy bear. Kellogg here takes us across the gutter, breaking out of the frame to the first completely full-spread illustration. And what a dazzler it is, as girl and teddy bear float through the window and past stars in the night-blue sky up toward the moon, while the goose flies right toward us, throwing his shadow on the moon.

* Kellogg takes us back to the realistic house, partially framed but far below us now, as the swirls and patterns of light and stars flow from the dark window, taking the girl and teddy with them. Again all overflows to cover most of the pages. Multiple images of geese flying here and there are superimposed on each other, including the one carrying the excited girl and her bear on the upper right.

* The goose flies them to a dreamland that fills the two-page spread completely. Around the mountain rising from the lake in the center, Kellogg has filled both sides with a sort of wonderland that includes characters from many of his other books. Children have great fun spotting the ones they know. For example, Pinkerton, the dog from *Pinkerton, Behave* and other books, sits in the boat at the lower left, while the sea serpent from *Ralph's Secret Weapon* rises from the lake on the right. The geese fly on above this magic dream kingdom.

* The story ends with a small and, for Kellogg, quiet picture. Girl and bear are snug in bed, wing of the goose (real or dream?) protectively around them, as the curtain flutters over onto the goose, and the moon shines through the window.

Exploring the work of Kellogg can involve just his re-creations of legendary characters like *Paul Bunyan* or *Pecos Bill*, or the series about

Pinkerton, or his alphabet books. Teachers have spent weeks on his work without the children tiring of his deft art and wonderful sense of humor.

SOME OF KELLOGG'S RECENT BOOKS

Aster Aardvark's Alphabet Adventures. New York: Morrow, 1987.
Best Friends. New York: Doubleday, 1990.
Chicken Little. New York: Morrow, 1985.
Jack and the Beanstalk. New York: Morrow, 1991.
Jimmy's Boa and the Big Splash Birthday Bash. New York: Dial, 1989.
Jimmy's Boa Bounces Back. New York: Dial, 1984.
Johnny Appleseed. New York: Morrow, 1988.
Paul Bunyan. New York: Morrow, 1984, paper, 1988.
Pecos Bill. New York: Morrow, 1986.
Pinkerton, Behave. New York: Doubleday, 1990 (reissue).
Prehistoric Pinkerton. New York: Dial, 1987.
Ralph's Secret Weapon. New York: Dial, 1983.

RELATED ACTIVITIES

Teachers report Kellogg inspires children to try to copy his characters and active pictures. I think they should just read and enjoy him, and copy if they will. Children who enjoy writing stories have been inspired to produce additional adventures of Pinkerton, or of Jimmy's boa. They have even made their own alphabet adventures with another character like Aster Aardvark. They or their classmates then can illustrate these in Kellogg's style.

I Want a Dog
by Dayal Kaur Khalsa

Before her recent death, Dayal Khalsa had produced a series of books that were unique in both their stories and their style of illustration. Several, like *How Pizza Came to Queen's* and *My Family Vacation,* seem to come directly out of her own childhood, while others, like *Julian,* are less specific. All her books seem to strike a responding chord in the children who read them. Her pictures have a simplicity that suggests folk art or an unschooled technique, but her perspective is sophisticated and her anatomy correct. She applies her opaque gouache or acrylic paint in flat areas, with just a hint of shading to round some of her figures. Her books are usually recognizable immediately by the style of her illustrations.

✳ The cover of *I Want a Dog* combines the setting and figure placement of Georges Seurat's painting "Sunday Afternoon on the Island of Grande Jatte," which is known to most adults but few children, with Khalsa's unique style and "doggy" subject. One doesn't need to know the painting to feel the serenity of the scene; the composition with its horizontals, soft curve of trees, and carefully placed verticals gives us this peace. For the pointillist dots of color that Seurat used, Khalsa has substituted her own style of flat areas of opaque paint. It takes a moment to notice the number of dogs in the picture, even a poodle on the woman's skirt, and the skates, which are almost at the center. The girl in the small framed picture on the back cover, one which is repeated inside the book, is working on a skate with shoe polish. This shows us, if we haven't noticed, that skates are also important in this story. Khalsa uses a lot of greens and some red on the cover, which suggest a happy rather than sad story. The letters of title and author information are framed off and backed with a different color, so they really stand out. The author is printed in simple black upper-case letters, but the title is in large blocks of red, with triangles on the *A*'s and *T*.

✳ The end papers pick up the yellow color behind the title and author.

✳ On the title page, the yellow title, as on the cover, emphasizes the "want," as do the dogs themselves. The clearly recognizable breeds are lined up in a straight, horizontal line by size along the regular verticals of the picket fence. The skate, pointed in the opposite direction, laces hanging loose, trails incongruously behind. The rest of the information is simply printed in black, matching the line that frames it all.

✳ We plunge immediately into the story. There are a lot of words here, but they are carefully framed off from the pictures, which still dominate each page. The capital letter that begins the text on each page is in the same style as the title, framed by itself and backed with the same yellow color as on the cover. On the left-hand page, we meet May, amid her pictures of dogs. Khalsa's use of color is clear here, as is her simplification. The shoes, clown, and stripes are clearly defined, but May's face is essentially two dots and two lines. On the right-hand page is a busy street, with stores, people, and of course, dogs. The cars add a vintage feeling that is in many of Khalsa's books. It doesn't seem to affect the children who read and look at her work; her stories have a universal quality.

＊ The schoolroom is entirely "peopled" with dogs by May. In every other way it is a typical classroom, even to the bulletin board. This is a favorite scene with children, who find the incongruity very funny. The picture on the right gives Khalsa a chance to paint a realistic suburban yard, with actual bricks on the houses and grass on the lawn. The sky has unusual clouds, however. They and the tree have a texture with the paper showing through that suggests the use of pastels or chalk for the original art. But in contrast with the details of the specific breeds of the dogs, May is painted with very little detail, except for her shoes. Khalsa picks what she puts in and leaves out very deliberately.

＊ Before we are tired of the text along the bottom, it moves to the side again for a picture focusing on May and a particular puppy at the pet shop. On the right-hand page, we have only mother's body, with not even fingers indicated, but the hands on hips convey her feelings. Khalsa centers the puppy again here, but adds the kitchen details, the birthday cake, and even the crossword puzzle with pencil pointing in.

＊ Back go May and the puppy, with the text now moved to the other side. Even through the window of the car we can see more dogs, and also the picket fence from the title page. On the right-hand side, mother and father focus on May, whose body language shows her angry determination. The details of the Faulkner book and the *New York Times* surely are placed there for adults to enjoy; they could easily be omitted and just shapes placed there for design purposes. Mother and father's body language is also shown by Khalsa with minimal detail.

＊ The next two-page spread is very different in design. The words still move along in the two boxes at the bottoms of the pages. But the small pictures go unframed across the top, with white space left for a blank at the upper left and all across the middle. They reflect and extend what the words say, using different dogs and different times and places. Do you find this size and arrangement effective?

＊ Back in May's room, this picture has a different focus. Khalsa uses diagonals to help depict the chaos caused by May's anger. On the right, the perfect balance and perspective of the staircase really focus on the skate, standing out clearly on the bright blue carpet, and leading to May's bright idea.

＊ Khalsa uses her first two-page spread to involve the reader in the intricacy of May's training course. The words remain in their boxes at the bottom. But the picture spreads with the carpet across the gutter. Khalsa has again put book titles in for the adult reader. Also note the art works on the wall. Some children may notice and recognize the Gilbert Stuart portrait of

George Washington. But how many will "get" the van Gogh on the left, or the Hokusai on the right? The lamps and the washing machine again are notes from another era for the observing to notice. Kids can just note and enjoy the details of the walkway, the Ping-Pong table, and the fish tank.

＊ Two pictures show May's first outside venture with her skate/dog. Realistic scenes of the outdoors and the playground balance across the page, with the diagonal tree branch on the left balancing that of the slide and swings on the right. May pulls the skate one way on the left-hand side, and the other on the right. Khalsa applies her opaque gouache or acrylic color very deliberately, unlike the wash of water color, over large areas like the trees and playground. But she also uses it for tiny details like the shoes, skate, and spotted dog. She also continues to favor green.

＊ The design changes again, avoiding monotony. On the left-hand page we have a positive indication that this is long ago from the details of the luncheonette, especially the prices. Some children may understand that this action is not happening now, but it really doesn't matter for the story. There is a lot to see in this picture, but the central focus is on the tiny skate tied outside, beyond the "No dogs" sign, and on the dog beside it. Back in the green kitchen, May is happily occupied. The scene is all horizontals, even May's legs and arms, and she's happy.

＊ Two more horizontal pictures take May through autumn and winter. The "trick or treating" picture centers the wonderfully costumed children, but adds the frame of the door and the witch on one side, with the patterned wallpaper and different-patterned rug as additional frames. The witch is balanced with the chair and the delicious details of the little packages of M & M's. This rather static picture contrasts with the activity amid the falling snow on the right-hand page. Many details, such as the store signs, snow shovels, and bags of rock salt, make this scene seem very real.

＊ We move on to summer and an active but still horizontal and peaceful double-page spread for the grand finale. The text here is minimal; the picture tells us more. That Khalsa shows us a multicultural neighborhood is an additional plus to the smiles all those skate/dogs always evoke.

＊ The publication and cataloging information is tucked in on the last page, in the black line frame. If you try to picture all this anywhere in the front, you can see why it is here. It would spoil the layout of the first pages and is not intrusive here.

RELATED ACTIVITIES

It is fun to compare May with another insistent girl, from Tony Ross's *I Want a Cat* (Farrar, Straus, 1989).

Photographs in books about breeds of dogs from the 636's in the library might be helpful to those children who want to identify what Khalsa has painted. A mini art lesson could be based on the famous pictures on the wall above the walkway in the basement.

BOOKS BY KHALSA

Cowboy Dreams. New York: McKay, 1990.
How Pizza Came to Queens. New York: Crown, 1989.
I Want a Dog. New York: Crown, 1987.
Julian. New York: Crown, 1989.
My Family Vacation. New York: Crown, 1988.
Sleepers. New York: Crown, 1988.
Tales of a Gambling Grandma. New York: Crown, 1986.

17 Kings and 42 Elephants
by Margaret Mahy,
pictures by Patricia MacCarthy

Patricia MacCarthy has illustrated posters and greeting cards as well as books. Her use of the difficult art of batik gives her illustrations a unique quality. In the batik process, the brilliant, saturated color is framed with the white of the silk that is wax-coated and left uncolored after the dyeing. The nature of the application of the wax and color leads to curvilinear designs rather than straight lines with corners, and to mainly flat areas of color rather than shading and modelling of forms.

✳ Some of the kings and elephants of the title appear to march from the upper left rear of the back cover across and behind the spine to the foreground on the front of the cover. The kings seem happy, even exuberant in stance and expression, as cheerful as the bright colors they are painted.

The clothes, crowns, and faces make them all different individuals. The black letters and numbers of the title have an unusual shape, with the *g* and *h* reminiscent of Arabic writing. The author's name stands out in bright red, while the illustrator's is printed in modest black.

✳ Brilliant green end papers echo the greens on the cover.

✳ Black print is used for all the information on these two pages, except for the repeated red for the author. Across the page near the bottom march the kings and elephants again, this time in a straight line, all riding sedately, with the angles of their umbrellas making a jaunty addition.

✳ Mahy's text is carefully placed in the open ground space designed for it. This text is worthy of being read through without interruption, while the listeners make their own mental pictures and enjoy the word play. It has a lilt and rhythm that stands repeating, with children joining in. But it is the pictures we will attend to now. MacCarthy shows a wet, wild night with puddles and slanting rain. Still the elephants march across the two-page spread like those on an Eastern temple frieze, while the bright colors keep the rain and night from seeming depressing.

✳ The kings have dismounted and appear above the bank where the crocodiles crawl, above the water that runs across the bottom of this two-page spread. The green of the crocodiles echoes the grass, whose jagged edges match the crocodiles' teeth. But again, the bright colors, as well as the smiling kings, lift this above any hint of menace; the crocodiles are "romping" after all. The white outlines left from the batik process here make the animals stand out almost as if they are cut from paper.

✳ Here come the elephants and kings again, across the two pages, spread in a composition much like the cover. Just a few puddles and blades of grass, and a dark blue sky, are all that is needed to make the simple setting believable here.

✳ On this two-page spread hippos, back and front, are simplified but anatomically correct. Again only a few puddles and grass clumps make the ground, but there are trees, birds, and foliage enough for a believable jungle behind the hippos, against the dark blue sky.

✳ Now the elephants are coming right toward us across the spread, with all seventeen kings singing "loud and happily." The elephants seem to sway to the rhythm as their trunks and tusks curl.

✳ MacCarthy has created startlingly real tigers here. The large one on the right-hand page looks right out at us, while the others across the two pages sit or stand quietly, or lap the water. The pattern of the tigers and their placement on the pages in the scene of land, water, flowers, and tree trunks all make an interesting and involving composition. The colors, shades of brown and tan against the blue and green of water and grass, are also very effective. Compare the land and water areas, and note the placement of the greenery.

✳ The golden tan and touches of brown carry over to this two-page spread, but the pages are dominated by the dazzling blues and greens of the peacocks. These blues and greens carry across the tops of the pages. The curves of all the different birds' bodies and necks are repeated in their eyes and the circles of the peacocks' fans. The feathers of the bird on the left lead the eye to the spread tail that is the focus of this stunning picture.

✳ The blue here pales to form, along with the greenery, a backdrop or frame for the ballet-like formation of rosy pink flamingos. MacCarthy has arranged the necks, bodies, and wings to make a balanced, but still interesting, composition.

✳ The jolly kings and a touch of elephants reappear at the lower right of this two-page spread so we don't forget they are out there watching with us. But this scene, with the continuing pale blue and intense green, is dominated by the imaginative and colorful birds with patterned wings, flying or perched in the trees. The kings and elephants share their colors.

✳ The kings continue their journey across the two pages, over the yellow-tan ground, with the greenery and a deeper blue sky again behind them. The black "gorillicans" anchor the lower left, large but smiling rather than menacing. The "baboonsters" are arranged on a horizontal branch, with the loop of vine adding to the composition. The baboon swinging or reaching on the left-hand page adds action, as does the upside-down one on the right.

✳ The kings become the focus again on the yellow-tan ground against the pale blue sky. Their anatomy makes their lively dance look real, as they form an abstract pattern of shape and color to match the "bibble-bubble-babble" of the verse.

✳ The colors darken with the "heavy night." There remain only touches of bright color amid the landscape and the gray rears of the elephants. The restful composition also matches the quieter pace of the words. The parade is over.

COMPARISONS

Other jungle scenes, such as those in Nancy Tafuri's *Junglewalk* (p. 48) will surely come to mind to compare with these. The different character that the batik process gives will be evident in the comparison with other techniques. The rain here is also interesting to compare with that in Peter Spier's *Rain* (New York: Doubleday, 1982).

A trip to the library should yield photographs of temple processions with elephants, carved on the walls of temples in India, Indonesia, or Cambodia. Try the travel guides. It is interesting to compare these processions with MacCarthy's depictions.

Another illustrator who has used batik for illustration is Yoshi. *Butterfly Hunt* (Picture Book Studio, 1990) is a stunning book, and a comparison of the illustrations should prove interesting.

ART ACTIVITY

Batik is much too difficult for young children in groups, because it requires the use of hot wax as well as many other steps. But a teacher can demonstrate, and perhaps let children try, a simple procedure that shows how the batik artist works.

Using a small piece of white cloth, or porous paper, make a solid shape or design with a white crayon on both sides. Then dip the cloth or paper into a small bowl of water and food coloring. Let the cloth or paper dry. Then scrape off the crayon. It is easy to see how the crayon kept the paper or cloth from picking up the dye.

If you want to color the design itself, you should use cloth (not paper), and you must really remove all the crayon. If you want the colored area to stay the same color, you must coat that with the crayon before dyeing the rest, or it will pick up the new color on top of the old.

BOOKS BY MacCARTHY

Animals Galore. New York: Dial, 1989.
Herds of Words. New York: Dial, 1991.
Ocean Parade. New York: Dial, 1990.
Mahy, Margaret. *17 Kings and 42 Elephants.* New York: Dial, 1987.

No Such Things
by Bill Peet

Children are attracted immediately to the wonderful creatures Bill Peet puts on the covers of his books, like *Jethro and Joel Were a Troll* and *The Kweeks of Kookatumdee.* They enjoy listening to his stories in prose or verse, smiling at the predicaments of the characters. His art is similar in many ways to the color comics, with a black, sketchy outline, filled in with color that may or may not be natural, and the use of the white background of the page. Years of drawing have given him the ability to draw, convincingly, imaginary or real creatures with humorous exaggeration.

＊ On the jacket cover of *No Such Things,* two fandangos from the text inside are set against a background made up of the black ink outline, filled in with chalk or pastels in similar shades of green. A textured paper gives roughness to the greenery. The colors of the animals are as absurd as their exaggerated smirks. Shadows and reflections in the water add realism to the otherwise fantastic scene. The fandangos are horse-like, but different. The yellow of the simple upper-case letters of the title is the same as that of the fandango on the right. The author's name is in equally simple black upper- and lower-case letters. The back of the paperback edition shows a character from another Peet book, framed in an oval frame. It is an engine with personality, even with a sort of eyes and nose, typical of what Peet can do to enliven even inanimate objects. Under the paper jacket of the hard cover edition, the cloth cover has the fandangos incised in outline.

＊ Unfortunately, the paperback edition is lacking the bright yellow end papers of the hard cover, which match the title.

＊ The title on the title page is in the same upper case as the jacket, but in blue this time, almost rising from the water. The author's name is the same as it was on the jacket. Peet has not stopped the water abruptly to make space for the title, but has gradually let it fade away. There is still a cartoon feel to the picture, but there is also a mock menace. The fish looks apprehensive, as the reefs seem to reach for him with clutching fingers. The rocks at the bottom seem to have eyes. The touches of yellow, green, and red brighten the more somber blue. The "fingers" reach diagonally right, as the fish swims right, into the book.

* The plain black print on white of the copyright and dedication pages gives the eyes a rest.

* We begin the lilting, rhyming discussion of a series of imaginary "things," with plays on words that may need some clarification, but certainly don't require it. The twumps are first. Against the white background, Peet gives us only butterflies and a grasshopper for atmosphere, while the baby twumps stand on the weeds on the mother, and she stands on some that look the same. Peet creates the characters with just eyes, nose, mouth, and expression.

* Across the two-page spread, the greenery on the bottom of the lake fades into the white space saved for the text. Peet has placed his glubzunks to balance the composition. The touches of red in their eyes add interest. Several frogs are merely sketched in black, but are obviously in motion. The only frog fully drawn is on the left-hand page. Small as he is, we can see his expression and body position clearly.

* Bright reds, oranges, and yellows contrast strongly with the blues and greens of the previous pages. Peet spreads the tree branches across the two pages with only the white of the page for background; yet we accept this as a tree branch against the sky. The pazeeks have many bird-like characteristics, but they still are absurdly funny. With very little detail, Peet manages to convey the delight of the larger ones on the left and the glum patience of the smaller on the right.

* The mopwoggins are ludicrous but still believable. With a minimum of color and line, and a few rocks, Peet gives us a landscape as well.

* Again a minimal landscape and a white-paper sky are background for a two-page picture of strange creatures, with text across the bottom. Using just eyes and mouth lines, Peet shows us flumpers who are rolling happily along, as well as those who are dismayed at going flat.

* Across these two pages, the cattails on either side lean toward the dragonflies. The juggarums are a particularly clever blend of jug and frog. The log is reminiscent of the glubzunks, as it anchors and balances the left-hand page against the rocks on the right. Shading gives three dimensions to the characters and the rocks, making this scene obviously more than a cartoon. The cobweb on the left is a nice touch of realism.

* Peet is playing with bright colors here as well as the words "flying into a tizzy." He can make the birds' faces show blankness or terror. A few dragonflies have flown in from the previous page, just for fun.

* A static, two-page spread works for static animals. Peet's drawings of their sad expressions make them convincing.

✳ Under the sea again, we meet a nonthreatening reef this time. Peet has fun with the twists and loops of the gullagaloops, as well as their faces.

✳ The fandangos really look snooty. Peet has colored them in wild and wonderful color combinations, then balanced them across the two pages, with water across the bottom, and greenery above, below, and around them.

✳ Now Peet gives us the terror and danger hinted at on the title page, with the grabnabbits. The colors are wild, and the fish really seem frightened.

✳ The white page is now used for snow, and the green of the trees goes across the top, as the snoof walks off to the right, fooling the hunters on the left. Peet has hunters walking down diagonally, while the tree on the lower left leans toward where they are walking. Some other tree trunks lean, or split, making the picture more interesting.

✳ These creatures really look absurd, not only because of their tiny heads, but their enormous feet as well. Peet balances the angles of the necks, and the simple landscape, across the two pages. The textured but drab magawks stand out against the pointed, textured, red and yellow mountains in the background.

✳ We have action and diagonals as contrast, with the white page as snow again. The trees are verticals and frame both pages, but the paths and mountain peaks, as well as the sky, are all in motion.

✳ Finally, the flumox fools the little fish in a fitting finale.

This is, of course, not a story, but a collection of related episodes in verse. It is also a sampler of Peet's art and humor.

ART AND IMAGINATION ACTIVITY

Designing imaginary animals, with names and related behavior, is a good mental exercise. Children can use textured paper and crayon to have their pictures look more like Bill Peet's.

If the children's drawing ability allows, they can draw the creatures by themselves, or a group can design and draw one. For younger children or less apt artists, outline heads, bodies, legs, or whatever can be copied and cut out, for the children to paste together and decorate to make their own animal. For an easy beginning, they could just try different or more elaborate designs on cut-out blank fandangos.

To start imaginations working, try giving students odd words like "pizzicato," "skinflint," or "gavotte," and asking them to picture creatures with these names and give them habits and habitats, in words or pictures.

BOOKS BY PEET

Big Bad Bruce. Boston: Houghton Mifflin paper, 1982.
The Caboose Who Got Loose. Boston: Houghton Mifflin paper, 1987.
Jethro and Joel Were a Troll. Boston: Houghton Mifflin, 1987.
The Kweeks of Kookatumdee. Boston: Houghton Mifflin, 1985, Sandpiper paper, 1988.
No Such Things. Boston: Houghton Mifflin paper, 1983.
Pamela Camel. Boston: Houghton Mifflin, 1984, Sandpiper paper, 1986.
Zella, Zack and Zodiac. Boston: Houghton Mifflin, 1985.

Children may also enjoy hearing parts of Peet's autobiography, *Bill Peet* (Houghton Mifflin, 1989) and seeing the illustrations; they also enjoy his older books, if you can find them.

Tooth-Gnasher Superflash
by Daniel Pinkwater

Daniel Pinkwater is perhaps better known for his zany word humor than his illustration, although some of his funniest stories, which he has told on the National Public Radio program, "All Things Considered," are about the days when he studied art. His chapter books involve strange characters who have adventures in and out of this world. Some of his picture books take place in normal locations like Alaska (*Aunt Lulu*), or Hoboken, New Jersey (*The Hoboken Chicken Emergency,* Prentice-Hall, 1977), with real people like Aunt Lulu the librarian or even Mozart (in *The Muffin Fiend,* Lothrop, 1986). But others leave the earth far behind (*Guys from Space*). Recently, Pinkwater has done some interesting experiments with computer-generated illustration. But otherwise, his pictures display the same arbitrary eccentricity as his stories. He likes to outline with a black felt-tipped marker and fill in with color, just like a kid. For this reason, kids like his work and try to copy it.

＊ *Tooth-Gnasher Superflash* is a hit with kids from the moment they hear the silly title. The front of the dust jacket displays the title in fancy white lettering with red and green circles, like traffic lights, inside the *O*'s. The author's name is in ordinary upper- and lower-case letters, in a mustard yellow that reappears as background on the title page of the 1981 edition. The background color of the jacket is a rich, royal blue. A rectangular picture under the title information shows us the Superflash, in a lighter blue, coming down a dark red road, with a yellow strip down the left and a chartreuse green one almost down the middle. There is white along either side, making the colors really stand out. The diagonals make the car really come at us. It's a car, we know, but a very stylized one. Its grille looks like pointed teeth, a "tooth-gnasher," of course. Two circular lines indicate headlights. A circular bubble atop the car reveals the family we will meet inside, all sketched with quick, black outline strokes of what appears to be a felt-tipped marker, and then colored in. Dots and lines make eyes, nose, mouth, and hair. It's minimal, but it works. On the back of the jacket is a black-and-white photograph of Pinkwater and a "friend," a typical silly note. The cloth cover is blue and yellow to match the colors on the jacket.

✳ White end papers neither add nor detract.

✳ The title uses the blue from the jacket and cover for the necessary words. The lettering of the title is the same as on the jacket, with the red and green *O*'s.

✳ More white paper is background for the copyright, dedication, etc., printed in plain black. Pinkwater uses the white paper as background all the way through the book.

✳ The text on the first and all subsequent pages is printed simply on the left-hand pages, leaving the action on the right. Above a broken-fendered green car (the old Thunderclap-Eight), which is in an outlined light green circle in front of an outlined orange line, floats an otherwise dignified-looking gentleman who, we are told, is called Mr. Popsnorkle. He can't miss getting a laugh with a name like that. Why he is horizontally above the car, arms stiff at sides and tie neatly inside jacket, is not clear, but children seem to accept him there without question.

✳ In the next picture, we are behind the kids, looking through the windshield. Using a few curved lines, Pinkwater makes the car. Five black circles with lines on top, filled in with yellow and orange, serve as the five children's heads. The black highway, stretching ahead with a white line down the middle, can be seen through the windshield. Over Mrs. Popsnorkle's head is printed the German word for "horse," an inside joke for Pinkwater's wife, perhaps, who raises horses.

✳ At the car dealer, the minimal car barely looks big enough for one. The five children are made up of circles and blobs. Mrs. Popsnorkle seems commandingly large. Unfortunately, her role in the story is that of a stereotypically empty-headed female, but the whole story is so silly that this stereotype seems like simply more silliness. Two thick red lines make the ground or floor, while a yellow area above could be sky, but Pinkwater isn't clear here. The salesman, Mr. Sandy, seems understandably uncertain as he eyes the Popsnorkles.

✳ The Superflash is again coming toward us, this time on a chartreuse-green ground with a lavender sky and red ground line. Kids only see the car, and everyone supposedly in it.

✳ The close-up of Mr. and Mrs. Popsnorkle, his hands on the wheel, is so simple children can easily copy it or draw a similar picture. Pinkwater has used a blue and a red broken horizontal line across the top here and colored in part of the blue background, but he chose to leave much of the picture white. Try covering the red and blue lines to see what they do or don't add to the picture.

✳ As Mr. Popsnorkle roars onto the highway, the background colors coming to a point, echoing the nose of the Superflash, seem to make the car speed as much as the clouds behind it. Kids love the five smiling faces in the back, and the worried look on Mr. Sandy's face.

✳ Only a happy Mrs. Popsnorkle and kids are visible as the car rises from a black line drawn on the strange red road. Obviously the car can't stay that way.

✳ Kids squeal with delight at the dinosaur-car, which matches its angle to the car on the previous page. Only five happy faces are shown here. Most of the road has been left white, with three other colors used in back.

✳ Pinkwater gives us the absolute minimum of Mr. Popsnorkle's view here. There are several places in this book where the changes in point of view can be explored, from the second picture page, where we are looking over the children's heads through the windshield to the road beyond; to the side and front views of the car and people; to this close-up. Kids love to guess what pushing the next button will do.

✳ The elephant-car gallops in the same direction on the white road, with a red area beyond, and a waving green ribbon-like line above. The passengers, except for Mr. Sandy, seem delighted. The children have raised their arms to cheer.

✳ Now we see a back view, and a puzzled Mr. Sandy. A strange red aura above the car seems to add something needed for the design of the page; try covering it with a cut-out piece of white paper.

✳ The chicken-car flies on in the same direction, with a really worried salesman and a happy Mr. and Mrs. Popsnorkle. Again, only what seems necessary is added for background.

* A bit rumpled, Mr. Sandy clutches "lots of money" as the Popsnorkles drive away on a chartreuse road, clouds on either side, into that same semicircular sky. The view from the rear is very simplified, but still quite recognizable.

* Mr. Popsnorkle may have been in the air in the first picture, but here all five children are pinwheels of delight in the air, as a smiling Mr. and Mrs. Popsnorkle drive the car toward us. Note the horizontal broken lines on either side of the car that seem to give a feeling of motion.

* The final picture matches that on the jacket, leaving every reader longing for his family to find a dealer that sells the Superflash.

ART AND IMAGINATION ACTIVITIES

The library has many books in 629.22 on racing cars, cars of the future, and other types of "super cars" for children to explore. Then they can imagine what else they would like their Superflash to become, or what the old Thunderclap-Eight did.

Individually, or in groups, have them design their own super car.

This is also a chance for them to explore the technique of drawing with felt-tipped markers. Have other Pinkwater books around for examples.

Some students might be interested in the similarity between the floating figures in this book and those in the paintings of Marc Chagall, in his "Me and the Village," at the New York Museum of Modern Art, for example. Reproductions are in books about Chagall and in most encyclopedias and histories of modern art.

BOOKS BY PINKWATER

Aunt Lulu. New York: Macmillan, 1988.
Guys from Space. New York: Macmillan, 1989.
I Was a Second Grade Werewolf. New York: Dutton, 1983.
Tooth-Gnasher Superflash. New York: Macmillan, 1990 (reissue), paper, 1990.
Uncle Melvin. New York: Macmillan, 1989.

Happy Blanket
by Tony Ross

Ross illustrates both his own stories and those of others. A very early work, *Admiral Mouse* (O.P.), is painted realistically in a meticulously detailed style, with every whisker shown and elaborate costuming. But now his exaggerated human and animal figures are loosely outlined, and filled in with thinly applied water color paint. His style is similar to Quentin Blake's, in *Quentin Blake's ABC* (Knopf, 1989) or *All Join In* (Little, Brown, 1991), for example, but less natural, more stylized, and drawn with a less nervous line. Ross also conveys humor and meaning from gesture and posture. Perhaps because he has several children of his own, Ross's pictures show believable children behaving very realistically.

----

* *Happy Blanket* is a book with a gimmick. Other books have tried to work forward and then back again, or from both front and back to meet in the middle. But Ross wanted to have two separate stories relate and really meet in the middle. The book has been printed so that either side can function as the front cover. The flaps, copyright information, and title page are the same. Even the spine works as well one way as the other. Arbitrarily we will start with Lucy, on the girl's side. She stands right in the middle of her cover, the blanket center stage. Ross indicates a floor, baseboard, and wall, but otherwise, no background to detract from the important characters. That Lucy's proportions are exaggerated is obvious; her head is a squashed oval and she has no neck. But she is appealing nevertheless. Ross uses bright pinks and golds to give a cheery tone to this introduction to the story. Simple black letters spell out the title and author.

* There are no end papers; the title page is the first page. Again, black is used for title, author, and publication information. In a cozy-looking, restful blue, circular picture, a shining crescent moon character sleeps happily and peacefully on a cloud, holding a piece of the cloud like the beloved blanket.

* The blue carries over to the first two pictures. Most of the pages of the book contain a few words top and bottom on the white background and a picture on each page framed with a squared-off line. On the top of the left-hand picture, Lucy huddles and shivers. She is sitting directly on top of a faucet. This is probably not possible to do, but it looks effective here. The lines of the tub and tiles slant toward the tiny spider in the lower left corner. The soap, sponge, duck, etc., sit solidly in the center. On the right-hand page, Lucy is peeking around the sofa at the right, while the cat, sardine snack handy, stares wide-eyed from the center of the chair, sitting as no real cat could. The TV they both focus on is at the center bottom. The shadows are, appropriately, dark blue.

✳ Pink and gold reappear as Lucy finds her Happy Blanket on the left-hand page. She also has the typical pink thumb that goes with it. This picture is interesting to compare with the cover for differences. On the right-hand page, Lucy and her blanket sleep in a bedroom that has to have been sketched from a real child's room. Children will recognize many of their own toys there. We almost lose Lucy in the clutter, but the blanket leads us to her.

✳ Dad comes out of the shadows to take the blanket away. Ross puts the cat there to see him, a realistic touch. But Ross makes the cats in the right-hand page picture not realistic, just funny, as the picture brightens with Lucy happy again. Blanket and the line it creates in the design are the focus in both pictures.

✳ There's that tense diagonal again, as Mom tries to pull the blanket away to wash it. Again Ross puts in one of those unrealistic cats, pulling with Lucy on the left. Why Ross puts the patterned ceiling on the left and not in the right-hand picture is a question. Kids usually laugh at the frightened cat on the right. See if they can tell you why he's funny.

✳ Lucy marches straight into the park. If there is a Henry Moore statue in your area, some children may recognize the style of the statue looming over her. On the right-hand page, Lucy visibly shakes in fear; even her hair quivers.

✳ Now, for the first time, Ross takes his illustrations across the two-page spread. From the blanket, and from Lucy's imagination, the benign-looking bear with yellow claws emerges dramatically, as the cat trembles near Lucy. The vertical solidity of the bear on the right is balanced by the base of the statue behind Lucy on the left.

✳ Suddenly, the bear becomes realistically mean-looking and frightening. This spread is quite complex in its design and point of view, as it spreads across the pages to join the two stories. The reader is looking down at Lucy, who is looking up at her bear from the lower left. Meanwhile, on the right, the boy and his blanket whirl in a circle echoing the bear's arm. Down below them on the lower right sits the startled lady on the bench. Also watching are a dog and cat in the upper right. Of course the children will want to turn the book around to see the picture the other way, but try not to read the end of the other story yet. It's time to turn the whole book around and start the other story.

✳ There is the same title and author, same print, but a different happy kid is holding his Happy Blanket. He seems to be outside, but just a suggestion of hills and trees show this.

✳ Ross uses the same title page and picture.

✳ The general format is again a squared-off picture on a white background on each side, with print above and below. On the left-hand side, Gregory is already happy. His blanket and the rosy wall and floor reflect this. He also has a tail-wagging dog with a very sharp nose. On the right-hand page, Gregory must contend with the dark, and his teddy bear seems as apprehensive as he does.

✳ Aunt Maggie is as crazy a caricature as one could imagine, even in eccentric-tolerant England. Ross has drawn her with multidirectional angles to her attire and body. Even the dog finds her amusing. Most children, with a little help, will "get" the fact that these folks who disparage Gregory's attachment to the blanket are doing the same sort of thing themselves. On the right-hand page, Gregory is already using his imagination with his blanket. His feet don't even touch the ground. Ross makes this ground with just green dabs of paint. Is the moon the same one we saw on the title page?

✳ Ross has fun with Grandpa's "dirty old thing" comment by having him smoke a repellent pipe that seems to endanger his nose as well. The dog expresses his feelings, while Gregory listens patiently. Then, on the right-hand page, imagination takes him off again toward the right, dog leaping after.

✳ Ross has more fun with Uncle Sid, quite a character. Perhaps he still isn't "too old" to be playing with models. On the right-hand page, Gregory has acquired a few more props for his imagination. Both he and his dog point back toward his uncle, matching the angle of Sid's table.

✳ Gregory and his dog approach the same staue in the park, but from a different angle. Compare these two pages with the same scene with Lucy to see the different point of view in the left-hand page scenes, and the similarities in those on the right.

✳ Gregory's blanket is flung across the two pages and becomes a magic carpet, as the dog leaps away. Again it is interesting to compare this with Lucy's blanket transformation when the book is turned over.

✳ Then it's time to put the two stories together and examine the final scene again. Has Ross successfully solved the problem he set?

Children may recall seeing examples of trick pictures that look like one thing but are something different when turned upside-down. Mitsumasa Anno gives examples of these in his *Upside-Downers* (Putnam, 1988). Several other illustrators have set themselves similar problems. Students may enjoy examining Ann Jonas's *Round Trip* (Greenwillow, 1983) and *Reflections* (Greenwillow, 1987), and Arnold Lobel's *The Turnaround Wind* (Harper, 1988), to see how they deal with pictures working in both directions in a story. Children might even try to make such pictures themselves.

RELATED ACTIVITY

Children who had a favorite blanket, or who have a sibling with one, love to talk about it. Then they can compare some other blanket stories, such as Ann Jonas's *Where Can It Be?* (Greenwillow, 1986).

BOOKS WRITTEN AND ILLUSTRATED BY ROSS

The Boy Who Cried Wolf. New York: Dial, 1985.
A Fairy Tale. Boston: Little, Brown, 1991.
Hansel and Gretel. New York: Random, 1990.
Happy Blanket. New York: Farrar, Straus, 1990.
I Want a Cat. New York: Farrar, Straus, 1989.
I'm Coming to Get You. New York: Dial, 1984.
Lazy Jack. New York: Dial, 1986.
Mrs. Goat and Her Seven Little Kids. New York: Atheneum, 1990.
Oscar Got the Blame. New York: Dial, 1988.
Super Dooper Jezebel. New York: Farrar, Straus, 1988, paper, 1990.
This Old Man. New York: Macmillan, 1990.
The Treasure of Cozy Cove. New York: Farrar, Straus, 1990.

Beach Ball
by Peter Sis

Readers of the *New York Times Book Review* or *Time* may recognize the unique style of Peter Sis from the drawings he has done for those periodicals. His pen and ink outlines are incorporated with tiny dots and/or lines to build texture, a technique which he admits is very tiring, but which is different enough to help him succeed in the competitive world of illustration. Although he lives and works in the United States now, Sis was trained in his native Czechoslovakia and in England and brings a European perspective to his work. Along with his simpler concept books for younger children, he has illustrated picture books and longer books written by others. In particular, his art has added distinction to some of the novels of Sid Fleischman, including the Newbery winner, *The Whipping Boy* (Greenwillow, 1986). When he adds water color to his precise black-and-white art, he seems partial to a particular clear blue, which is evident in *Beach Ball*. Also obvious there is his ability to portray distinctive characters with a minimum of detail. The faces of the girl and mother on the cover are perfect examples. Because of the precision with which he works, Sis's art is difficult for large groups to appreciate. Especially for the puzzles in this book, multiple copies and/or small groups are essential.

✱ The principal characters are introduced in their setting on the cover. The stretch of beach, with sky and horizon on top and the matching blue waters below, forms the area for the picture, while the printing appears in the sky and sea sections. The title letters are as multicolored as the blanket and ball below. The letters are both upper and lower case, perhaps for more roundness like the ball, and are edged in the black used for all the upper-case letters of the author information below. The title letters undulate, like the shore and the curve of the blanket, as opposed to the straight horizon and author information. Perhaps the title is being pulled by the airplane. The multicolored ball of the title is the central focus of attention. The many-colored and patterned blanket or quilt incorporates images from inside the book. The angles of the umbrella and bag on the left and the duffle on the right point toward the ball. The picture of sand, sea, and sky continues on to the back cover, where a striped umbrella stands at attention on the beach, deserted by all but a few shells and a disappearing fish. The cover works as two separate pictures, front and back, or as one long one with the book open. The colors tell us this will be a light-hearted book.

✱ The front end papers show us the sea, sky, and deserted beach, with only rubbish cans and sandpipers, as the beach would be at the start of the day. We see it from further away than the scene on the cover, however. The back end papers are the same view, but colored by the setting sun of evening, after the adventures of the story.

* The title page gives us a view of the cover scene from as far away as the end papers, as if Mary and her mother have just moved onto the deserted beach, which stretches across the two-page spread here and throughout the book. The title and author information has shrunk accordingly. But there are slight differences in the positions of Mary, her mother, and the duffle, and the ball has not yet appeared. The cover picture was for the cover; here the story actually begins.

* The fish, perhaps from the back cover, surfaces on the left-hand page for some action with the dedication and copyright. Sis, and the sister of the dedication, come from a landlocked country, Czechoslovakia, so the fascination with the beach is understandable. On the right, the ball appears, blown up by Mary. The angle of the umbrella and duffle both point the way mother and Mary are facing, into the story.

* The text is written in letters that reflect the wind, which is clearly shown in the blowing towel and umbrella on the left and the blanket, picture, hat, and scarf on the right-hand side. Sis has used his same sky blue for the artist's picture. The chase after the ball is on.

* Mary chases the ball across the edge of the shore on the first puzzle page. The helicopter pulling the alphabet is our clue that these pictures are of people or things beginning with the letters *A* through *Z*. Through all the puzzle pages, Sis has used the same setting, but with different action. Yet we never get bored, because of all the different items and activities he places in front of that backdrop.

* Up in the sky again appears the puzzle message. The absurdity of some of the items on the beach contrasts with the reasonability of the others. Mary and the ball are constants. The horizontal pattern of the background contrasts with the many diagonals Sis uses for the action.

* Now it's numbers of objects from one to ten we must find, along with the fun Sis has built into the situations portrayed. Kids sometimes do better than adults at this. I stopped looking for the four-item picture when I found the four babies and their bottles on the left, but the children noticed the four fish pictures under the double umbrellas. Then we decided that there was more than one picture for each number, and the competition was on.

* Sis tells us "shapes" on both the left and right sections of the sky on these pages, so we don't miss the point. Mary and the ball sail on.

* The opposites are a real challenge. I find more each time I look. The boat sailing in on the right continues onto the next two pages, and sails off on the next, making these pages like an unrolling scroll of Mary's chase.

∗ The boat is the Circus Line, so we can have more animals to name. Sis's humor is everywhere; he even puts in a Beach Boys Rock Concert. We don't lose Mary or the ball behind the ship.

∗ Sis moves hordes of people back to form the maze. He also goes wild with pattern here, building to a climax. Mary loses her hat, but the ball seems to have settled.

∗ Mother has finally caught up and found the hat, but amid all the members of the girls' camp, Mary is lost. When we find her, however, we see that she finally has the ball. Note the title of the book being read at the far right on the pink float.

∗ The whole world seems to cheer as all attention centers on the joyous reunion on the right-hand page. Sis has emphasized the letters and even the exclamation points with his tiny pen-strokes. Note the many curves and circles, even the raised arms.

∗ Now the color of both sky and water changes, as the semicircular orange sun sets on the again deserted beach. Sis centers the ball, this time against the sun, with the cavorting figures of Mary and her mother balanced on either side, on the left-hand page. Sis touches in their lengthening shadows, and that of the trash can on the right-hand page, which balances their figures. Along with a few shells, they are all that is left of the masses that filled the pages earlier.

∗ As mentioned above, on the back end papers, we have pulled away for the view of the beach at the end of the day.

Children have as much fun with this book as they do with the Waldo books, or other puzzle books like Mitsumasa Anno's, for example, *Anno's Journey* (Philomel, 1978). It certainly sharpens perception, while introducing a different technique. Some children may even try some drawing with the tiny dots and strokes, but most find it tedious at this age.

There are some interesting and strange items to be found in the beach scenes by Anthony Browne in Annalena McAfee's *The Visitors Who Came to Stay* (Viking, 1985). Another book about a lost beach ball that might be fun to compare, both story and art, is Molly Bang's *The Yellow Ball* (Morrow, 1991).

BOOKS WRITTEN AND ILLUSTRATED BY SIS

Beach Ball. New York: Greenwillow, 1990.
Follow the Dream: The Story of Christopher Columbus. New York: Knopf, 1991.
Going Up! A Color Counting Book. New York: Greenwillow, 1989.
Rainbow Rhino. New York: Knopf, 1987.
Waving. New York: Knopf, 1987.

PICTURE BOOKS BY OTHERS ILLUSTRATED BY SIS

Banks, Kate. *Alphabet Soup*. New York: Random, 1988.
Livingston, Myra Cohn. *Higgledy Piggledy*. New York: Macmillan, 1986.
Mayper, Monica. *After Goodnight*. New York: Harper, 1987.
Rice, Eve. *City Night*. New York: Greenwillow, 1987.

Daisy
by Brian Wildsmith

Brian Wildsmith's brightly colored, wildly patterned, expressionistically painted illustrations have delighted children for years. Although people appear in his books, it is his animals and birds, in richly textured landscapes, that have dominated his art. In 1982, Wildsmith published the first of a series of books that have explored the challenge of split or half-pages that change half of the scene at a time, and of cutouts in pages that reveal part of the upcoming page. Children enjoy playing the game with these "toy books," but don't realize how difficult it is to make these work. Although Wildsmith continues to use bright colors, he has toned down his painting and made the paint more transparent and less splashy; he has refined his technique to make his newer books more detailed and realistic. His stories have become more complex, with levels of meaning. Both story and pictures have proved to be favorites with the children.

———————

✻ Daisy's name arches above her on the cover in rather fancy black letters, with Wildsmith's name simply printed above. The cow, with a bright yellow parachute strapped to her back, is, incredibly, just riding along tied to the top wing of a biplane, flying straight across the cover from back to front over a sketchily indicated, undulating landscape. Behind the pilot sits a motion-picture photographer, making Daisy's position a bit more understandable. Daisy herself, the men, and the landscape are little more than sketches when compared to the intricately detailed engine and incredible colors and patterns of the plane flying through the blue sky.

✻ The end papers are the purplish pink of the band of color behind the engine of the plane.

✳ The title and author reappear printed as on the cover. Framed against the white page by the beams is a view of what appear to be Daisy's eyes looking out at us from above the doors of her stall against a textured green background. Wildsmith gives us wood grain and knot holes, even hinges of the top halves of the door that are open. Daisy seems really confined here.

✳ The two-page spread of Farmer Brown's house is centered on the farmer and on the tractor he admires on his television screen. Stone wall, ground, shutters, and hinges are all painted in, in color. Around the central scene, Wildsmith has sketched the boards of the exterior, as if they framed a stage set. On the left, standing out against the white boards, is a multicolored rope which will lead to our heroine. Bright against the boards on the right-hand side is a collection of round wheels and colorful patterned carts, with boards and tools standing up for the TV-watching rooster's perch. The fact that there is only a half-page on the right is hardly noticeable, because Wildsmith has matched the pictures so perfectly. Only the bottom bluish stone is cut off by the page.

✳ The picture works with the half-page turned as well. Now Daisy, at the other end of the rope, is watching far-off places on the TV. The rest of the scene is the same. Daisy's rear has hair and muscles, but we really haven't met her yet.

✳ A multicolored and textured landscape spreads across the two pages. The farmer stands framed in the open gate, colorfully costumed, with a profusion of plants and flowers around him across the foreground and the landscape and text above. Daisy stands far away, seemingly unimportant in the field. The half-page cut matches almost perfectly.

✳ The same basic scene, with half-page match on the left, now seems very different, as Daisy walks through the open gate into her starring role in the story. Note how realistically detailed Wildsmith has painted her here as compared to the cover picture and the previous one. She matches the rear view we saw as she looked into Farmer Brown's window.

✳ The village sits on the slope among the mountains, with the sharp steeple pointing up at the right. It looks foreign, with the stucco walls, red-tile roofs, and pump in the courtyard. See whether the children think it is American. Cats are all the life we see, except for Daisy, making her way down the green hill, with the gray rocks coming down from the left almost beside her. The half-page again is almost a perfect match.

✳ The scene remains the same, with another fine match on the left, but Daisy has moved on to the roof.

✳ Now Wildsmith gives us a strong, black horizontal foreground on which a group of assorted people, in colorful but nonspecific costumes, have gathered to look at Daisy. He puts in deep, recessed stained-glass windows of different shapes to punctuate the white church and red roof that fill the two-page spread. Central to the picture are Daisy on the roof and the priest gesturing below. The television camera focuses in from the lower right. Wildsmith leaves large areas white, even more than the text requires.

∗ The camera now films Daisy in mid-flight toward the firemen's net, with Farmer Brown centered on the roof above.

∗ Wildsmith leaves a large area white, above for the sky and below for the dock and the text. The crane is only sketched in, but all the working parts are there. So are all sorts of parts to the boat, which dwarfs the multicolored carts and crates on the right. Daisy's arrival at the bottom left is also overshadowed. Aside from the bold red of the ship's stern, Wildsmith uses touches of bright red all over the page.

∗ Up goes Daisy on her way to boarding the ship.

∗ Wildsmith knocks our eyes out with the reddish wash that flows over the outlines of the buttes and plateaus of the West. It covers more than half of the top of the two-page spread. Below, the white page becomes the ground on which the familiar scenes from Hollywood westerns are sketched in. Daisy pulls a wagon as another cameraman films from the lower right. The red fades to realistic color on the right where the town is seen.

∗ The half-page reveals more typical western action, as Daisy is filmed while being ridden in the opposite direction from before. Note all the tiny details Wildsmith manages to fit into these small sketches. As usual, he particularly enjoys the machinery.

∗ Daisy is now a paler, sleeker cow than the hairy one who walked out the open gate. She is placed on a platform to be photographed under the lights at odd angles, like any model or Miss America. The stark white boards behind her, the black boards of the floor, and the black area she stands on are in contrast to the colored flowers, the array of lights, and the costume of the photographer. Wildsmith has had his color fun with the pillow, in particular, and with the color decoration on the platform. Even the poster has multicolor stripes at its lower edge.

∗ The pink bathtub with the ornate gold feet makes the situation seem even more absurd.

∗ Notice again how Wildsmith has used large areas of white, and here of black and white, to contrast with his bright colors. Here he is also playing with traditional perspective, which he can do skillfully, but he does not use it in every picture. With mere strokes rather than individual details, he gives us the intricately modelled walls and painted ceiling of this huge, palatial room. He also indicates a decorative tablecloth, many people, and in greater detail, lots of fancy food. The footmen's red jackets really stand out.

* Daisy makes a shambles of the table and food, as the crowd pulls back. Wildsmith has chosen to make the setting still dominate here, so children have to get a close look to see that this is really an action picture, with food flying and glasses tumbling down.

* After all the activity on the last pages, here there are just the two figures standing fairly statically, joined by the multicolored rope. They stand on a grained and textured floor, with a horizontal white baseboard and the textured yellow-gold wall behind. Daisy again looks different. Compared to earlier pictures, does she look pale and sad? She is still, however, a cow, and not anthropomorphized. The producer certainly does not look like a typical Hollywood character. Wildsmith has obviously enjoyed designing him a decorative and colorful suit. He does look worried about Daisy, however. On the right, against the white page, Wildsmith has drawn medical tools and equipment, then filled the horizontal shelves with colorful bottles and books, a real contrast to the left-hand page of this spread.

* The white is picked up in the doctor's coat. But Wildsmith can't resist giving him red socks, what look like buckles on his shoes, and a purple stethoscope. We can tell Daisy is not well by the way she stands. The half-pages, as all through the book, continue to match beautifully.

* The cover scene is repeated here, with the plane further away and climbing, making room for the text, and for a less static picture. The central hill is different; it is the grassy pasture in which we first saw Daisy grazing.

* Daisy descends under a beautifully colored (of course) parachute on the left, as the plane flies away and Farmer Brown drives up the hill in his new tractor.

* Now we see the entire farmhouse, roof turned red by the setting sun, against the pink and red-washed sky with the crescent moon appearing on the left. Wildsmith distracts us with all the details of the house that were missing the first time we saw it, and with the many more items of farm paraphernalia. Does it perhaps appear different from the first picture because Daisy sees it differently? Finally our eyes are drawn to the slanting yellow light from the window. Daisy stands there, watching the TV from outside while Farmer Brown does the same from his chair inside.

* This time Daisy is watching herself, as a sort of closing joke.

* A small vignette closes the story with Daisy peacefully grazing. No fence or boundaries are needed now, since she is content. A partial page is used on the right for the dedication and publication information, in keeping with the page design of the rest of the book.

Children may or may not "get" the moral of the story without help. A reminder of Dorothy and "There's no place like home" from *The Wizard of Oz* may work.

Other illustrators have used half-pages. John Goodall is known for his wordless picture books, many of which are half-page. Among them are a series about Paddy, *Naughty Nancy Goes to School* (Macmillan, 1985), and historic re-creations of the changes in places over years, such as *The Story of a Castle* (Macmillan, 1986), *The Story of a Farm* (Macmillan, 1989), etc. Children become more interested in how a book is bound after seeing this kind of book and may want to do some simple bookmaking, even with half-pages, but they need a lot of help at this age.

RECENT WILDSMITH BOOKS

Carousel. New York: Knopf, 1989.
A Christmas Story. New York: Knopf, 1989.
Daisy. New York: Pantheon, 1984.
Give a Dog a Bone. New York: Pantheon, 1985.
Goat's Trail. New York: Pantheon, 1986.
Ikeda, Daisaku. *The Cherry Tree* translated by Geraldine McCaugheran. New York: Knopf, 1991.
Pelican. New York: Pantheon, 1982.
Python's Party. New York: Oxford, 1987.

(There are many others)

Cherries and Cherry Pits
by Vera Williams

Vera Williams does more than tell stories that children delight in hearing; she illustrates them with pictures that show both skill and originality, in a style uniquely her own. Her characters tend to be multiracial and are not always from the typical middle-class suburban family. So discussions of her books can lead to talk about what it's like to live with grandma but no dad, or to have a mother who works hard and comes home tired, or to not be able to afford a comfortable chair to sit in. Williams is also concerned with nature and conservation of our natural resources. Teachers have taken off from her books to units as varied as a mock canoe trip overnight at school from *Three Days on a River in a Red Canoe,* to a geography unit based on post cards brought from home, designed by the students, and from *Stringbean's Trip to the Shining Sea.* We will be primarily discussing her art, but Williams offers her readers so much more.

＊ Some typical characteristics of Williams's art are apparent on the cover of *Cherries and Cherry Pits.* Her colors are usually bright and cheerful, except when the story indicates otherwise. She enjoys making patterns and borders. She applies her water colors loosely, and not flatly, within outlines. Bidemmi, a young African-American girl, is smiling at us from the cover. She is holding two important items from the book: the cherries of the title, and her favorite felt-tipped markers. Williams has made a pattern of marker strokes for the background of the front and back covers. She has separated a space across the top with a border of red hearts and "kisses" on orange. On the bright pink background, Williams appears to have signed her name in black. The title letters are shades of cherry red, outlined in black. The cherries are falling or have dropped all over the back cover. Here another strip of bright pink for the ISBN numbers is separated by two borders of red and pink "kisses" on white.

＊ The bright pink is used again for the end papers. Williams has even put her dot-and-line border on the flaps of the dust jacket.

＊ A cherry-shaped border of cherries, in shades of red, with leaves and stems of green and blue, surrounds the title. Some children see this as heart-shaped. The author and title are printed the same as on the cover, but arranged differently within the frame.

＊ On the left-hand page, the black print of the copyright and other information on the white page is accented with two horizontal red lines. On the right-hand page, Williams has painted two real-looking cherries next to an envelope and note, apparently written and signed by her, with two more cherries. First graders understand this dedication and are quite moved by it.

＊ Bidemmi opens the door on the right-hand page. We recognize her from the cover, although her blouse and hair are changed. Children who have used water color paint can see how Williams has applied it more and less opaquely here. Having the horizontal panels of the door cover almost half the page, Williams makes a very different picture from one that is all Bidemmi. But the face is certainly very appealing. On the left-hand page, she has made her dot-and-line marker border, with extra strokes in the corners, typical of the way kids use markers. The text is printed in simple black type, but the initial capital letter is made up of tiny red dots, like cherries.

✳ On the left-hand page, a realistically intent Bidemmi, back in the blouse from the cover, holds an almost impossibly large marker, perhaps big for emphasis. Our attention is focused on her, with no details beyond her and the table. The text on the right continues with the same border and letters.

✳ Now Bidemmi is supposedly illustrating her own story with markers. Children see immediately the change in style. But there is still a Williams-style border of hearts, etc., within the picture. Williams (Bidemmi) uses a lot of white background here, with the white of the bag standing out in the picture. The subway is only slightly indicated and may require some explanation to noncity children. On the left-hand page, the text has only a thicker-line color frame.

✳ Intense, bright colors and happy faces leap out of the next right-hand page. The cherries flow out of the bag and decorate the background, which has no wall or floor. The rug and the children's clothes include typical Williams riots of pattern. On the left-hand page, the border has gone from a simple rectangle of color to breaks in the lines, with the "pretty lamp" inserted. Here the text begins the theme the children love repeating.

✳ Bidemmi moves to crouch on the floor over a smaller piece of paper. Depicted in Williams's own style, she is believably realistic and natural. On the right-hand page, the text is now framed with lines embellished by roses, while some of the articles from Bidemmi's new story appear as drawn by her.

✳ Williams gives us another very realistic view of an involved young artist on the left-hand page. On the right, Bidemmi has drawn her character, complete with paper bag inside, on brownish paper placed on the white page. The border has trains running on the bottom and outside edge.

✳ Before we tire of the format of text on one side, picture on the other, Williams moves to a series of scenes, like frames from a film, done in Bidemmi's style. She places them on a white background, sprinkled with colored dots on the left and blue-outline stars on the right, with text under the pictures. The three pictures on the left-hand page get gradually larger and brighter as the woman comes up from the subway. They get still larger on the right, and get framed, although the sink is only black on white. Perhaps sinks do not interest Bidemmi; the parrot and flowers are in vivid color.

✳ We return to text on one side, with a frame of colored lines, and the picture on the right. Bidemmi here uses corners and points for decoration, bright colors, and a lot of white background, on which the single cherry really stands out, with pit clearly depicted. The listeners get to repeat the refrain.

* Now Williams has painted a pensive Bidemmi in close-up, looking toward her story on the facing page. Children enjoy the shoe and shoelace border, as well as the sheet that looks like yellow lined paper.

* Bidemmi now uses the yellow paper and markers to draw a very active boy striding across the left-hand page and up and down the stair border around the text on the right. Why Williams put a white border on the right and not on the left is an interesting question. It may relate to the text, or to the size of the boy.

* A fancy border with bows in the corner, like that in the sister's hair, surrounds the text on the left-hand page, with a cherry inside a heart at the bottom. Fancier still is the cherry-filled border Bidemmi puts around the bright picture on the right. The characters stand stiffly as they would in a child's drawing, but the perspective in the floor pattern is probably too sophisticated for a child to do.

* Now both styles appear in one picture, as the Williams-painted girl draws herself with markers; her other pictures are on the wall behind her as well. Like the other Williams water color pages, this scene fills the page with no borders. The text on the right-hand page, under the self-portrait, has its own marker border, however, on a lot of white space.

* Bidemmi is using a piece of textured pink paper here on the left-hand page, surrounded by white and with its own blue marker border. Notice the torn edges at the top of the paper. Bidemmi is leaning over at an angle that matches the slant of the cherries spilling from the truck. Note the different sun in the two pictures on these pages. On the right-hand page, the frame of small circles might be the pits. The refrain changes slightly to "saving the pits."

* The story becomes more serious. The frame of the text on the left is not bright. The frame on the right is simply the white page. Only the bright yellow dress and other small touches of color enliven the expanse of brown. The drawing of Bidemmi's body is really too well done for a child, but we accept it because it is childlike.

* We are back to Williams's real Bidemmi, clutching her bright markers. The text on the right has a double border, as she prepares for the climax to her story.

* On the left-hand page, the story and pictures grow and progress with the pit, within the borders. Whether the choice of colors has significance can be discussed.

✳ Both pages are filled with bright colors, and both include the tree in a rectangle within an irregular octagonal frame, full of Bidemmi and her activities. On the left, this frame is simply surrounded by bright green, with text underneath. On the right, there is plain blue background and text on the bottom, but the tree has burst through the frame over the top and sides.

✳ We return to the cherry frame of the title around the text on the left-hand side. On the right, framed in bright pink, are so many scenes of happy people and cherries that children need time to study them individually later. The design is carefully balanced, but with touches like the bird flying into the picture in the upper right, and the boy kicking out in the upper left.

✳ Finally, Bidemmi presents her marker-drawn self on the sidewalk, amid the cherry tree forest she hopes to see.

✳ The back end papers are a ripe, cherry red, brighter than those in the front, perhaps showing they will ripen in time.

RELATED ACTIVITIES

Discussion of the two styles Williams uses can be enriched by adding the Quentin Blake illustrations for *Monsters*, by Russell Hoban (Scholastic, 1989), for consideration. Children can do their own pictures, first with water color-type paint, and then with markers, to see how differently these work. They may also remember the marker illustrations of Daniel Pinkwater (p. 83) discussed earlier.

BOOKS BY WILLIAMS

A Chair for My Mother. New York: Greenwillow, 1982, paper, 1984.
Cherries and Cherry Pits. New York: Greenwillow, 1986.
More More More Said the Baby. New York: Greenwillow, 1990.
Music, Music for Everyone. Greenwillow, 1984, Morrow paper, 1988.
Something Special for Me. New York: Greenwillow, 1983, Morrow paper, 1986.
Stringbean's Trip to the Shining Sea. New York: Greenwillow, 1988.
Three Days on a River in a Red Canoe. New York: Greenwillow, 1981, paper, 1984.

The Napping House
by Audrey Wood,
illustrated by Don Wood

The Woods have collaborated on many successful and popular picture books, like their recent *Piggies* and the Caldecott Honor Book *King Bidgood's in the Bathtub*. They also occasionally work alone or with someone else. Don Wood's distinctive style of illustration is characterized by his use of textured, shadowed, rounded, three-dimensional forms; realistic people in situations with strange or erratic twists; and an overriding sense of humor.

✳ On the dust jacket of *The Napping House*, only the letters of the title are bright enough to stand out. Almost everything else is dark, or in shades of blue, with author and illustrator printed in black. Just touches of pink and yellow, and brown wood, brighten the quiet scene. Framed by a thin white line, the rectangular, almost square, picture on the cover puts us in both a napping and a smiling mood. The rain is coming down vertically outside, but almost everything else in the picture, including the bed, has curves. Don Wood has painted, in thin oil paint on pressed board, a scene that has characters you feel you could touch. We look down on a bed with sheets and pillow that have shadows and dimensions, and bed posts that are solidly rounded. On the bed, at the bottom of the pile, snores a lady in an old-fashioned ruffled nightgown and cap, feet akimbo. A child is smilingly, blissfully asleep, completely upside-down to the viewer, but perpendicular to the snorer and atop her. And on top of the child rests a furry dog. The painting of the hair on the dog, and the fur on the slippers at the lower right, really shows the texture.

On the back of the dust jacket, the casually posed and dressed Woods are photographed in black and white in front of a house, which may be their own. The similarity between this house and the house in the story may not be coincidental. Children may spot this, or may have to be asked to compare. Think about how a color photograph would look here as opposed to the black and white. Do you think the photographer deliberately placed Don Wood's arm at that angle? Is the pose as casual as it looks? The cloth cover is bound in a harmonious shade of blue textured cloth, with the printing and a vignette of the curled-up, sleeping cat stamped in a metallic color similar to the color of the title on the jacket.

✳ The end papers are the dark gray of the storm clouds that produce the rain we saw on the jacket.

✳ On the title page, the white letters of the title stand out clearly against that slate blue sky and the vertical rain. The other words are printed in the same simple black as the jacket. But compare this page with the jacket to see how the different placement of information works in the design of the page. Vertical pickets of a white fence march across the bottom of the page, but each picket is pointed rather than straight, and the fence itself is not a straight horizontal, which would have been boring. Wood has also softened the lines with the profusion of leaves and flowers, and with the rounded post and newel on the left. He has also added just a touch of green and lavender to the almost all blue page.

✳ The sky, the rain, the fence, and the flowers continue across the next two-page spread, with the copyright information on the left and the dedication on the right, in black. On the right, we have come to the slightly open gate between the two posts. In case we have any doubts, the also slightly open mailbox tells us we have indeed come to the Napping House. Again, Wood has given just enough variation in design and color to keep us interested, but not excited.

✳ Now we see the whole house, with the fence around it, on the right-hand page. Although the focus is on the right-hand page, the scene extends across the two pages. The rain is slanting here, and there is more action in the design. The trees have gnarled and twisted trunks. The path in front of the house is mostly horizontal, but twists off to the lower left. The brick path to the house is vertical, but curves out at the top and bottom, and narrows in perspective, as do the sides of the fence. Although "everyone is sleeping," the abandoned tricycle, swing, and treehouse show that there are activities at other times here. A word about the text is appropriate here. This is a typical cumulative "House that Jack built" type of tale. But the words are so well chosen that they can bear the repetition. Children love to join in as this story grows. For this reason, it is better not to analyze the pictures at all during the first reading, but simply to take time for the children to see what is happening, and then move along. Additional trips through can examine the changes of point of view, position of characters, and color.

✳ On the next two pages we are inside the house. The rain is dripping straight down on the outside of the window. The restful blues predominate, with just touches of brown wood. There are restful curves everywhere in this picture, including the ends of the bed and the chair, even the edges of the cloth on the table and the ruffles. All the important characters but the last are visible, if the viewer looks carefully. (The mouse can be tricky to find on top of the mirror.)

✳ The blue gets deeper, becoming lavender in places. The movement begins. Granny has turned over so we can see her, sleeping. The child is moving from the chair, seemingly sleepwalking. The chair curves have straightened, the bed posts at the foot have straightened a bit also. A pillow has fallen on the dog.

✳ The child has taken the pillow, but the dog is now stretching. The child's weight bends the bed frame further. A comparison with the previous page shows a slight brightening of the color. Rain still runs down the window pane.

✳ Another comparison will show a touch more brightness on this two-page spread. The dog is sprawled in a silly upside-down position atop the child, while the cat yawns and stretches awake, tail up like the dog's. Not only does the bed frame curve more, but we seem to be moving up above floor level, seeing more of the top of the bed, chair, and table. The chair top leans off the page on the left.

✳ The dog is down, while the cat is curled up asleep on top of him. Granny is almost off the bed, which really sags under all the weight. More white spaces make the scene a bit brighter, although it is still dark and rainy through the window. We are viewing the scene from a still higher point. Viewers may not notice that the mouse has now moved. Few will note the appearance of the final character, on the arm of the chair.

✳ We have moved still higher. The colors of items like the rug, now almost a complete circle, are becoming clearer. Everyone's back is toward us except for the mouse, topping the pile of bodies on the curves of the bed. The last player has moved to the pitcher.

✳ The colors brighten a touch more, we move a bit higher, and we meet the flea atop the mouse. The picture on the right-hand side makes an interesting comparison with that on the jacket, as to point of view, characters, and color.

✳ We are now almost completely above the scene, as the reactions begin with the mouse and the almost invisible flea. The colors are brighter, but blue still predominates, and the rain continues outside.

✳ Colors are brighter still, our point of view begins to descend, and the cat really leaps. Every hair appears on end, paws and claws extend, and the eyes almost pop out in a comic exaggeration of reaction. Granny's feet flex, but the rest of the group sleeps on.

✳ As we move down in our view, the colors get lighter and brighter. Even the rain seems less heavy, as the outside turns greener. The dog and cat are both in mock comic positions in the air, while the mouse and flea bring action to the left-hand page.

✳ Yellow touches the wall as the child, with pillow and blanket, and arms out, joins the dog in the air. The cat leaps diagonally from off the bed on the left-hand page, as the mouse slants in the opposite direction. Mirror and pitcher have been knocked aslant as well. The flea has returned to the right-hand page.

✳ Now everyone and everything, including the bed clothes and the sneakers, are in motion, in every direction. We are descending to a floor-level view. The flea and mouse are both back on the right again, while sunny yellow light bathes the wall.

✳ Sunlight fills the room, which we view from floor level. Through the window, we can see the trees and garden in the sunshine. Creatures and things are moving all over the place, in bright, intense colors. Granny and child are smiling through it all.

✳ Back outside is the house we saw on the first page; the rainbow is only part of the color added to the scene. All the characters, except the flea, are also added in action and contrast to the first scene.

✳ Finally, the back end papers are the blue of the jacket, not the gray of the front end papers, to match the change of mood.

As noted above, this book requires several trips through for children to see all that is happening. They love to reread it themselves as well.

After this book, children should be much more aware of points of view, and how they affect pictures. They might practice drawing their own room, or the classroom, from high above, from the floor, or even just areas from close or from far away.

BOOKS BY THE WOODS

Elbert's Bad Word. San Diego: Harcourt Brace, 1988.
Heckedy Peg. San Diego: Harcourt Brace, 1987.
King Bidgood's in the Bathtub. San Diego: Harcourt Brace, 1985.
The Little Mouse, the Red Ripe Strawberry, and the Hungry Bear. Sudbury, MA: Playspaces, 1990.
Moonflute. San Diego: Harcourt Brace, 1986.
The Napping House. San Diego: Harcourt Brace, 1984.
Piggies. San Diego: Harcourt Brace, 1991.
Quick as a Cricket. Sudbury, MA: Playspaces, 1990.

Chapter 5
Grades Two to Four

INTRODUCTION

Because children are sharpening their reading skills, this age is an appropriate time to make sure that they learn the fables, folktales, and fairy tales that form the underlying base of so many of the important works of art and literature. Even students who know all these tales from previous hearings can begin to think about them differently as they hear different versions. They may also perceive the stories in new ways when they see the various depictions of the same or similar characters by different artists. Children can begin to exercise their critical thinking skills by comparing and contrasting both words and art.

By second grade, students can also appreciate parodies and take great pleasure in recognizing "take-offs" and twists of the familiar fable or fairy tale. Such "take-offs" can be introduced and discussed separately, or in conjunction with the story they parody. An entire unit can be based on fables, introduced by one of the collections or by individual tellings. A single fairy tale can also be used to introduce an illustrator's works, or can be part of a yearlong study of such stories.

These years, as children become more aware of the world around them, are also the time to explore the folktales and art styles of other countries and cultures. Again, these books can be read individually or form part of a larger multicultural unit. Each tale becomes the beginning of the study of a country, its people, its history, and its arts and crafts. Differences are obvious, but amazing parallels in story, hero, and even occasionally in art form can be drawn from comparisons.

Because the choice of what to read when, and how, to each group is so arbitrary, and because the range of ability is so wide at this age, the books discussed in this chapter are simply listed alphabetically by illustrator, as was done in the previous chapters. The order and arrangement are up to you.

Anno's Aesop: A Book of Fables by Aesop and Mr. Fox

by Mitsumasa Anno

Anno's picture books have had a worldwide impact. Aside from his simple alphabet book and other visual challenges for the very young, he has produced pseudo-travel tales rich with puzzle clues for further exploration and a provocative series on mathematics and logic to lure young thinkers far beyond what teachers and parents might think them capable of understanding. In all his books, he provides pictures that do more than simply illustrate. His deft drawings of both people and architecture, replete with tiny details but simplified when he chooses, and his carefully applied transparent water color are placed on the pages purposefully, to add dimension to the words.

We will examine the visuals of only a few of the 63 closely packed pages of *Anno's Aesop*. But all 63 have something worth pondering, even if it's simply considering what Anno puts in versus what he leaves out. To complicate the analysis, the actual fables and pictures fill most of the tops of the pages, while a parallel but related group of stories runs along the bottom. Supposedly those on the bottom are being read, or told, by Mr. Fox to little Freddy Fox, from a book that he found at the edge of the forest. The interrelationships of stories and pictures offer many opportunities for discussion, making this an Aesop that offers a way to introduce the traditional tales, with more to ponder for those who feel they already know them.

✳ On the dust jacket, the title is written in decorated upper-case letters of a blue that really stands out. The heavy black outline gives the letters more emphasis. Similar smaller letters are used for the author's name, colored an even sunnier yellow than the sun itself. The subtitle is in simple black. Over the parchment or handmade paper-like color coming from around the spine, Anno has placed a white rectangular frame, inside which he has painted his cover picture. He gives this picture a gray, ink-outlined frame, which seems in turn to be placed inside another ink-lined, reddish frame with fancy corners, like those once used to hold photographs in albums. Perhaps he felt he needed this much framing to hold in all the creatures and other things he has depicted in the sectioned-off portions of this illustration. The children and animals in it are realistic and recognizable, but details are not there, although expressions are, even on the faces of the ants. The trees, foliage, and flowers are stylized, more from Anno's fertile imagination than botanically accurate. The characters are those appearing in the stories in the book. He has built these sections up from the bottom, so they are not symmetrical or equal, but do balance: the goat climbing lower right against the girl swinging lower left; the plants, trees, and flowers on one side versus those on the other. The red triangle roof above the lion is the brightest spot among the subdued colors, pointing us toward the fox reading to Freddy, and to the title itself. The donkey stands solidly in the center above the horizontal piece of the chimney. Arching above the title fly the birds, picking up the brown and the white colors in the rest of the picture. The sun shines above, one ray breaking through the two inner frames Anno has so carefully drawn.

On the back of the jacket, more characters are shown, but there are fewer sections or scenes, perhaps because it is night, with the moon shining above rather than the sun. Here a roof at the lower right, plus a cat and a mouse, points us up, as do the flowers lower left, while the cow there looks down. The pattern of vegetation and characters flows back and forth, but always up to the wolf baying at the moon. Here the colors are similar to those on the front, but with more touches of red, with a wash of that brighter blue across the night sky. Under the dust jacket, the cover is the same parchment color as the spine of the jacket in some editions. The spine of the cover is bright red. An impressed drawing of the fox and the grapes on the front makes a neat rubbing for the children to try.

＊ In some editions, the end papers are a darker tan, in keeping with the tones on the jacket and cover.

＊ On most of the top of the title page, Anno has drawn and painted a picture of the book within this book, that is, the one found by Freddy Fox and read to him by his father. Note the different lettering of the title on the smaller book, but the use of the top half of the pictures from the front of the jacket, from the red triangle roof to where it must be cut off to remove the author's name. The sides have also been eliminated. It is interesting to speculate why Anno chose to use this part, and this part only, of the jacket picture, and to frame it as he did. The choice of red and black for the cover of the other book is also interesting. On page 60, the last picture in the book is the simple back cover of the book within the book. It makes a stark contrast to the other illustrations and gives a sense of finality to the book itself. The letters of the author and title on the title page are like those on the jacket, but the blue is used for both, perhaps to distract less from the illustration.

✳ Against the tan or parchment background that is used throughout the book, Anno brushes a white, paint-textured rectangle across the two-page spread, covering three-quarters of the pages. He adds a black line inner frame. He will use these white areas throughout for the illustrations and for the retelling of the fables of Aesop. Across the bottoms of the pages, in a different print, will run the tales of Mr. Fox. For these pages, Anno has painted a series of imaginary flower bunches, all different, above multicolor triangles forming a ground line or border, just to decorate the table of contents. Below, on the tan, Mr. Fox's Fables begin.

✳ The fable about the fox and the grapes is all that is told in the upper section. But the picture and the tale below add more: the tale of Scaramouche, a story that relates to Tomie de Paola's wordless *Sing, Pierrot, Sing* (Harcourt Brace, 1983). Anno has made the grapevine central, then curved and twisted it across the top left, with the fox reaching up toward a tempting bunch of stylized, not realistic, grapes. No grapevine ever looked exactly like this, but the essence is there. The singing Scaramouche is the fox's counterpart on the right. The curves of the vine carry us into the house, which is cut away like a stage set, with homey details like the pots and spider web. The curves of the grapes reappear on the girl's dress, while those of the vine are on her grandmother's dress, in the arch of the fireplace, and on the instrument that Scaramouche is playing. The hearts on his hat might well be symbolically on his sleeve. Anno chooses here to put no furniture or other details in the scene with the two women, but to draw all the bricks in the fireplace. Throughout the book Anno makes interesting choices in respect to detail, and it is fun to speculate why. The fox and Scaramouche stand on no ground at all. The colors used are few, and not intense.

✳ On pages 6 and 7, Anno again uses few, pale colors. The grass is indicated, but the sky left bare. The tree is a realistic, gnarled oak tree, with acorns included for the story on the bottom. It is very different from the stylized trees on the jacket. It centers our attention, making the essentially horizontal picture with its undifferentiated bears more interesting. Anno thinks nothing of inserting numbers into his illustration for his lesson, something few artists would do.

✳ Anno continues his parallel stories throughout the book. Occasionally, as on pages 40 and 41, he breaks the white rectangle at the gutter and gives us two separate pictures to analyze, but even here the two balance as well as contrast, in design and even in ground line.

This is, of course, only one of the multitude of Aesop's and other fables available in collections or singly in picture books. One second grade language arts curriculum began the year with a unit on fables that lasted almost two months and incorporated a study and comparison of the illustrations along with that of the stories and their meanings.

I will mention here just three other collections that I have found useful: Heidi Holder's *Aesop's Fables* (Viking, 1981), for succinct retellings with intricate illustration; and two liltingly retold by Tom Paxton and elegantly illustrated by Robert Rayevsky, *Aesop's Fables Retold in Verse* (Morrow, 1988) and *Belling the Cat and Other Aesop's Fables Retold in Verse* (Morrow, 1990).

RECENT BOOKS BY ANNO

Anno's Aesop: A Book of Fables by Aesop and Mr. Fox. New York: Orchard, 1989.
Anno's Alphabet: An Adventure in Imagination. New York: Harper, 1975, paper, 1988.
Anno's Britain. New York: Putnam, 1982.
Anno's Counting Book. New York: Harper, 1977, paper, 1986.
Anno's Counting House. New York: Putnam, 1982.
Anno's Flea Market. New York: Putnam, 1984.
Anno's Math Games. New York: Putnam, 1989.
Anno's U.S.A., New York: Putnam, 1983, paper, 1988.
In Shadowland. New York: Orchard, 1988.

PARODIES

Children enjoy the following parodies:

Heide, Florence Parry. *Fables You Shouldn't Pay Any Attention To* illustrated by Victoria Chess. Philadelphia: Lippincott, 1978.
Ross, Tony. *Foxy Fables.* New York: Dial, 1986.

Where the Forest Meets the Sea

by Jeannie Baker

The "collage constructions" that Jeannie Baker makes are not just done as illustrations for picture books but have also been displayed in art galleries. Both art and stories can be understood and appreciated by kindergartners, but older children, who have seen many types of pictures, are really intrigued by Baker's unique style. They are also better able to receive the urgent message of conservation conveyed in her recent work. Baker uses a wide variety of materials, such as cloth, wood, feathers, sand, twigs, and leaves, along with modelling clay and paint, to build her relief pictures. These must then be photographed to be reproduced in her books. Careful photography produces pictures that are so textured and tactile that we seem to be able to feel them.

---

* *Where the Forest Meets the Sea* gives us the added dimension of the Aborigines and the other creatures who once inhabited the tropical rain forest of North Queensland, Australia, where the story takes place. The jacket/cover opens to a large scene of forest, shore, and water, with a just-visible boat holding our two main characters. The white-lettered title on blue that runs along the spine interrupts the picture, which "works" when viewed as a whole or just from the front or back. Baker uses many shades of blue for the sea and sky. Her almost white sand is the color of Queensland area beaches, and she adds many textures and shades of green foliage. On the front, in addition to the boat off in the distance, two multicolored birds fly across the scene, adding life and a touch of bright color. Their red and yellow is used to shade and color in the black-outlined letters of the title. The author's name is the blue of the sky. Baker places lattice-like branches, leaves, and vines across the top, through and below which we are looking at the scene. The vines mark off the left of the picture. From there, a point of the shore leads our eye to the boat.

On the back of the jacket, more vines form verticals. Try to picture the scene without them; do they tie it together or just break it up? Do they make you feel closer to the picture? Baker has foliage on either side of the top, which also helps balance the picture. The river or creek zigs and zags its way toward the front of the jacket and the sea. Two arms of the shore also seem to point us back to the front. Do you find the ISBN number an intrusion on the picture? Some designers won't allow it on their books.

* The end papers are the deep blue of the sea.

* The lettering of the title is repeated from the cover. It stands out more against the white page and the other black letters.

* The simple black print of the publication and dedication gives the eyes a rest.

* This comparatively simple construction by Baker contrasts with the complexity of the cover. The flat horizon and sea give a sense of rest. But the angle of the boat and the action of the father show that movement is imminent. Children may speculate on the meaning of the name of the boat now, and again when the story is over. Baker has chosen to use only one page here, with a solid white page on the other side and white lettering on the picture itself. How would black text on the left-hand side change the way the spread looks?

* Baker chooses a two-page spread here, with the father and son far out from (or above) us, on a vast expanse of blue, with one decorative fish and scenery in the foreground and forest, sky, and partial rainbow at the top. The text, lower left in black, is balanced against the ocean life lower right. This picture is an interesting one to use to discuss point of view. We seem to be standing on the shore, with the water changing color as it does when it gets deeper, but it's also possible we are at the bottom of the sea. The shore reveals typical coral formations and fish of North Queensland. Again, the strong horizontals of boat, water, and horizon make this a quiet picture.

* Now Baker places the text on the left-hand page and uses the entire right-hand page for the illustration. Here, father, son, and boat are dwarfed by the complex jungle of foliage. The flying cockatoos make the scene come alive. The tall palm reaching on the right against the intense blue sky balances the flying birds in the composition, while the rocks, sand, and shore anchor the picture.

* Baker now concentrates our attention on father and son, and on the ghostly crocodile, which may be painted in or perhaps is a superimposed photograph. We are not told how she gets this ghostly effect. A vast area of sea blending into sky is left untouched. Sand and some beach debris spread across the two pages. How would the effect change if the text were on the left-hand page? Boy and father become tactile and real here.

* Father waves from the upper left of the two-page spread, from the beach that points us toward the creek and the exploring boy. Baker has made the tree roots almost like clutching fingers but has added friendly looking fish and colorful butterflies.

✳ Baker uses two-thirds of this spread for the picture she wants, leaving the words on the neutral-colored part of the left-hand page. She has built a complex forest scene that children love to study, with trees arching over the boy. Again, a ghostly creature is painted or photographed behind a tree trunk.

✳ Boy and stunning blue bird are dwarfed by the tree trunks, roots, and foliage of this very realistic forest. The trees almost lead him in as they lean.

✳ With another switch of page design and point of view, Baker places the text on the right-hand page, with a vignette of the boy crouching by a sprouting tree. On the left, filling the page, trees reach up against the sky and join together at the top. The snake forms a sort of wiggling link.

✳ The wonderfully intricate ancient tree trunk almost fills the two pages with another change of design. The entering boy gives us a sense of scale. The Aboriginal children are more than ghosts here; they are there with him.

✳ In a striking and daring picture, Baker has almost covered the two pages with the textured, dark brown-black of the tree, and has put us inside with the boy, looking out through the "window" and the spider web at the forest and the brightly plumed bird. The text stands out in white contrast on the left.

✳ The boy starts back through the double-page spread. The trees, still real, stand more vertically here. The Aboriginal shadow behind him is almost not there, except for his body paint.

✳ We see the father through the trees as the boy does, crouching over the fire, with beach, sea, and sky peaceful and clean behind him.

✳ Baker uses both pages to give us the full sweep of the beach, water, and forest, all still safe. Two ghosts remind us of the past, as does the "Time Machine" on the boat. Father looks happy enough, but the boy seems sad.

✳ On the same scene, Baker has projected what has happened to so many places and could easily happen here. In particular, note the children watching television instead of what little beauty is still left around them.

✳ The information on the location of the story and on the construction of the relief collages is of great help in appreciating this book with children.

COMPARISONS

Another book that deals with the destruction of the rain forest is Helen Cowcher's *Rain Forest* (Farrar, Straus, 1986). Many factual studies of rain forests have been published in the last two years and can be easily found in the library by interested children in several places in 300's, 500's, and 900's.

This book also gives us a picture of a particular area of Australia, with some hints on its unusual animals and some history. It can be the spring-board for a study of Australia, with trips to the library for more on all the areas Baker introduces. An amusing introduction to two of the special animals is Kerry Argent's *Wombat and Bandicoot: Best of Friends* (Little, Brown, 1990). Argent is one of Australia's many fine picture book artists with a particularly Australian point of view.

Two other picture books give an idea of the art of the Aboriginals. In one, John Alfred Rowe illustrates Rudyard Kipling's *The Sing-Song of Old Man Kangaroo* (Picture Book Studio, 1990) in typical Aboriginal style. Dick Roughsey, one of the first Aboriginal picture book people, has done many books of Aboriginal legends, including *The Rainbow Serpent* (Gareth Stevens, 1988). More serious students might find the parallels between the plight of the Aborigines and the history of the Native Americans in our country of interest.

ART ACTIVITY

Children can try making their own collage constructions with the additional materials and dimensions that Baker demonstrates. They need to make some sort of plan or design first, then decide what kinds of materials will work in it. They will appreciate Baker's work more when they realize that these pictures need to stand up, so the pieces have to be securely attached. They find that not everything they choose will stick. If cameras are readily available, try taking photographs of these collages to see how difficult it is to get a clear picture, and how the photograph changes the picture.

BOOKS BY BAKER

Home in the Sky. New York: Greenwillow, 1984.
Where the Forest Meets the Sea. New York: Greenwillow, 1988.
Window. New York: Greenwillow, 1991.

Goldilocks and the Three Bears

by Jan Brett

Jan Brett's picture books have become popular with children for their brightly colored, opaquely painted pictures, their appealing characters, and their intricately detailed settings. Children love finding all the different items Brett uses to build her illustrations, while they enjoy the whimsical fun she manages to have with the stories she tells. She draws on her travels around the world for the costumes and architecture that appear in her work. Frequently her borders have an important role in her books; they can even tell a second story.

✳ *Goldilocks and the Three Bears* is not only a fine example of Brett's work, but it is also a good version to compare with the others available of this old favorite. The jacket/cover has an intricately carved wooden frame around the picture and the title information. In a sort of oval insert in the top of the frame, Goldilocks sleeps above her name, clutching a bunch of pink snowdrops. She is a beautiful girl in the fairy-tale tradition, dressed in a Tyrolean-type peasant costume that seems in keeping with the wooden frame. Her name is in fancy red letters, with the tail of the *G* wrapping around the "the" in the rest of the less fancy title letters in black. A thin black line separates the italic letters of the author information, also in black, from the title. All this is set against the pale green-washed background of the picture of the three bears. They are hairy, realistic, three-dimensional bears. But they walk on their hind legs and are dressed in costumes reminiscent of medieval heralds. Brett uses dark outlines; bright, opaque, jewel-like colors; and more patterned borders. Papa and baby are jauntily belted, while papa's hat sports a tassel waving behind. Mama wears a peasant headband and carries a birchbark purse. They swing baby bear happily between them as they walk through the curling ferns beneath their feet. Birch tree trunks form a slanted border on either side.

The back of the jacket/cover is almost startlingly white, with a diamond-shaped, more simply carved frame in the center. From the exact center of this, baby bear looks right at us, the vivid colors of his tunic forming a background for another bunch of snowdrops in the paw at the center bottom point. Flower and insect details decorate the jacket flaps.

✳ The end papers are a latticed pattern of diamond-shaped frames like that on the back cover, which alternate areas green-washed like the front cover background with sections having very realistically painted plants and/or insects of the woods. Each plant is growing or sitting on a green, flower-patterned mound in the center bottom of the frame. Green predominates, but there are partially open pinkish-purple snowdrops, like Goldilocks's and baby bear's. Obviously, this book will be filled with flora and fauna.

✳ The active half-title page has a black print title underlined with a green-outlined, patterned band. Under it, a butterfly hovers over a beehive on a log, on green grass. A mouse peers out of the log, while bees fly from the hive.

✳ The two-page spread of the title is framed, top and bottom, with the same simple twisted carving of the end papers. But the sides include carved leaves and mice, with real mice joining the carved ones, and a doorway on the left through which mother and father bear are exiting. On the right, the baby is marching off. Inside the frame, the title and author are the same as on the cover but spread across the two pages. Under them, in a green landscape, Goldilocks is leaning over in the right foreground to pick one of the flowers. Brett has placed a birch as another inner frame on the right, with the shapes of girl, rock, and ferns balancing those of the trees across the page.

✳ A different, simpler carved frame surrounds the information page on the left, with an interior frame formed from the patterned ground, draped ferns, and rocks and tree trunks; a mouse and flowers are added for lively touches. The story almost begins inside the similar frame on the right-hand page, where Goldilocks, flowers in hand, sees the cottage in the mist. It is made up of marvelously intricate details, with a row of flowers along the path that leads to it. Here again, there are frames within frames, made up of tree trunks, twisted roots, and rocks.

✳ But the story must begin with the bears. So Brett gives us two more pages, each framed with another carved design. On the left, we have a close-up of the front of the fanciful cottage, with greenery all around it, and the mice playing here and there. On the right-hand page, an arch with bees in the corners and a window make a backdrop for the bears we have already met on the cover. Here the papa helps the delighted baby with a somersault. They stand on a gaily bordered white rug with space left for text. Yet another mouse emerges from a peasant boot or slipper.

✳ An elaborately framed two-page spread here shows us the important components of the story. Set on carved shelves along the left are the three distinctive bowls, along with a carved flower, repeated across the page, and carved mice amid bulbs. And what delightful, original and different bowls they are! On the right, we see the beds we will hear more about later, and a different carving of mice and bulbs. Within a simple wood border across top and bottom is a frieze, with stylized hills and running animals. Along the bottom is a grass-green rug, on which it is difficult to distinguish the pattern of nuts and leaves from the real bugs crawling out of the fallen jar. Tree trunks and stone steps on the right form additional side borders. Dominating the left-hand page is father bear, seated on a rough-hewn chair, spooning honey on bread from an elaborately decorated jar on the floor by his feet. Two overstuffed mice lean against it. The beautifully decorated coffee pot and cup contrast with the rough carving of the small table. On the right-hand page, the baby bear is playing under the fancily carved chair, while multicolored butterflies fly up from the dumped jar in this realistic domestic moment.

✳ The family sets out on its fateful walk across this two-page spread, framed simply top and bottom, and more elaborately on the sides. The mice are busy with the bulbs in the carvings on the lower left and right, with toadstools topping both sides. In the centers of the frames, Brett reminds us visually of Goldilocks by putting her eager face in the center of the left border and her body deep in dark woods in the center right border. Meanwhile, the text is framed on the left with greenery, flowers, and a tree trunk. With the cottage centered in the back of the left-hand page, baby bear leans over the fallen, angled tree, away from his parents, to pick mushrooms. Under glorious golden sunflowers that match father's tunic, mother and father march right, mother looking back to keep an eye on baby. Children love the details on this page, like the patterns of the sunflowers and the dangles on the tunics.

✳ Differently carved but matching frames border the two pages here. Inside the left-hand frame, with a mouse on a tree and a green plant bordering the text, Goldilocks peers into the cottage window, behind the wonderful carved bear and flower pillar. The thatched roof arches above. Goldilocks enters through another archway on the right-hand page, looking at the chair, table, and rug we saw previously. On her right is the fancy door we saw on the cottage before, while on the left is a chest carved with the sunflowers and topped by a fancy throw and an owl-held candle. Horizontal floor boards in the foreground are balanced by decorated beams above.

* Now the side borders of the two-page spread have the tops of carved pine cones, while the carved mice are planting the bulbs at the bottom. In between, Brett shows us the baby bear involved with a beehive on the left, while the animal frieze runs across the top, and sunflowers on a white tablecloth border the bottom. A mouse peeks out to watch on the lower right, as Goldilocks lifts the lid to peer into the steaming large bowl. The other two bowls stand covered and waiting in line on the table.

* Two matching, simple, carved frames border the two pictures of Goldilocks in action. Brett leaves white space in both frames for the text. On the left, the squashy red chair with blue tassels is tried. The other two chairs are visible on the sides. On the right-hand page, the animal frieze and tree trunks with stone steps are repeated as inner frames. Goldilocks falls realistically as the baby's chair breaks around her. Do her positions in the two pictures balance? Should they? Note that she still clutches the flowers.

* Different matching frames are used again; each has an inner border or borders, with space for text. Goldilocks enters left foreground on the left-hand page as if onto a stage with arches and framed sides. The mouse has crept out to watch from the lower right. On the right-hand page, the elaborately carved bed fills the scene, with Goldilocks perched uncomfortably at the too-high head.

* Carved strawberries top the side borders of the two-page spread, while the carved mice are busy watering the sprouting bulbs on the lower sides. In the center of the left border, Goldilocks sleeps, while in the center right, we have a close-up of the flowers still in her hand. The bears have returned, and each is surveying a bowl, as we have a clear picture of their dismay. Two of the bowls still sit on the table, but the baby bear has picked his up to look inside, only to find it all gone. Father leans over and in from the left, while the baby leans the other way on the right.

* The outer frame of this spread has carved bees and their hives on the tops of the side borders, while the carved mice deal with the insect life around their growing flowers on the bottom. In the center of the left border, mother examines her chair, while in the center of the right border, the baby peers through the broken bottom of his. In the center, we have the room framed with the animal frieze, tree trunks, and carpet. A furious father roars as he tilts his chair and almost breaks the border; mother looks timidly over his shoulder. Baby sits on the floor on the lower right, sadly contemplating the wreckage of his chair.

* Two frames and pictures show two different beds. From a side view, the carved bed fills the left-hand page. Father leans over amid the pillows, while two mice watch next to the fancy fur boots. On the right-hand page,

mother's bed makes an interior frame, inside which she sits center stage with her elaborately patterned pillows. Two mice watch from the top here.

✳ Another two-page spread with carved side borders appears on the next pages. This time the frame has flowers on either side at the top, and mice with the blooms about to open on the bottom sections. In the center of the left border, father bear's head appears looking in amid his covers, while in the center of the right border, mother looks in over her pillow. The carved arch of the baby's bed forms the backdrop for him looking at Goldilocks, peacefully sleeping on the right, flowers in hand. A mouse peeks through the carving.

✳ Now the borders have carved butterflies on the tops, and mice frolicking around the open flowers on the bottom. Other real mice watch, or can't bear to, in the centers of the borders. In the two-page spread, a frightened, awake Goldilocks pulls back in the lower right, as the mother and baby watch her from her left, and father bear looms, enormous, above her.

✳ Flowers forgotten, she runs off to the right in the left-hand framed picture, as the bears watch from the other side of the bed, and the mice from underneath. On the right-hand page, we see how cleverly Brett has designed the house so Goldilocks can jump out of the window without being hurt. She carefully picks her way along the thatch as the bears watch, framed in the window; baby is now clutching the flowers. The picture has balance and stability, as does the life of the bears now that Goldilocks is leaving.

✳ And indeed, the last picture, framed inside with an arch and with the circles set in the window, shows us the comfortable huddle of happy family togetherness, with the flowers as a central focus. Goldilocks is faintly disappearing, seen at a distance through the window, as the mice watch her go.

RELATED ACTIVITIES

Children interested in the costumes may want to search in books on the history of costume, or of Switzerland or Bavaria, to see where Brett found her ideas for the attire of her characters.

When comparing versions of the story, in addition to discussing variations that add a lesson on naughty Goldilocks, compare the ways that different illustrators have depicted the bears, Goldilocks, the cottage, and, of course, the bowls, chairs, and beds.

VERSIONS TO COMPARE

Cauley, Lorinda. *Goldilocks and the Three Bears*. New York: Putnam, 1981.
Marshall, James. *Goldilocks and the Three Bears*. New York: Dial, 1988.
Stevens, Janet. *Goldilocks and the Three Bears*. New York: Holiday House, 1986.
Watts, Bernadette. *Goldilocks and the Three Bears*. New York: Holt, 1985.

BOOKS ILLUSTRATED BY BRETT

Annie and the Wild Animals. Boston: Houghton Mifflin, 1985, paper, 1989.
Beauty and the Beast. Boston: Houghton Mifflin, 1989.
The First Dog. San Diego: Harcourt Brace, 1988.
Goldilocks and the Three Bears. New York: Putnam, 1987, paper, 1990.
Lear, Edward. *The Owl and the Pussycat*. New York: Putnam, 1991.
The Mitten: A Ukranian Folk Tale. New York: Putnam, 1990.
The Twelve Days of Christmas. New York: Putnam, 1990.
The Wild Christmas Reindeer. New York: Putnam, 1990.

Once a Mouse . . . A Fable Cut in Wood
by Marcia Brown

Over her long career as illustrator, Marcia Brown has worked in several styles with different media, telling all kinds of stories and fairy tales with her pictures, winning prizes like the Caldecott medal along the way. Her skill is apparent, whatever medium she chooses, as is her sincere attempt to express the emotions as well as the factual or historical context of the tale. Although it is thirty years old, *Once a Mouse* . . . was chosen for several reasons. First of all, it is an authentic fable "from ancient India," as the title page states. It is illustrated in a manner that native Indians feel captures the spirit of their country and its folk art. And finally, the original illustrations are done with color wood cuts, which are rarely used now for illustration. Children can get an idea of the characteristics of this kind of art and perhaps be inspired to try some kind of printmaking themselves.

✳ Brown has used three colors (ochre, dark olive green, and a brick red) and, of course, the space left uncolored on the white paper. In using the wood cut technique, she had to cut a separate block for each color, allow for the effect of overlapping color, and carefully place each color block on the paper. The grain of the wood adds to the texture, but otherwise the color is simply pressed from the wood onto the paper and is not shaded or made darker in some parts than others. Brown uses large, uncut areas of color but still manages to get enough movement and interest because of her solid design and anatomy. The front jacket shows the areas of color and the use of the white paper to form vital parts of the tiger's head. The white also goes around the tiny, barely recognizable mouse and the hand-cut letters of the title. Past the spine, the picture continues around to the back of the jacket. Here the back of the tiger is covered with plants that are like stripes, so he doesn't need any. The face of the hermit appears mysteriously over the vegetation, again using the white of the page for definition. Brown has left little white on the back, making the picture dark and more jungle-like. The reproduction is good enough to see the grain of the wood and where Brown printed one color block over another. The cloth cover is tan, with a frieze of dark green plant and animal shapes from the end papers going across the lower part of the back and front of the cover. The title is lettered in the same kind of lettering as on the jacket, but in brick red.

✳ Brown obviously looked at either photographs or the actual animals and plants to depict the striking action scene on the end papers. Here, the plant and animal frieze goes across the bottom, while gazelle-like creatures leap across the center against the brick red background. Above them, birds fly and monkeys swing through foliage. Even the ripple of the horns implies action, and the leaves bend and sway in different directions. Brown uses a minimum of detail, but the creatures all have identities.

✳ All this action contrasts with the title page, which is mainly white, with simple lettering and a picture of dark green with only touches of ochre. The very simplified but recognizable mouse at the lower left looks toward the hermit squatting under the tree. Brown has used just the trunk, two branches, and a few leaves; yet we accept this as a tree with a bird in it. How do the ochre leaves and grass change the picture from what it would be if they were the same color as the rest? Each leaf has a place in Brown's design.

✳ All the print will be in the olive green, like the dedication and copyright on the left-hand page. The first *O*, however, is printed in red, which also brightens the picture on the right-hand page. Brown has made this illustration an active contrast to the title page. The mouse is running here, the bird is flying, even the tree trunk has those active lines. Compare the hermit's position and the angle of his legs with the picture on the title page.

✳ More action spills across the two-page spread. We get just an indication of trees and grass on the left as the hermit runs, so fast his beard blows back. Brown leaves a large portion of these pages white, but makes a ground of sorts from the jagged-edged area of ochre, with two points framing the running mouse, like the shadow of the crow's beak. The crow dominates the scene and the mouse.

✳ Brown chooses to confine the text to the left-hand page here and uses only the right-hand page for the illustration. Again using two colors, and only a touch of ochre, she fits the hermit into the confined space, carefully placing his arms and body as he reaches over to grab the crow and cradle the mouse in his hand. Do you miss the red in this picture?

✳ Now there is little white, as Brown covers most of the two pages with ochre, with the green making shadow-like trees and grass. The hut forms a sort of frame for hermit, mouse, and food. The cat emerges lower right.

✳ The hermit and mouse are in opposition to the cat. Against a textured, circular, ochre background, the hermit bends over and curls his arm and hand protectively around the mouse, even as his other hand reaches for the bowl. On the right-hand page, the cat is almost a horizontal weapon, with even the whiskers pointing at the mouse. The setting is just a suggestion of vegetation that stands up like the tail, but Brown brings the red back here, perhaps for the danger.

✳ The newly created cat confronts the other cat, now in quite a different body position, across the gutter of this two-page scene. Brown leaves just enough white for highlights, especially for the text and the new cat, who fairly bristles. The trees around them are sketched in. The hermit stands watching, straight up, parallel to the gutter, between the cats.

✳ Now the red washes over almost the entire two-page spread, perhaps for the danger in the night. The silhouette of the dog as the remaining white, really stands out against the red, while the new cat, mainly in ochre and white, is easy to see. Bed, hermit, and cat are all horizontals under the thatched roof, contrasting with the active images on the left-hand page.

✳ Brown places the hermit in the upper left, gesturing to surround the page with swirls of magic that extend across the gutter. He thus produces a new dog to turn and snarl with jagged teeth at the other dog, who stands with only vegetation behind him and suggestions of stones underneath. He no longer threatens.

✳ The red color of menace returns for the tiger and his shadow and also, interestingly enough, for the book the hermit is reading. Vegetation frames all the characters here. Brown has curled the tiger above the dog, building his body with suggested rather than real anatomy, for example, drawing no outline for the bottom of his belly. But we still believe this is a tiger.

* The red is gone, and a magnificent new tiger now stretches across the two-page spread under the exaggeratedly long outstretched arms of the hermit. The shadow seems to remain dog, however. Note the textured lines in the background that suggest the waves of magic. The hands of the hermit curl up, like the tiger's tail.

* What a wonderfully rich forest scene Brown depicts here, with tall trees, white left for the ground, many kinds of foliage, so many animals above and below the stalking tiger, and the fleeing gazelles of the end papers. The red here may simply be used to give more dimension to the picture, or it may represent the fear the tiger inspires in the other creatures.

* Several animals watch from in and around the tree at the left, as the hermit circles his arms and points at the tiger, filling the right-hand page under the text. The tiger's expression is not one of pleasure.

* The angry tiger sprawls straight across the two pages, which are almost completely red around him. Only some tall grass frames the picture on the right. Imagine how unbalanced the picture would be without it. Countering it on the left-hand page, reading his book, sits the hermit. He looks very small compared to the tiger.

* But see how Brown has moved the hermit into control again. His strong face dominates on the left, and his pointing arm and finger come across the page and are above the tiger completely.

* Although smaller here, the hermit still controls in this wordless, two-page picture. His arms stretch out towards and above the foliage, as the tree limbs reach toward him from the right-hand page. The red washes over most of this picture; pick your reason. Far on the right, in a white area surrounded by red, the mouse is running. Brown adds animals watching in the tree, and clouds crossing the sun at the upper left. Or is it the moon at night?

* The hermit sits much as he did on the title page, quietly thinking. Here Brown surrounds him with foliage, including the bird back in the tree. The white space on the bottom of the page continues up into the forest a bit at the right, and there is, surprisingly, a mouse. Is the bird about to attack and start the story again?

If interest in India is aroused by this tale, research into Indian history, art, and culture can reveal much of importance for children about this large, but frequently ignored country.

In addition to many fairy tales that she illustrated years ago, which are still popular, Brown did handsome wood cut illustrations for *All Butterflies: An ABC* (Scribner, 1974), now out of print, but still available in some libraries. Her award-winning *Shadow* combines cut paper, painting, and wood cuts for illustrations that older children really appreciate. *Of Swans, Sugarplums, and Satin Slippers* by Violette Verdy. is not really a picture book, but it is filled with Brown's dancing water color, pastel, and pencil illustrations of scenes from ballets.

ART ACTIVITY

Although they cannot make real wood cuts, children can use various materials into which they can cut or incise designs or patterns. Styrofoam meat trays from the supermarket can be easily incised with pencils or ball-point pens. A material called Polyprint that has an adhesive back and is available at art supply stores can be incised with the desired picture and stuck to blocks of wood for a more professional effect and easier handling for stamping. With care, children can cut their illustration into old stand-bys like soap and potatoes. Such incised designs then have to be inked or colored in some way, then stamped onto paper or cloth. All kinds of ready-made stamps and stamp pads are also available for experiments.

The next step is practice with more than one color, using separate pictures for each color and seeing what happens when you place one on top of the other.

AVAILABLE BOOKS BY AND/OR ILLUSTRATED BY BROWN

Cendrars, Blaise. *Shadow*. New York: Scribner, 1982, Macmillan paper, 1986.
Once a Mouse . . . : A Fable Cut in Wood. New York: Macmillan, 1961, paper, 1989.
Verdy, Violette. *Of Swans, Sugarplums, and Satin Slippers*. New York: Scholastic, 1991.

Snow-White and the Seven Dwarfs

translated by Randall Jarrell,
pictures by Nancy Ekholm Burkert

Nancy Ekholm Burkert is an artist who spends much of her time painting for gallery exhibitions and has illustrated only a few books. If possible, it is interesting to compare the original 1972 printing of *Snow-White,* which was a Caldecott Honor book but never satisfied Burkert, with the 1985 printing, which made her happier. Obviously she is a perfectionist, researching her costumes and settings until they resemble period stage sets with props; she works her compositions until she feels moving anything would spoil them and makes her characters three-dimensional human portraits in dramatic, real-life action. With its long text translated by the poet Randall Jarrell, this is probably not even a picture book by strict definition, having six two-page spreads with no words and one other illustration. But Burkert's work is worth examining for its quality, and also for comparison with other versions of the story.

✳ On the dust jacket, Snow-White herself seems so realistically alive that we almost hear her breathing through her parted lips as she looks back over her shoulder. There is anxiety rather than peace in both her expression and the angle of her neck. Burkert uses the white of the background as part of the girl's complexion, just touching it with color. The face is framed on two sides with the leaves of the forest she must flee into, and on the third side by her hair only. Burkert uses some opaque paint, but provides texture with colored pencils. The arresting face is framed with a thin white border, then by a black line that is further out into the brick red background of the jacket. The title, in upper- and lower-case letters, is white like the area around Snow-White's picture. The rest of the information is in upper-case black letters, matching her hair. The cloth cover is also black, relieved only by the metallic lettering on the spine and the incised, medieval-like medallion of birds and flower, nice for rubbing, on the front.

∗ The end papers are elaborately designed reflections of the banners and shields of the Middle Ages and early Renaissance, with borders like those in medieval manuscripts.

∗ By contrast, the title is printed on the half-title page in the same type as on the jacket, in pale gray on white.

∗ The title and other information on the title page are in black but with the same print as on the jacket. The publisher information is punctuated, however, by two red triangles similar to the end papers, and all the information is framed by a blue border. The focus of our attention is on the elaborate frame around nothing, that is, of course, the mirror that is so important to the story. What a marvelous design it is, even to the Latin motto on the top! Let the students look the words up in a Latin dictionary later. Just tell them the form under which to look for the second word is *veritas; veritatis* is the genitive or possessive form, meaning "of." Burkert has touched the mirror frame with a blue that matches the frame of the words below.

∗ Two more plain white pages with black print rest the eyes.

∗ The small amount of text begins on the right-hand page on a large expanse of white, which also serves as the snow of winter. A pale gray frames the page, while the initial letter is part of the winter scene, just like those seen in illuminated manuscripts. On the left-hand page, bordered in gray-blue, red, and a thin black line, a mullioned window in a stone building right out of a picture from the Middle Ages frames the queen at her sewing. Her costume, hair, and background designs are also true to the pictures from those times. Burkert uses more white snow here, with vast expanses of gray stone. There are only touches of gold, red, and blue, concentrated in the window around the queen.

∗ Two pages of text are carefully placed on the white pages, with a gray line frame going across the gutter and around the two-page spread. The text ends by telling us that Snow-White is terrified in the forest with the wild beasts.

∗ Within the gray, dark green, and white frame around the two-page spread, Burkert has frozen a moment in time. This forest has real trees and animals, accurate in every detail. Take time with the children to spot all the animals and birds that are lurking there. As mist filters through the trees on the left-hand page, Snow-White runs left, anxiously looking back to the right. The jacket portrait might be a close-up of her in this scene. The animals on the left all look right also, as the vegetation leans toward her. Most of the other birds, animals, and plants look and lean toward her as well, but the fierce wild boar could be safely charging away. The darkness on the right seems to be changing into brightness on the left as she runs. Note how few colors Burkert has used for all this detail, and how sparingly she has used them. Only the girl's yellow undergarment and the yellow bird are really bright.

✳ Another balanced, framed text fills two pages.

✳ We are inside a hut that is right out of the period, from the pots and broom by the fireplace to the lion-shaped ewer to pour water for hand-washing, to the early knives and forks. Burkert has framed the two-page spread with gray, red, and black, and then used the elements of the room, such as eaves, fireplace, bed, and table, to frame the people. This frozen moment shows the dwarfs coming home from work. Far from the caricatures of Disney, these dwarfs are seven individual, separate people. Snow-White herself has become a composed homemaker rather than a frightened girl. Although there are angles and some action in this picture, essentially it is a peaceful one. Burkert has used rich reds and yellows and patterns here to warm the scene.

✳ Two more pages of text are framed in gray.

✳ Burkert moves here from realistic scenes back into the pages of an illuminated medieval manuscript. Framed in white and black, low on the left-hand page, is a realistic scene. We cannot see the wicked queen's face, here or elsewhere, but her black-clad figure strides off to the right, leaving Snow-White, hair again loose, crumpled on the ground and trailing down to the left. The outside of the house here is rendered in complete detail. The rest of the background is sketched in a darker blue against the light blue of twilight, but if you look closely, every detail is there. Burkert sets the queen's head against the pale pink patch of sky and has the colorful ribbons trailing against the black, leading to the patch of red that is Snow-White's dress.

All around the small, realistic picture is a mystical, medieval one. The outside frames, pale green top and bottom, blue on the sides, are succeeded by white, then green, then elaborate traceries of reverse blue and green, with winged faces in the corners. Then another green and white frame surrounds the picture that goes across the two pages. The bottom is an undulating hill of green, mainly pointed trees, and the top is the same blue of twilight, with the setting sun personified on top with the touch of fiery red. A white path winding up and a line of white on the horizon stand out from the blue, within which rise hills, mountains, castles, towns, farmers, animals, and knights. Colored shields also appear. On the lower right, balanced against Snow-White and the queen, a reddish dragon curls around, as it symbolically seizes a white rabbit in its jaws. The reds, blues, and greens are used for effect here, rather than realism. The figures, designs, and scenes are reflections from those in medieval art.

✳ A great deal of text on the same framed white pages takes us to the making of the poisoned apple.

✳ We are back to a frozen moment, but this one could be in a nightmare. All the items on the table might have come from an alchemist's workshop. Curious students might want to research what some of the herbs are. Burkert has put them in the foreground, with the ominous dark background relieved by pale light through windows on either side. The pestle on the lower left points to the fatal apple in the book, while the outstretched arm of the queen holds the real apple upper right, as she swirls away to do her mischief. The bats, bugs, and skull add to the evil atmosphere. The pink of the queen's dress and hat is almost incongruous in this setting. We still are not allowed to see her face.

✳ Two more framed white pages filled with text bring the king's son to Snow-White's coffin.

✳ The black and gray of the frame, the rocks, and the cloaks of the dwarfs, as well as their attitudes, are in keeping with their mourning. But Burkert gives us a touch of light and pink on the upper left-hand page that spills down and leads to the bright colors and opulence of the coffin. The prince's entourage bears all the trappings we have seen in the medieval paintings. I don't feel this prince has much character in his face compared to the dwarfs, but fairy tale princes always get their princesses, however dull the princes may be.

✳ The text ends on these two framed pages, with a pale gray, stylized leaf to mark the end.

✳ Although this is one picture on the two-page spread, it is divided neatly with a column and arch on each side. A bright frame with blue and white inside goes around it all. On the left, the white dog we saw at the dwarf's house looks at the empty black and arched area where stairs are going down. There, all that remains of the wicked queen are her burnt-out shoes in the darkness. Above the arch, an angel symbolically weighs what might be justice. There is no softening of the queen's fate in this version, as there are in some others. Meanwhile, on the right, the prince and Snow-White, her hand outstretched, climb up stairs toward the bright yellow light, the colorful floating banners, the waiting king and dwarfs, and the sounding trumpets. The tapestry on the wall also symbolizes their "happily ever after."

RELATED ACTIVITIES

The library is full of books about the Middle Ages, with pictures of the costumes and settings Burkert has depicted. Students will appreciate her work more if they can see the sources.

Books on medieval art will show the students her other sources. Look especially for the handsome reproductions of the Books of Hours that are now available. The illustrations in these are what Burkert is frequently echoing.

Burkert has completed only one book since she did *Snow-White,* and it also has too much text to be called a picture book. The illustrations, however, are stunning, and worth bringing to the attention of students who like her work. It is *Valentine and Orson* (Farrar, Straus, 1989), which is also full of the flavor, spirit, and details of the Middle Ages.

VERSIONS TO COMPARE

Barrett, Angela. *Snow White* retold by Josephine Poole. New York: Knopf, 1991.

Burkert, Nancy Ekholm. *Snow-White and the Seven Dwarfs* retold by Randall Jarrell. New York: Farrar, Straus, 1972, 1985.

French, Fiona. *Snow White in New York.* New York: Oxford, 1986.

Hyman, Trina Schart. *Snow White.* Boston: Joy Street, 1974.

Iwasaki, Chihiro. *Snow White and the Seven Dwarves.* Natick, MA: Picture Book Studio, 1985.

Jeffers, Susan. *Snow White and the Seven Dwarfs* retold by Freya Littledale. New York: Four Winds, 1981.

Watts, Bernadette. *Snow White and the Seven Dwarfs.* Winchester, MA: Faber and Faber, 1983.

Rumpelstiltskin
by Donna Diamond

Donna Diamond has illustrated many books that are not picture books, and even *Rumpelstiltskin* is a borderline picture book in its relation and balance between text and pictures telling the story. But she offers a very distinctive style of drawing that children find fascinating. It is also particularly interesting to compare her drawings with other versions of the same characters and with the pencil drawings of other illustrators. Her work has the reality of black-and-white photographs but with an added air of mystery and luminosity.

---

* The paper jacket is white, with the title and illustrator printed in plum letters: italic upper and lower case for the title, simple print for the illustrator. On the front of the jacket, Rumpelstiltskin seems to be introducing himself to us with a deep, deferential bow. He looks incredibly real, three-dimensionally modelled and throwing a shadow, one arm pointing up toward his name, the title. On the back of the jacket, a small vignette of the vital spinning wheel of the story is also drawn with solidity, casting its own shadow. The cover under the jacket uses black for the spine binding. The remainder is a lighter shade of the plum used for the lettering on the jacket. The title is incised in similar letters on the cover. There is no other color anywhere in the book. You must decide whether you think the book is successful without it.

* The end papers are all white.

* The half-title page repeats the title again in black.

* The title page repeats the title again in black, but larger. The spinning wheel from the back of the jacket is repeated under the title. The other information is also printed in black.

* Simple black printing is used for dedication and copyright.

* Solid tree trunks are drawn on the left, with real-looking blades of grass growing at the base. The leaves and shadows are indicated. But in this picture, which uses part of the page as a white frame, what really catches our attention are the central figures. The girl pulls and leans away, one fist clenched, obviously reluctant. The older man, her father we understand, holds her wrist tightly and looks away from her. He is not happy, but he will do as he is told. Both figures are solidly real, dressed in period costume with actual folds and wrinkles. We would almost say that they were photographed, but the book tells us that they were drawn in pencil by Diamond on Mylar. Perhaps the Mylar accounts for the luminous, almost glowing, quality of some of the white areas in these extraordinary drawings. The text is printed simply in black on the right-hand page, with a lot of paper left white.

* Two pages of text still leave quite a bit of white space and room for a vignette on each page. One shows the spinning wheel again; this is where it enters the story. The other is the traded necklace, an unimpressive string of beads.

* The picture here goes across the two-page spread, framed in white, with no text. The girl sits dejectedly on straw that looks very real. One hand hangs limp and useless, as she hopelessly contemplates the straw pieces in her other hand. The spinning wheel is directly opposite her, amid its own pile of straw. The whole scene is dramatically lit by the full moon shining through the window. The squares of the window contrast with the triangles on either side formed by the eaves, and with the triangles at the spinning wheel. But the patterns are secondary to the girl, the dark, and the light.

* Two more pages of text and white space contain two more vignettes, a pile of the spun gold and a ring—a real contrast to the large pictures.

* The white-framed picture across the two pages offers a jet black background, which makes us wonder how Diamond does this with a pencil. Against this, the girl and Rumpelstiltskin look at each other, behind the arc and spokes of the vital wheel that seems to join them. He takes the ring; she clutches her breast anxiously. They look so very real.

* Another contrasting two pages of white and text have two views of the little man in action. He kneels and gestures in from the left, then leans in and offers a hand on the right. Would the pictures work as well reversed?

* We are in a grand-looking room, with the spun gold stacked on either side. Central, and just visible in the gloom, is a carved and decorated fireplace with the wheel centered inside it. Here the light pours in from a castle-type window with a drape, throwing a shadow on the floor. In the light, the king kneels to kiss the girl's hand. She seems happy enough. Note the dragon picture on the castle wall.

* With the text, Diamond balances a chest and bags of coins on the left with a hand-waving baby on the right.

* Against another black background, the girl and the little man gesture at each other from the ends of the bed as they bargain. Diamond lights this scene from a cathedral-type window behind the girl. A drape cuts across the corner. The light plays with the folds of the bedclothes and puts highlights and shadows on the contrapuntal characters.

* Diamond varies the format on these two text pages. A wolf and a rabbit gaze at each other on a line of grass under the right-hand page text. Is this a reflection of the confrontation of the girl and man on the previous page?

* This two-page picture is strange in its arrangement. An expanse of moonlit grass runs all across the bottom. Huge tree trunks cast shadows. Other trees stand and lean. Far over on the right, under the full moon shining on his cottage, dwarfed by the trees, Rumpelstiltskin dances around the fire. How else might you design this page?

✳ On the name-guessing page, Rumpelstiltskin cavorts in four different positions. Would you arrange this page differently?

✳ We see him last on two pages, spread across against a black background, illuminated by light from somewhere. He grimaces as he is about to, as the text tells us, tear himself in two. The children don't believe that. But they enjoy this version anyhow.

ART ACTIVITY

If any express interest, children can be encouraged to try to get the effect of realistic solid shapes by using pencils and shading. They might want to look at some of Chris Van Allsburg's black-and-white illustrations for *The Garden of Abdul Gasazi* (Houghton Mifflin, 1979) and *Jumanji* (Houghton Mifflin, 1981) for inspiration. But they should know that Van Allsburg created some, if not all of these illustrations by doing more than simply drawing with a pencil. He also scratches or files the graphite used in drawing pencils to obtain graphite dust, which he then applies to the page with a brush.

BOOKS ILLUSTRATED BY DIAMOND

Clifford, Eth. *The Remembering Box*. Boston: Houghton Mifflin, 1985.
Duncan, Lois. *Horses of Dreamland*. Boston: Little, Brown, 1985.
Hodges, Margaret. *The Arrow and the Lamp: The Story of Psyche*. Boston: Little, Brown, 1989.
Rumpelstiltskin. New York: Holiday House, 1983.
Swan Lake. New York: Holiday, 1980.

VERSIONS TO COMPARE

Galdone, Paul. *Rumpelstiltskin*. New York: Clarion, 1985.
Wallner, John. *Rumpelstiltskin*. Englewood Cliffs: Prentice-Hall, 1984.
Zelinsky, Paul. *Rumpelstiltskin*. New York: Dutton, 1986.

The Tale of the Mandarin Ducks
by Katherine Paterson,
illustrated by Leo and Diane Dillon

Choosing just one of the books illustrated by the Dillons was almost impossible. Not only have they produced a consistently fine series of picture books on a multitude of subjects over many years, but each book reflects the particular cultural background or flavor of the subject and is quite different from all the others. For example, *Two Pairs of Shoes* retold by P.L. Travers has all the richness and intricate detail of Persian miniatures, while the Dillons' Caldecott-winning *Ashanti to Zulu* by Margaret Musgrove reflects their careful research for both the accurate landscape of Africa and the tribal dress of the characters. Their recent illustrations for *Aida* by Leontyne Price combine Egyptian style and patterns with elegant operatic pageantry. But *The Tale of the Mandarin Ducks* is such an interesting interpretation of eighteenth-century Japanese wood cuts, and is such a well-told story, that it became the choice.

✳ The Dillons have painted a picture, framed with the yellow-tan color of the jacket, with water colors and pastels that imitates a wood cut, with its areas of harmonic, not intense, opaque color, black outlines, and traditional design and subject matter. The textured paper of such wood cuts is also evident in these pictures. A kimono-clad couple in the doorway of their traditional house look fondly at a pair of ducks. A few chrysanthemums form a sort of canopy over the ducks. The colors used are mainly shades of yellow and brown, with touches of blue and purple. The author and title information is set in a frame of its own, against a background the color of the house. It is almost like a signboard there, with the flowers in front of it. Author and illustrator information is printed in simple black, upper-case letters. The title, however, is in an unusual, decorative print or type in a rich plum purple. On the back of the jacket, more of the traditional chrysanthemums in yellows and browns, with green stems, almost fill the picture, which is set on the yellow-tan background. Two blue birds fly off together at the upper right. The blue touched in across the top of the picture blends into the rosy orange, an effect seen in woodcuts, but difficult to achieve. In the composition, the birds are balanced against the flowers that come across to the center and lower right, and against an area of black on the lower right. The ISBN number here is a glaring intrusion. Under the jacket, the spine of the cover is golden yellow. The cover itself is the plum purple of the title letters, with the ducks incised in elegant gold.

* The end papers, in black, gray, and blue, take us dramatically into the forest that is an important part of the story. The vertical tree trunks are depicted in lines that are reminiscent of Japanese paintings. The foliage across the top and the trees seen in the distance are simply indicated in solid black. The subtle shading of the blue and the shining moon are again not typically like wood cuts. The tree branches break the monotony of all those verticals, as does the soft roundness of the tree tops.

* Throughout the book, the Dillons have chosen to place their rectangular illustrations on either side of the gutter, putting a white frame around each, even though the two-page spread usually makes what is really a single picture. This eliminates problems of lines crossing the gutter and gives a consistency to some otherwise quite differently designed pages. But that white space in the middle does sometimes break the pictures in two at a disturbing place. On the half-title page, the two ducks appear at the lower left of the left-hand page, with just a few pebbles and blades of grass sketched in for the setting. Both pages are washed with a textured orange-brown that is shaded from top to bottom and seems very bright after the dark end papers. On the right-hand page, the title appears in the same purplish letters. More chrysanthemums grow up to form and fill the lower right triangle.

* The colors and mood change again on the title page. A transparent water color landscape of lake, shore, and mountains spreads across the bottom of the two pages. The sky goes from dark blue across the top to pale pink behind the hills. Fronds of weeds grow up and lean in from the left foreground, while a Japanese-style tree grows on the right foreground, spreading out at the top. The title and author information matches that on the jacket.

* The landscape here continues from the previous page, showing the end of the lake. We see, on the left-hand page, the rest of the tree from the previous page, spreading across the top here to the other side. In the hollow of the tree is the duck; the drake swims in the pond. On the right-hand page, with the text, the hunting party enters from the right, amid trees like those on the end papers. Note the triangular form of the tree at the upper left and the triangular shape of the men and trees lower right. There are also horizontals, verticals, and diagonals galore to trace in this picture.

⁎ The text moves left, as the action comes to the foreground. All through the book, the Dillons have allowed ample space for the text in the background. Here, we can see the details of pattern and costume with which the Dillons have enriched the scene. More yellows and reds brighten the picture. The men all have faces and expressions. The angles of their arms and tools add to the action. On the far right, Shozo's hands stretch up as he pleads with the adamant master.

⁎ Costumes, faces, and gestures dominate on these pages. The vase of flowers, the translucent screen or window, and the table on which the cage sits are added typical touches. The arms, hands, and folds of garments are all carefully designed. On the right-hand page, the focus is on the caged drake.

⁎ The drooping body of the drake clearly shows his decline from the previous page. The picture of the duck in the oval frame above his head is a nice touch. The maid coming toward him on the right-hand page could have stepped right out of a Japanese wood cut. The scene behind her is also typical. Does the breaking of the bowl of fruit and plate by the white frames and gutter lessen the impact of the picture here?

⁎ This dramatic depiction of the angry lord confronting the pleading Shozo is set in a period room, with screen, platform, etc. Balanced against a box-lantern on the left, the cage has already been pushed almost out of the picture on the right.

⁎ We are back in the blue night and black trees of the end papers. In the foreground, Yasuko tenderly cradles the obviously ill drake. She again looks like she belongs in those wood cuts. The break at the gutter is particularly noticeable here.

⁎ The Dillons take this opportunity to show us a Japanese garden, as the lord shakes his fist and points his finger on the left-hand side, while Shozo bows his head from the far right. The black of the bridge and lantern connect him to the other picture, with its black doorway and branches. Note the differences in the tree branches above Shozo's head and those at the upper left.

⁎ Now we see part of the kitchen with the typical baskets and jars. The pictures, as well as the text, are fleshing out the two main characters for us. The colors here continue mainly in the yellows and browns.

⁎ The lord's wickedness is apparent in his face and in the way he clutches his scabbard. The couple flow together as they confront him. At the lower right, under the text, the tree by the pond appears in a circular frame. Are they thinking of this, or does it symbolize the ducks? Only the Dillons know. It does form an important element in the design of the two pages, however, balanced against the head of the lord.

✳ On the textured orange background without scenery, the two oddly costumed figures at the right stand against the spears and the raised sword driving the couple toward their death. The block of text on the left is balanced against the two figures at the right. The patterns on the fabrics add to the texture on the page.

✳ Back in the dark woods of the end papers, with the moon shining through the trees, the tiny figures are almost lost. The Dillons have used more color here, and more shapes and lines in their composition, than in the end papers. The text is framed here, and placed on a different color, rather than simply put in the sky or background. It might not be readable on the dark background.

✳ Shozo and Yasuko, hands bound, are in the foreground now, between the vertical trees. The two ghostly figures can scarcely be seen. Again the text is framed and on a different-colored background, set off from the darkness.

✳ Still in blue tones, the characters emerge from the darkness with their costumed mentors. Some children will already be guessing who they are. The scene shows the typical Japanese bathing setup, including a lantern. Under the text on the left is a framed picture of the cottage they have come to, as described in the text. This has its place in the design, a rectangle there opposed to the large rectangular screen at the right. Do you miss the floor line?

✳ The couple lie on their futons, in the blue darkness, across the two pages, covered with patterned quilts. Again a frame surrounds a readable text. The table at the upper left counterbalances the text frame upper right.

✳ The colors return to rich oranges. The couple in their doorway fill the left of the left-hand page, with the chrysanthemums at the lower left reminding us of the jacket and half-title page. The duck and drake fill the right-hand page with their splendor. Their colors can now be related to the costumes worn by the so-called messengers.

✳ The yellow-oranges and the blues blend in this "happy ever after" picture. On the left-hand page, the cottage is now surrounded by activities, even Japanese kite flying. The text must be framed here, for it really can't fit anywhere. On the right, the couple walk off through the vertical trees into old age together. Although aging, Yasuko holds a spray of blossoms, perhaps to show that their love still blooms.

✳ The dedication and copyright information at the close are printed on the same illustrations as the half-title pages at the front.

This tale contains many of the usual elements of traditional fairy tales for children to notice. It also introduces many items of Japanese life and culture, some of which can still be found in Japan today. An entire project on Japan can be launched with this book.

Materials on Japan's history, and its life today, can be found in the 915's and 950's at the library. Students should also look at wood cuts by such famous artists as Hiroshige and Hokusai and at Japanese paintings in books on Japanese art history for both style and subject matter.

Alan Say uses Japanese wood cuts as his inspiration for the humorous legend *The Boy of the Three Year Nap* (Houghton Mifflin, 1988), an interesting book to compare with the Dillons'. Contrast the art of both these books with the Japanese painting technique used by Suekichi Akaba in Katherine Paterson's retelling of *The Crane Wife* (Morrow, 1981, Mulberry paper, 1987).

ART ACTIVITY

Experiments with printing, such as those described in the section on Marcia Brown, can be used to help the students understand the qualities of a print versus a painting. (See p. 121.) More mature or adventurous students might want to try their hand at Oriental painting. Special brushes and ink blocks used for this type of painting are available at art supply stores. The dry ink block is moistened to make liquid ink. A brush of the desired size then is used to apply the ink to paper with large or small strokes using the tip or flat part of the brush to obtain the effect desired. No corrections or changes are possible, so make sure you try it yourself first.

PICTURE BOOKS ILLUSTRATED BY THE DILLONS

Aardema, Verna. *Who's in Rabbit's House?* New York: Dial, 1975.
———. *Why Mosquitoes Buzz in People's Ears: A West African Tale*. New York: Dial, 1977.
Aida as told by Leontyne Price. San Diego: Harcourt Brace, 1990.
Brenner, Barbara. *The Color Wizard*. New York: Bantam, 1989.
Hearn, Michael Patrick. *The Porcelain Cat*. Boston: Little, Brown, 1985.
Musgrove, Margaret. *Ashanti to Zulu*. New York: Dial, 1977.
Paterson, Katherine. *The Tale of the Mandarin Ducks*. New York: Dutton Lodestar, 1990.
Travers, P. L. *Two Pairs of Shoes*. New York: Viking, 1980.

Walter, Mildred Pitts. *Brother to the Wind*. New York: Lothrop, 1985.
Willard, Nancy. *Pish, Posh, Said Hieronymus Bosch*. San Diego: Harcourt Brace, 1991.

Come a Tide
by George Ella Lyon,
pictures by Stephen Gammell

When Stephen Gammell's impressionistic black-and-white drawings for *Where the Buffaloes Begin* by Olaf Baker (Warne, 1981) won a Caldecott Honor Award, his draftsmanship and ability to create real animals in believable landscapes began to be appreciated. Two other qualities have emerged in his work since then to add to our admiration. One is his use of colored pencils and water colors, handled deftly to add to the meaning of his illustrations. The other is a wonderful sense of humor that children respond to immediately. It keeps us smiling even when he deals with serious or potentially frightening situations. Gammell usually illustrates the words of others, but always brings to their work his distinctive style and the added dimensions of his illustrations. Gammell has illustrated two books about mountain life by fine Appalachian writers: *The Relatives Came* by Cynthia Rylant (Bradbury, 1985) and *Come a Tide* by George Ella Lyon. For both stories, his pictures give us a feeling for the people and countryside, as well as a sense of fun and delight.

✳ Rain splashes in through the blue line frame onto Grandma and the girl who will be telling us the story. They are just about to set the cloth down for a picnic. Gammell has used his colored pencils sketchily for grass and hair, more precisely to show us the indomitable face of Grandma turned toward the coming rain. He applies his water color paints transparently and splashily for effects the pencils do not give. He also leaves a lot of white space for part of the picture; in fact, the back of the jacket is all white, except for the splashes of rain that carry over to the front. Grandma stands resolutely straight against the rain, which comes in at an angle. The cloth and basket form an opposite angle. Against the blues and greens of rain and grass, the line of golden sunshine, the yellow hair-ribbon, and the touches of pink and red brighten the picture. The dark red of the shaded letters of the title seems an odd choice; they do not match anything else. The slant of the letters works against the slant of the rain. Author and illustrator information in black italic letters also does not blend with the picture. But the first water of the tide has come before we open the book. The cloth cover under the jacket is a cheery bright pink, close to colors on the jacket, with an umbrella outlined on the front.

✳ The end papers are deep blue, reminding us of the water.

✳ The page before the title page has Grandma and the girl fleeing down the hill, leaving the basket. The shaft of sunlight is almost gone, as the rain increases. Girl and Grandma are still connected by the tablecloth as they run off into the book. Note the touches of pink, red, and yellow that brighten the rainy scene.

✳ The picture and the rain extend across the two pages, as a man and a boy join the girl and Grandma atop a hill. Gammell draws and paints hills and rain very simply, but realistically. No one seems very upset by the rain. Grandma holds the girl's hand as it emerges from the cloth atop her head. We are led by the slant of rain and hill across the gutter to the title page, where the information matches that on the jacket. Here Gammell has added the slant of sunlight, with which he has also touched part of the left-hand page. He has also tilted the basket back into the picture at the lower right, with a plump pink pig nosing inside, and food spilled behind him. We can't help smiling.

✳ Gammell has splashed snow or rain above the dedication, as well as on the scene of the mountain houses where the story begins. He winds the fence down to connect the houses of this tight-knit community. He also uses the white of the page extensively for snow, but adds the warm touches of yellow lights and red truck and wagon.

✳ Grandma is back on the left-hand page, square on her rocking chair, arm protectively around the girl. There is a lot of togetherness in this story. Gammell has drawn a frame and painted behind it at the top but then splashed the paint/rain on top of it all. Here it slants one way; in the full-page picture on the other side, it slants the other or runs straight down. The trees are bent in by the driving rain. Gammell shows us the water going into the creeks that wind into the river, flowing toward us.

✳ The rain continues to come down in the pictures on both sides here, but the water flows differently. On the left-hand page, people are trying to cope with a rake and a pitchfork, leaning over into the water. On the right-hand page, the water cascades toward us again, carrying pigs and chickens, as parts of houses crumble on top. But still, bad as it seems, Gammell gives us the bright yellow and red touches. The pink pigs, especially one happily doing the backstroke, keep this from seeming a disaster.

✳ A crowd of characters on the bridge look this way and that amid the rain and flowing water. But they don't seem worried. The pig is having a wonderful time. On the right-hand page, inside the smaller frame, the dark tones may seem more serious; the light shines as a sign of watchful waiting. Gammell has spilled and dripped the drops of blue just like the water that is soaking this story.

✳ The warning is serious for those by the light in the otherwise dark house. Note how close to symmetrically balanced this picture is. On the right-hand page, the family must wade to the truck. But still, the girl seems to dance, and the colors and patterns keep us from concern. Gammell almost has us searching for a towel by this time.

✳ The truck headlights shine across the two-page spread of people and rain-soaked landscape. The pig and the indomitable Mrs. Mac show no worry.

✳ The Cains' situation is certainly grave. The truck perched on the hill leans back toward the house on the other side, as John chases the duck in the rising water. The lights from the house and the crooked headlights shine brightly through, cheering the scene up.

✳ Papa Bill, another typical character, has gathered what is important to him and lifts his hat in salute. Below the truck, the waters carry furniture, coffee pot, and another happy pig. Gammell has anchored this busy scene with the tree and the fence at the center.

✳ The artist has placed the hill and security of Grandma's house in a frame, from which he again splashes out, perhaps to separate it from the text. Note the angles of the headlights, hill, and fence, and, of course, the happy pigs. On the right-hand side he chooses to fill the page with Grandma welcoming the family as they come up the steps. Yellow light shining from the house and headlights adds warmth to the family togetherness.

✳ Around the classic scene of mother changing baby, Gammell gives us a series of vignettes of all the activities as Grandma settles everyone in for the night. Water is still dripping, but it has at least stopped falling. This activity leads directly to the almost framed-in bed on the right, where some water has splashed and still drips, but mainly where the kids are finally at rest under the cozy, poofy cover.

✳ Grandma and father have driven down to see the flooded house. Yellow light streams in behind the path as the rain seems to slow down on the left, but still pours on the right. The truck is sliding into the water, as father points to the mess. All sorts of things float in the water, which dominates the two pages.

✳ But folks seem to know how to cope. Gammell still spatters some rain about, but he has more fun with the mud in the foreground. Action and patterns abound on these pages.

✳ Another scene rich with characters, patterns, and action is touched by the shaft of sun and splashed with a few more raindrops and a lot of water color paint. Gammell has designed a series of triangles here, from the roof of the "rescue wagon," to the group being fed and those watching, down to the overturned wagon and those working on it.

✳ Drying-out items surround the text on the grass, while Grandma, the girl, the banjo-playing Papa Bill, and an African-American friend stand atop the hill in a ray of sunshine. But a few drops of rain are a warning of what may happen again, as the children splash around the frame Gammell has put on the right-hand page. The frame separates or emphasizes the dog, children, and cart careening down the hill and out of the frame.

✳ The mother holding the baby, dripping as she wades through the water, still smiles as she waves goodbye. The cheery touch of bright yellow behind her is a symbol of the courage and cheer of all the folks in the story.

Read alone, the spare, almost poetic text has wry country humor. But Gammell has really added so much more with his art.

Children may enjoy reading and comparing some of the many other books about Appalachian and mountain life, in particular Cynthia Rylant's books, like *When I Was Young in the Mountains* illustrated by Diane Goode (Dutton, 1982). Mountain music is always a favorite. One music teacher combined music and clog dancing with a study of other Appalachian crafts, like quilting and basketry, along with readings.

BOOKS WRITTEN AND ILLUSTRATED BY GAMMELL

Git Along, Old Scudder. New York: Lothrop, 1983.
Once Upon Macdonald's Farm. New York: Macmillan, 1985, paper, 1990.
Wake Up Bear... It's Christmas. New York: Lothrop, 1981, Greenwillow paper, 1990.

BOOKS BY OTHERS ILLUSTRATED BY GAMMELL

Ackerman, Karen. *The Song and Dance Man.* New York: Knopf, 1988.
Baker, Olaf. *Where the Buffaloes Begin.* New York: Warne, 1981.
Birdseye, Tom. *Airmail to the Moon.* New York: Holiday, 1988.

Blos, Joan. *Old Henry*. New York: Morrow, 1987.
Hoopes, Lyn Littlefield. *Wing-A-Ding*. Boston: Little, Brown, 1991.
Lyon, George Ella. *Come a Tide*. New York: Orchard, 1990.
————. *A Regular Rolling Noah*. New York: Bradbury, 1986.
Martin, Rafe. *Will's Mammoth*. New York: Putnam. 1989.
Rylant, Cynthia. *The Relatives Came*. New York: Bradbury, 1985.
Woodruff, Elvira. *The Wing Shop*. New York: Holiday, 1991.

Rapunzel

retold by Barbara Rogasky,
illustrated by Trina Schart Hyman

Because she has frequently stated that she believes in fairies, elves, and other fairy tale folk, it is not surprising that Trina Schart Hyman chooses to illustrate such stories. But beyond the rich store of her imagination, Hyman draws on meticulous research for the details she includes in her illustrations. She is also fond of borders and frames, sometimes elaborately decorating them or placing other borders within them. Her heroines are usually appealingly romantic, frequently with a wild profusion of hair, which contrasts with Hyman's own neatly trimmed curly cap. Many of the characters show spunk beyond that usually found in fairy tales. *Rapunzel* is an arbitrary choice from a wealth of possible Hyman child-pleasers.

✳ Our heroine looks directly at us from the dust jacket, her hair swirling madly and improbably behind her. The pale yellows and browns of her hair and dress stand out from the warm reddish brown of the background. Rich green foliage is visible behind her, with green also in the lines within the frame around her and in the leaves of the lilies she is picking. These flowers have the yellow of her hair, with bright touches of red added. One frame of mustard yellow, with green and white, goes around Rapunzel, with flowers breaking through it. It also borders the title and author information. Another border of green with white leaves separates her from the printing, which is in Gothic-like letters. These are upper case only for the title, printed in the same rich, red-brown as the background. The upper- and lower-case letters for the author and illustrator are in lighter brown and tan on a white background.

The similar mustard, green, and white frame surrounds the mysterious picture on the back of the jacket. Similar flowers to those on the front are in the foreground, but most of the red is gone. These flowers lean into the picture rather than bursting out of it. Amid abundant foliage similar to that behind Rapunzel, an old, witch-like woman leans on her cane at the left, her gardening basket at her feet and her bony hand reaching up. One black crow flies in from the upper left, while others fly down toward her reaching hand. Branches protrude in from the upper right. A pale, orange-pink sun shines in the pink sky, and a pale fuschia-pink scarf trails in curves behind the woman, both adding a touch of warmth to the dark birds and foliage, as does her bright red hat. All is not gloomy in this story; if this is a witch, she is not too menacing. The hardback edition has a cloth cover of the same rich brown as the jacket, with the Gothic letters of the title incised. If possible, compare the colors of the paperback and hardback pictures on the jacket and cover; the paperback's are more intense: another example of how the choice of paper can affect the illustrations.

✳ The hardback has end papers of a mustard yellow to go with the jacket colors. Unfortunately, the paperback does not have these.

✳ The half-title, in the Gothic-style letters, is black on white within an elaborate frame of pictures, themselves framed in mustard, on the red-brown background that is used, with slight variations in color, throughout the book. Hyman puts realistic flowers in the corners, tall birches on either side, pines and mountains on the bottom, and clouds with the sun across the top. White squares mark all corners, picking up the white of the center and the birches. The touches of pink brighten the woodsy colors.

✳ On the left-hand page, framed in red-edged, darker brown, is a sort of old-fashioned frontispiece, with a scene from further on in the story. In the border across the top, in hand-drawn letters, is a quotation that makes this clear. The scene itself is framed again on two sides by the birches in the foreground. The two ghostly figures are moving toward mist and dark green and brown trees. But off in the distance, the glowing sun and pink clouds assure us that all is not gloomy. The perky mushrooms in the bottom border, especially the red with white polka dots, add to this lightening of mood. On the right-hand page, the necessary information appears in the same style as on the jacket, on white again, but this time as part of the sky. We see the pines and mountains of the half-title page's border and the crows from the back of the jacket, but the border pictures have changed. Different realistic flowers and strawberries are in the corners and across the top. The bottom is a border of pine cones, while along the sides are elfin faces and more stylized strawberries. On this page, touches of red again cheer the dark colors.

✳ Hyman gives us decorated large and small borders and frames on the dedication and copyright page, leaving oval and white space for that information. A peasant-like design motif is added here to the other elements we have seen before. It is repeated as an interior frame for the right-hand picture. A decorated *O* begins the text on white, flanked by the first two characters. A typical peasant cottage is at the top, with branches tucked in across the bottom. The costumes seem authentic down to the wooden shoes.

✳ On the left-hand page, the text continues on white down the left side, fancily framed, with extra pictures top and bottom. The right half of the illustration shows the peasant chair and bed, with a typical Hyman cat adding interest. Although it is in a separate frame, the picture on the right-hand page belongs with that on the left. It shows us more of the same room, including the other end of the bed. Again, all the furnishings are believably peasant-like. The angle of the curtain pulled back over the bed goes with that of the scarf over the woman's shoulders as she leans out the window. Note the touches of red Hyman uses throughout.

✳ Hyman changes the point of view, so from close behind the woman, we have moved far out into the garden. We now see her contemplating it from the distant window. On the left-hand page, in a decorative frame, Hyman paints a garden full of flowers and fruit, although only the lilies we saw on the jacket are in detail in the foreground. Again she breaks the total picture into two parts, with a break, like a pillar, between them. We can tell by the pink scarf, which crosses the break, that the two pages form one scene. We do not see the face of the witch, and because she has picked pink roses, she does not seem so threatening, despite the crows in the picture. The extra borders above and below the text on the right include ladybugs, which also lighten the mood.

✳ The scene on the next two-page spread, despite the rosy, flowering borders and touches of red, is sad. The woman really looks ill; her husband is brooding and concerned. Only the cat seems content. The picture on the right-hand page is broken, continuing on the left with the waiting cradle. The section of text with white above the chair and cradle balances the design above the text to its left. The stove forms an extra border along the right-hand page.

✳ Hyman changes the page design here, with text on the upper right of the left-hand page and the lower left of the right-hand page. A sequence of pictures tells the visual story. Tall, unframed pictures on the far left and right show the first dangerous night climb over the wall and the second night's foraging in the garden. The smaller interior pictures are brighter. On the left, we see the overjoyed wife contemplating her full salad bowl, with appetite. On the right, she watches anxiously out the window.

✳ Of course, her husband is caught. The story is told here in two framed white rectangles on the left-hand page. Additionally bordered mushrooms are in the upper left-hand corner, while nighttime leaves and flowers are on the lower right. The confrontation is framed on the right-hand page. We almost can feel the husband reel backward from the angry witch, who has crows perched on her shoulders. The angle of their wings, their bodies, her elbow, the wall coming to the corner, and the tree limbs on the upper right all add to the uneasiness in this scene, although the witch herself stands there as straight as her stick.

✳ All seems well in the cozy scene on the left. Even the crows do not seem threatening, while the witch just looks like any old woman. She and Rapunzel form a cozy circle together. Leaves form the borders here, while everything in the garden blooms, roses in one corner, lilies in the other. But on the right-hand page, the text and pictures tell a different story. Above the left text, the mother is bent with grief over the cradle, now empty of her baby. Below the text on the right, the witch has already taken Rapunzel into the woods we saw in the picture opposite the title page and is arriving at the famous tower. One birch tree arches like the doorway, while the others go straight up like the tower.

✳ The gloom of the forest around the tower is relieved in the pictures by the pink sky beyond and by the strawberries flourishing in the borders. Tree limbs twist like Rapunzel's loose hair. The text is set off on the left here, while the action is at the tower on the right. Only a section of the forest is next to the text. The witch's pink scarf flies as she climbs. The scarf, her hat, and Rapunzel's dress add the color here.

✳ Enter the prince, alert and darkly handsome, dressed in a bright red tunic, in a full-page portrait framed in stylized flowers. On the right-hand page, two blocks of text on white, with the same frame all around, are topped on the left by violets with a checkerboard inner frame, and below on the right, a wistful and lonely Rapunzel looks out the window.

✳ A sort of hardware design frames the full-page picture on the right-hand page, along with the text and sunset scene on the right side of the left-hand page. At the left the prince, unframed (!), stands amid the tangled roots, staring eagerly up the tower as the braids tumble down. On the right-hand page, amid the cluttered details of her tower room, Rapunzel looks thoughtful as the prince argues his case. She seems neither "terribly frightened" nor smiling as the text suggests. The prince is suggestively circled by one of her braids.

＊ On the left, under the text, we here see the smile that wins the prince. Note the arch and circle of glowing pink sky behind her head. The borders on these two pages are, appropriately, hearts and flowers. On the left side of the right-hand page, a block of white and text is above a scene of Rapunzel weaving. Hyman uses a curtain from the upper right down the right side to oppose the figure of the intent girl. She is curved around the lower left, almost using the frame to lean against. Unframed on the right is a romantic embrace that some boys find just too much, while the girls sigh. Hyman has hair tendrils, silk, and scarf all waving in the breeze. Pink roses have replaced arrows in the prince's quiver. All the pictures here share warm, bright colors.

＊ Gloom returns. The text and pictures are framed in a simple twined and crossed pattern. Again this is really one picture with the frames and gutter cutting through. Gray rocks and a black crow are on the left-hand page, while the witch drags Rapunzel away on the right. This time there is no pink sky, no vegetation, only gray clouds, twisted roots, and dried leaves.

＊ On the left-hand page, a frightening witch confronts the prince. Hyman has posed the bodies to show action; the angry eyes and raised, claw-like hands of the witch, with the crow next to her, seem to attack the prince. The prince brings one hand up opposite the witch's to defend himself, while the other drops the flowers he has brought. Her pink scarf flutters, as does his blue sash. The very angles of their bodies confront. On the left side of the right-hand page, the white block of text is above a symbolic picture of the braid, curling at the bottom, touched by the fateful scissors. The jug on the stool may be for design or may have another meaning. The right portion of the text on white is topped by a moth with the moon behind it, surrounded by a decorated pink frame. Again the significance is unknown. All the sections are framed in rich red and gold. Pinks and reds occur on both pages, in contrast to the pages before. Perhaps this is foreshadowing happier times to come.

＊ Within pink and blue borders, with extra pink ribbons around the text, the lovers are reunited. The picture portion of the left-hand page includes the chubby babies, covered with Rapunzel's pink and white apron. Although they are surrounded by gray rocks, the tree along the right reaches up toward the pink clouds, the setting sun, and the pair of birds symbolically together on one of the branches. On the right-hand page, under more pink clouds amid gray rocks, Rapunzel leans protectively over the kneeling prince, taking his face in her hands. A rock leans in from the upper left in both pictures. A waterfall almost parallels the vertical tree. From the center of the bottom of the picture, a tree winds up and curves behind Rapunzel's back.

✳ The small family walks off into the mist toward the sunset, framed by the trees. The peasant-design border from the first page of the story returns to frame the center white portion of the end of the story, as well as two side landscapes with framing birches and more pink clouds. Interestingly enough, the witch remains in the picture on the left, her cane as upright as the tree trunk behind her.

As with the work of Vera Williams (p. 98) and Jan Brett (p. 116), children become fascinated with the borders of these pictures. They can compare the very different borders of these artists. Teachers report that for a while after studying these illustrators, all the pictures the children make have elaborate borders. It is amazing what the children sometimes put into them.

For children who want to know more about this artist, she has written *Self-Portrait: Trina Schart Hyman* (Harper, 1981).

VERSIONS TO COMPARE

Basile, Giambattista. *Petrosinella: A Neapolitan Rapunzel* illustrated by Diane Stanley. New York: Warne, 1981.

Ehrlich, Amy (and Grimm). *Rapunzel* illustrated by Kris Waldherr. New York: Dial, 1989.

Rogasky, Barbara (and Grimm). *Rapunzel* illustrated by Trina Schart Hyman. New York: Holiday House, 1982, paper, 1982.

SELECTED BOOKS ILLUSTRATED BY HYMAN

Fonteyn, Margot. *Swan Lake*. San Diego: Harcourt Brace, 1989.

Grimm Brothers. *Little Red Riding Hood*. New York: Holiday House, 1983.

———. *Sleeping Beauty*. Boston: Little, Brown paper, 1983.

Hodges, Margaret. *The Kitchen Knight: A Tale of King Arthur*. New York: Holiday House, 1990.

———. *Saint George and the Dragon*. Boston: Little, Brown, 1984.

Kimmel, Eric A. *Hershel and the Hanukkah Goblins*. New York: Holiday House, 1989.

Rogasky, Barbara. *The Water of Life*. New York: Holiday House, 1986.

Cinderella

by Charles Perrault
retold by Amy Ehrlich,
pictures by Susan Jeffers

The work of Susan Jeffers elicits "ooh" and "wow" from children, because they recognize and appreciate her attention to naturalistic detail and can see her painstaking technique of tiny strokes and cross-hatching. Much of her work is filled with the plant and animal life she seems to enjoy depicting, but her human characters are also portrayed realistically in gesture and character. Her clear, bright colors come from inks and dyes and stand out from the white of the pages, which she frequently incorporates into her pictures. Many of her books are personal interpretations of traditional tales.

✳ Jeffers's Cinderella dominates the cover, as really beautiful as we expect a fairy tale heroine to be. We are told inside the book that Jeffers has drawn detailed pencil drawings, then erased them after using a fine-line pen with her inks and dyes. Close examination reveals all the strokes of the pen that built the lines of the face, the shadows that add the third dimension, the details of the flowers twined in the separate strands of hair, and the feathers of the bird who will follow her through the book. Jeffers has Cinderella looking out past the flowers into the book, as her hair also flows off the front of the cover and onto the flap of the jacket. But the angle of the bird's tail, and its beak, lead us back to Cinderella. The bird sits on a patch which, along with the unkempt hair, reminds us that this lovely girl is also poor and possibly mistreated. The title and author information is all above the picture. Would it change the impact if it were below, or half above and half below? The title, in black, decorative, upper-case letters, is underlined with the red color of the bird. The illustrator is placed above the title here, while the author and reteller are below. The back of the cover and jacket are a pale blue, which is also used extensively inside the book.

✳ The end papers are a darker, richer blue, which also appears inside.

✳ The half-title repeats the cover lettering in a smaller size. Underneath, on leaves and flowers, perches the red bird, in a smaller vignette on the white page.

✳ The information from the cover is repeated on the title page in the space left for it in the double-page picture that sets the stage for the story to come. Jeffers has used the white of the page as a sort of frame, but breaks it whenever she feels it appropriate. A real fairy tale castle on the left is reflected in the peaceful, still water. Hills frame the title and are also reflected in the lake. In the foreground, the mother swan and her babies are quietly settled among the flowers. Only the blue hummingbirds seem to be moving, along with the swing of the pennants atop the castle towers. The curves of birds' bodies, hills, outlined flowers and leaves and pennants and the flat horizon line all add to the quiet of the scene. Jeffers has used very little color, but she balances the warm reds and yellows in the lower right with the mainly cool blues and greens in the upper left, using orange cross-hatching to tie it all together.

✳ The left-hand page simply offers information. On the dedication page on the right, our very human-looking heroine sits in front of the gate in the wall, mobcap by her bare feet, flowers around her, red bird on her shoulder. Because her face is so much smaller here, it has less detail, but we can certainly recognize her from the cover. Jeffers has set Cinderella in the center, putting some vertical flower stalks and the gate and wall behind her. Then Jeffers has curved the top of the gate and the stones, the rest of the flowers, plants, and basket to match the curve of Cinderella's head and body. Cover the bunches of flowers and leaves at the lower right to see how they add to the composition and balance the words of the dedication. Notice also how Jeffers uses bunches of circles to give the impression of foliage and flowers.

✳ The story begins as we meet the major characters in a picture that starts on the left-hand page but sweeps across the gutter at the top. Jeffers places them in action on the stairs by the castle window, framed by the arch, the bannister, and the sweep of railing. The character of the stepmother is clear from her gesture and facial expression. The sisters are simply shown as remote and haughty. They will be told apart more by the color of their dresses than by their faces. Cinderella's dejection is clear from her posture and face, as she leans away from the scolding, holding her broom. The little red bird is watching her. Note the placement of the orange-yellows, reds, and blue.

✳ Jeffers contrasts two scenes on the facing pages above the text. On the left-hand page, Cinderella huddles by the fireplace, her broom leaning above her. The sparse corner holds only the brightness of the cooking pots and the bird. Jeffers adds a shaft of light behind Cinderella, perhaps a ray of hope? On the right-hand page, we see the excited sisters on the stairs, in different dresses of their colors of red and blue. In the arched doorway, the stepmother, dressed in her characteristic yellow, receives the important invitation from the bowing courtier, whose horse is seen behind him through the door.

✳ In a vignette above the text on the left-hand page, Cinderella helps one sister dress, while the other admires herself in the mirror. On the white right-hand page, Jeffers gives us a full picture of the sweeping departure for the ball. The stairs and background with the chandelier form a balanced, almost monochrome frame for the delighted, dressed-up ladies. Cinderella stands quietly watching from the top of the stairs, while the bird perches across from her.

✳ The magic begins. The elaborate red coach tops the right-hand page against the night-blue sky. The fairy godmother smilingly touches it with her magic wand, as an astonished Cinderella is eclipsed by the other upraised arm. But the action and wonder of this double-page spread is in how Jeffers moves from the tiny mice coming out of the cage around and across the pages to the prancing horses at the bottom, galloping over to stand under the text on the left-hand page. They move amid the blades of grass and tiny blue flowers that bring a touch of the real world to the fantasy of the picture.

✳ More grass and flowers frame the right and left and spill over to sit under the text on the left-hand page, as the delighted Cinderella finds herself beautifully costumed for the ball. Note the cascade of purple flowers that grows from behind the godmother to a point above Cinderella, and then into the archway where the coach and horses are waiting.

✳ In this white-framed, two-page spread with no words, Jeffers represents Cinderella's excitement in the riot of flowers through which we seem to be watching her, and in the galloping horses with flying manes and tails. Her expression is more one of watchful anticipation. Jeffers adds the oval multicolor garden on the lower right, the castle on the upper right, and the pebbles on the road; all of which make this picture almost too busy and complex to find Cinderella.

✳ The picture sweeps above and below the text here, and across the gutter, to give us the roofs, windows, and night sky above as background to the radiant Cinderella, being helped out of her coach into the courtyard by the conventionally handsome prince. The candelabra-holding footmen lead us up from the lower left to the couple, while the horses anchor the right foreground.

∗ Now the dancing prince and Cinderella are center stage on the left-hand page, while the crowd watches behind them and spills across the gutter to the right-hand page under the text. The disapproval on many faces is evident, but others seem to enjoy the sight. Jeffers has given the characters authentic costumes, hair styles, and other period details. She also has included some architectural background on the left.

∗ The illustration is confined to the left-hand page, where the dreaming, ragged Cinderella dances on the colorful carpet under the chandelier, watched by the ghostly godmother. The horses in the picture on the wall remind us of those that pulled the coach. Framed in the arched doorway, the sisters seem to chat animatedly.

∗ Jeffers uses another wordless, double-page spread for one of the crucial moments of the story. Against the shadowy blue night and castle walls, with swans quietly drifting, Jeffers sets the action on the staircase. The prince reaches out, framed in white in the doorway, from far back at the top of the stairs. Amid the jewel-like glitter of the chandeliers, Cinderella runs frantically past the watching guards; she is coming apart as she goes. Note again how little color Jeffers needs to use amid all the texture. Would the picture be as effective if Cinderella were simply centered on the staircase, as the sisters were when they left for the ball?

∗ Jeffers runs a series of vignettes of trying on the slipper, under the text on the left-hand page and around the right-hand page, like frames from a movie. She individualizes these characters and their movements, making each distinct and different.

∗ A dramatic but realistic scene fills the two-page spread. Jeffers gives us a solid building, flagstoned courtyard, prancing horses, liveried attendants, the sparkling slipper on a pillow, and the stepmother and sisters framed by the window arch on a balcony. Cinderella, with her broom and bird, is almost lost over on the right.

∗ Above the text on the left, the sisters watch in dismay as the courier, having placed his cloak on the chair, leans over to fit the slipper on Cinderella's foot. Across on the right-hand page, the little dog seems to smile as the godmother watches approvingly. The stepmother tears her hair in anguish.

∗ A costumed courtier leads the "happy-ever-after" couples diagonally down, as he points diagonally up with his sword. The godmother, wings at the same angles, happily brings up the rear. We do not know what has happened to the stepmother, or the red bird, although some children suggest that the bird was the godmother in disguise. Other versions of this story have less happy endings for the sisters.

VERSIONS TO COMPARE

French, Fiona. *Cinderella*. New York: Oxford University, 1987.

Galdone, Paul. *Cinderella*. New York: McGraw-Hill, 1978.

Grimm Brothers. *Cinderella* retold and illustrated by Nonny Hogrogian. New York: Greenwillow, 1981.

Karlin, Barbara. *Cinderella* illustrated by James Marshall. Boston: Little, Brown, 1989.

Knight, Hilary. *Hilary Knight's Cinderella*. New York: Random House, 1981.

Perrault, Charles. *Cinderella* illustrated by Diane Goode. New York: Knopf, 1988.

———. *Cinderella* illustrated by Roberto Innocenti. Mankato, MN: Creative Education, 1983.

———. *Cinderella; or, The Little Glass Slipper* illustrated by Marcia Brown. New York: Scribner's, 1954.

BOOKS ILLUSTRATED BY JEFFERS

Andersen, Hans Christian. *The Wild Swans*. New York: Dial, 1981.

Brown, Margaret Wise. *Baby Animals*. New York: Random House, 1989.

Lindbergh, Reeve. *Benjamin's Barn*. New York: Dial, 1990.

———. *The Midnight Farm*. New York: Dial, 1987.

Longfellow, William Wadsworth. *Hiawatha: Selections*. New York: Dial, 1983.

Mohr, Joseph. *Silent Night*. New York: Dutton, 1984.

Perrault, Charles. *Cinderella* retold by Amy Ehrlich. New York: Dial, 1985.

Sewell, Anna. *Black Beauty* adapted by Robin McKinley. New York: Random House, 1986.

Wells, Rosemary. *Forest of Dreams*. New York: Dial, 1988.

Princess Furball
retold by Charlotte Huck,
illustrated by Anita Lobel

Active, brightly colored, patterned pictures are characteristic of the illustrations Anita Lobel has produced over the years for many writers. There is frequently a touch of the absurd, a poking of fun, and a sense of joy in her work, whoever the author may be.

∗ Charlotte Huck's retelling of this tale, although the text is long, offers Lobel a chance to both expand and embellish the story with her illustrations. On the cover, on a pale pink-beige background, the title is printed in dark blue, unusual upper-case lettering above the illustration. The names of the author and illustrator are printed in smaller, similar letters that are purple. At the center of the picture on the cover, one that is repeated in the book, is the brown-shaded Furball of the title. The fur is topped with Furball's circular, troubled face, with her eyes looking apprehensively over her shoulder. She dries a bowl, another circle, while many other circular patterns in objects depicted add balance and a sense of peace amid the kitchen chaos. Two white-clad figures flank Furball. One smiles pleasantly, the broom in his hand pointing at her, while the other does not. The gloomy one carries a platter of chickens, with a head also pointing at Furball. A third white-clad figure peers happily at her from behind a basket of lobsters. Lobel, as usual, has filled all the space. Although they are not photographically real, her people are realistically drawn, and everything in the picture has three dimensions. Lobel applies her water colors and gouache paint opaquely rather than transparently, modelling forms with shadows and linear black overstrokes. She places her white and brown areas in a balanced way, adding touches of the brighter oranges and greens.

On the back of the cover is an interesting choice, a small part of another illustration from inside the book. The wistful, sad expression on the girl's face, framed in white, may give a clue to the fact that she is the same girl as on the front, but, of course, much younger. She stands straight on the slanting black-and-white pattern of the floor. There is black and white behind her as well, but there is also that line of red that matches the roses drooping, perhaps symbolically, from her hand.

∗ The end papers are a dark silver-gray, leading appropriately to the gray gloom of the first illustration.

∗ The story begins with no words, but with a picture that sets the stage. Dark, vertical tree trunks lead to intricate patterns of branches against the pale sky. From the castle behind the trees, the road winds down to the scene before us. All the light faces are surrounded by black, and all the bodies are covered with it. Four bearers carry a black-draped shape with a crown drawn upon it. The poles they carry point to another crown, on the head of the man in the foreground. The tombstones around him reaffirm that this is a funeral.

In the left foreground, amid all this darkness, the woman in red holding the baby in white really stands out. That the king's child has lost her mother is apparent. We guess that the child is the princess of the title. The picture is framed by the white page it is placed on, as are all the illustrations in the book.

＊ On the left-hand page, we meet the girl from the back cover. Now her expression is easier to understand. Without words, the picture tells us all. On the right, draped and shadowed with the black of the funeral, the portrait of a lady much like the child must be of her dead mother. The flowers in the bowl under the portrait droop appropriately. The child seems lost and alone. Behind her, within the white marble arch and scarlet drapes, we see her father, the king, occupied with others, his back symbolically turned to her. On the right-hand page, the title is printed in type similar to that on the cover, within the sky of the picture. A column flanking both sides, and the window behind, remind us of the scenes in some Renaissance paintings, although the style is, of course, quite different, lacking all the detail and more modern-looking. Between the columns and the distant trees stand the people who are the focus of our attention, the young princess from the previous page and the woman in red who was holding her as an infant in the first illustration. Lobel makes clear the loving, caring relationship between them, not only by their expressions and the very look in their eyes, but also by the position of the arms and hands, all making a circle of comfort. The position of their heads is a reminder of the Madonnas with Child from Renaissance paintings, as are the costumes.

＊ On the plain white left-hand page are the copyright and other information. Above the dedication, Lobel tells us another part of the story, without words. Despite the loss of her mother and the indifference of her father, the young princess has happy playtime with ordinary children, watched over by the faithful nurse. Lobel gives this picture warmth and joy not only from the fun the children are having, which is obvious from their faces and dancing bodies, but also with her use of bright color and general design. The children are playing in a circle, both the river and the wall wind in curves rather than corners, and even the fishing rod is curved. Flowers abound, while round apples fill the tree on the upper left. The princess stands out from the other children because of her blue dress and cap, and her hair. The nurse is also a focus of attention in her dress, the same red as the apples. She sits in her curved chair, typical of the time, holding flowers as blue as the princess's dress. Blue also flows from the sky at the top, along the river and to the bottom of the picture. Cover the foreground flowers and the children in the river to see how much they add to the design of the picture without detracting from the major characters.

✳ The text finally tells us what we have already learned from Lobel. Above it, on the left-hand page, the princess and a kitchen worker smile at each other in front of a fireplace much like that in the picture on the cover. But the atmosphere is so very different, from the facial expressions and body postures to the absence of points and diagonals in favor of curves and circles like those we also saw on the cover. To the right, an arched window looks out on a peaceful landscape from an old painting. On the left, the nurse watches protectively. On the right-hand page, Lobel's exuberant characters have found it impossible to stay within the picture. They have danced out on the right and at the top. The princess sits on her curved chair, with the curled quill used for writing; her chair arms and table are solidly horizontal on the checkered floor. The hall on the upper right has straight, vertical columns, but ends in an arch. Black curtains, reminding us of the dead mother, are draped over an arched window. Between the window and the princess stands the solid, black, period-costumed figure of the tutor, while the dancing master, in green and gold with red-ribboned staff, seems to dance away with the red-clad nurse. This picture is full of many contrasts to ponder.

✳ The text is above the picture on the left-hand page. Would it look better below? The picture shows the princess and the king confronting each other. Her stance, expression, and clasped hands convey her anxiety. By size and position, the king dominates the picture. His crown even breaks out of the picture. He leans away from the princess as he tells her of her fate. It is interesting to speculate on the possible meaning of Lobel's use of the same blue for the king's inner sleeves and the princess's dress. On the right-hand page, the king, with a self-satisfied expression, stands straight at the right, while the portrait of the ogre and his silver looms over the cowering princess. It looks strangely like the king himself. A figure dressed in the same brown as the ogre holds the portrait. As a counterpoint, in the upper right we find the black drapes again, behind which the princess's mother, in the portrait, watches. She seems to have a touch of dismay in her face that we did not see there before.

✳ The weavers set to work, in a scene for which Lobel must have researched pictures of actual weavers. These looms have all the necessary pieces. The arched windows and costumes set them in their time. On the right-hand page, Lobel gets a chance to fill her picture with animals and people in action. This scene, and many of the landscapes to come, seem to be Lobel's adaptations of pictures from the period, such as those from the illuminated Books of Hours from the Middle Ages, or of Pieter Breughel.

✳ On the left-hand page, Lobel gives us vivid contrasts of black night against white columns, arch, curtains, and pillow; and of beautiful dresses next to brown fur and ordinary boots. The checkered floor and columns seem to lead the princess out into the night. Under the text on the right-hand page is a winter scene of dark tree trunks and white snow, through which the princess's footprints march as she walks out of the picture.

✳ Under the text, the picture shows us the trees and snow, but our focus is on the cozy oval made by the tree, in which the princess has fallen asleep. On the right-hand page, we have moved back from the tree to see a hunting scene right out of a Book of Hours. The dogs in the foreground focus our attention on the tree and its contents. Lobel's decision to paint white dogs on white snow is an interesting and challenging one. The hunters' green suits add a touch of color, as well as symbolize their king's colors through-out.

✳ Below the text, Lobel's picture is squared only at the upper and lower right, by the tree, and for a small part of the lower left. Otherwise, she seems to have cut the background away. This gives more importance to the figures and their action—the curve of the feathers, the coil of rope, the princess's hand flung up. Lobel does this, interestingly enough, only in this picture. On the right-hand page, the princess, now called Furball, is taken back to the castle, trussed-up like a captured animal. Lobel has her characters marching in a circle, around and through the trees onto the path. At the top of the picture, she uses the pattern of the bare trees against the snow and winter sky, while the active dogs, gesturing people, and a few winter weeds pattern the bottom.

✳ The pictures fall below the text on most of the rest of the pages. Here the arm of the hunter curves right out of the picture, as he holds the rope with one hand and pushes the apprehensive Furball with the other. Another hunter smiles as he watches. What does his face add to the picture? The feather curling from the hat on the left, and the curves of the sleeves, contrast with the angles of the shed Furball must inhabit. On the right-hand page is the cover illustration we have already discussed. Compare the colors of the two versions to see the difference the paper can make. The picture also gains something from being juxtaposed with that on the left-hand page that it misses on the cover.

✳ The rich, bright gold of the dress excites the princess so much that her hand breaks out of the picture. The angles of the shed behind her reflect this excitement. On the right-hand page, Furball and the king stand front and center, framed on the sides by carved panels and the row of pillars stretching back with arches above. The two courtiers in the foreground left and right add to the formally balanced picture, even to the feathers in their hats. By their stance and expression, the couple clearly care about each other already. The green the king is dressed in has a touch of the gold of the princess's dress.

✳ Off and out of the picture runs the princess, as the king reels back off the other side. The guards stand centrally between them. In another picture below the text on the right-hand page, Furball is back in the kitchen, in front of the fireplace. She furtively slips the ring into the soup, as the cook stands guard on the left with a broom. A similar handle matches the broom's angle on the right. The familiar jars, barrels, and vegetables relate this to the other kitchen scenes.

✳ In the full-page picture on the left-hand page, the anxious cook looks up at the king, seated at a high table that is almost like a dais. Lobel drapes a rich, red curtain above the king, perhaps for more emphasis, perhaps for royalty. Behind the ever-present courtiers, a window arches above a moon curved in the night sky. On the right, under the text, two arms point to Furball, who leans out of the picture away from them, holding a broom that is the counterpart of the stick held by the courtier. The cook's dismay is evident.

✳ Furball huddles, hand over face, as the king towers above her, his toe and arm breaking the picture. The ring is center stage. Lobel has placed the red drape behind the king again and has added the picture of bright red flowers in a pot. This castle floor has a different checkered pattern; perhaps the added brown relates to Furball's fur. Behind, to the left, stand the guards, with the columns and arches stretching behind. On the lower part of the right-hand page, the king seems thoughtful. The courtiers stand in the middle, staves crossed. This time, Furball looks back at the king and seems to hold the edge of the picture as she leaves. Above her, the moon is yellow amid the clouds seen through the arch, which matches the arch behind the king's head.

✳ The lamp throws an odd circle of light as the princess leans over the round tub to wash. There are fewer angles and less haste in this picture than the last one of preparation. Just a bit of a moon like the one in the previous picture is visible in the upper left. On the right-hand page, the king, dressed in elegant gold that reminds us of the princess's last dress, dances his elbow right out of the frame at the left. The princess prances, barefoot, off to the right, on the patterned floor. Musicians play under the red drape; the crowd watches. Arches, columns, and the moon are in the back again. Lobel has swirled the princess's dress to match the king's golden suit as they dance together.

✳ Both pictures are under the text. On the left-hand page, we are back in the kitchen, but Furball is less hunched, perhaps more sure of herself, while the cook seems less menacing. We even see the moon outside the window. The moon is also in the picture on the right-hand page, along with the two guards, and the arched windows. The king, under his red drape, is on almost the same level as Furball, and she seems less afraid.

✳ The musicians under the red curtains have come close to us, as the king and Furball dance close to each other, gazing into each other's eyes, while he slips the telltale ring onto her finger. He is now dressed in the blue of the dress she wore the last time. His distress, and that of the musicians, is evident in the small picture under the text on the right-hand page. Furball has already all but left the scene.

✳ This time in the kitchen, the cook is not there. Furball works with intense concentration, oblivious to the hair and dress still visible. On the right-hand page, Lobel sets us again by the tall table under the red drape, with the guards, columns, and arches. Now, however, the moon over the king's head is full. He smiles as he bends toward Furball, who leans out of the picture to get away. But both the ring and the dress are clearly there.

✳ With one hand, the king pulls the fur away, while he gestures happily through the frame with the other. The emerging princess still looks dubious. But on the right-hand page, she smiles happily, leaning toward the king, hand in his. He is kneeling to her, on top of the furs, hand on heart. To the left, another couple embrace as they watch. Under the centered arch at the end of the columns, even the two guards put their arms on each other's shoulders under the shining full moon.

✳ The picture is above the text here, for the cake is so magnificent it breaks through the top. The cook gestures toward the top, while on the right, through the window, a path curves between two trees toward the bright orange sun. The right-hand picture is a classic, balanced design. The flowers underfoot in the foreground are matched by those on the arched trellis above. Between the white figures of king and princess, hands joined, the patterned path goes straight up to the cake. Columns on either side lead to the central arch and the cloudless blue sky beyond. The guests on one side balance the musicians and people on the other. All is peaceful, bright, and joyous.

✳ The final "happily ever after" portrait, in its elaborate frame, shows a classic happy family in front of the columns and arches. Furball's dress is now red, while her little girl wears a paler version of her former blue outfit. The boy wears the green we saw on the courtiers, and that we see on the hills outside the door. The king has on a purple robe reminiscent of the one worn by Furball's father. Is that significant? And isn't that checkered floor pattern from his castle, not this one? These are questions only Lobel can answer.

This story has certain parallels with Cinderella, as well as many classic fairy tale motifs like the three dresses, and three nights, for children to find.

VERSIONS TO COMPARE

Jacobs, Joseph. *Tattercoats* illustrated by Margot Tomes. New York: Putnam, 1989.
Sage, Jacquelyn Ilya. *Many Furs*. New York: Celestial Arts, 1981.
Steel, Flora Annie. *Tattercoats: An Old English Tale* illustrated by Diane Goode. Scarsdale, NY: Bradbury, 1976.

BOOKS ILLUSTRATED BY LOBEL

Huck, Charlotte. *Princess Furball*. New York: Greenwillow, 1989.
Kroll, Steven. *Looking for Daniela*. New York: Holiday House, 1988.
Lobel, Anita. *Alison's Zinnia*. New York: Greenwillow, 1990.
———. *The Dwarf Giant*. New York: Holiday House, 1991.
———. *The Straw Maid*. New York: Greenwillow, 1983.
Lobel, Arnold. *On Market Street*. New York: Knopf, 1986.
Nichol, B. P. *Once: A Lullaby*. New York: Greenwillow, 1986.
Ziefert, Harriet. *A New Coat for Anna*. New York: Knopf, 1986.
Zolotow, Charlotte. *This Quiet Lady*. New York: Morrow, 1992.

The Patchwork Quilt
by Valerie Flournoy,
pictures by Jerry Pinkney

Depicting African-Americans realistically, in both their legends and their lives today, has become a special preserve of Jerry Pinkney. He draws from real people and their photographs, often using a soft black pencil. His water color paint is then applied, transparently or opaquely, depending on the effect he is seeking. The results are illustrations in which believably real people move through settings that are as detailed as Pinkney feels necessary for the story he wants the pictures to tell.

✳ *The Patchwork Quilt* is a particularly appealing story of strong family relationships. The quilt itself, of course, is worthy of comparison with Ann Jonas's. (See p. 37.) It spills from Grandma's lap at the center of the jacket/cover, down to cover the bottom half of the picture filled with the multicolored and patterned squares. Grandma sits in the armchair, looking down at the quilt, as her finger pulls a quilting knot. Seated on the arm of the chair, one hand on Grandma's shoulder and the other on the quilt, Tanya leans over so her head almost touches her grandmother's. Caring shows in the faces and postures of these very real people. Pincushion and thread are readily at hand, but otherwise the living-room setting is only sketched in. The title is printed in black, decorative, upper-case letters, with double underlining. Author and illustrator are in simpler black. This information has been placed within a green and red frame, on a peach-colored background, at the bottom of the picture, atop the quilt. We might want to see more of the quilt, but where else could this information fit? On the back of the cover, we get a close-up of the quilted squares, framed in a thin black line and set on that peach background as an outer frame. Note the green squares in the corners, like the red squares in the corners of the frame of that same green on the front cover. Try to picture these quilt squares placed parallel to the sides and top of the book, rather than diagonally. The picture would have much less visual interest, despite the attractive patterns and colors of the squares.

✳ The end papers are a quiet, medium blue found in the quilt.

✳ A paler shade of that blue makes a frame for the title and author information, which matches that on the cover. The background here, however, is lavender, and the corners are green like those on the back cover. Below and around this, Pinkney has washed the page with a pale beige, like the background on the front cover. The sewing basket, center left, spills out spools of thread, tape measure, and scraps of fabric toward the right. This vignette has no real setting, but it is anchored on the page by the bright red pincushion on the lower left, the open scissors with blades pointing in on the lower right, and the publisher information at the bottom.

✳ The copyright information and dedication are simple black printing on white. But under the dedication, Pinkney has placed one diagonal, blue-flowered quilt square.

* Pinkney uses the beige-washed background for most of his illustrations throughout the book. Sometimes the text is fitted into the pictures on this background. When the text has a page to itself, however, it is printed on the white paper. See if this bothers you as the story progresses. The picture here goes across both pages, with the right-hand side having a curtain and shelf setting off the text. On the left-hand page, Mama is putting the baked biscuits on the counter but looking at Tanya. The girl is sitting by the window but turned toward her mother. There is obvious family affection in this homey kitchen scene, brightened by Tanya's blouse, the curtains, and the basket of oranges. Pinkney includes details, like hanging plants and kitchen tools, that add to the realism.

* The left-hand page is white, with text. On the right, Grandma sits in the armchair, with Tanya again leaning over to her from the arm. This scene is interesting to compare with the picture on the cover, to spot the similarities and differences. When we finish reading, we can speculate on where in the story the cover picture would belong, because the new quilt has already been made there. The love between Tanya and Grandma is also apparent here. Note the placement of the basket and its contents.

* We can see more of the living room in this two-page spread, where Pinkney has nicely arranged space for the text. Although we don't see every part of the rug, or every leaf on the plants, we can certainly feel at home here. This is a middle-class African-American family rather than one in the inner city, a fact to consider if this book is used for multicultural study. It is also a family where three generations live together, a family structure known to many children. One from each generation is shown on the right, drawn and modelled with Pinkney's usual care and grouped to show their close relationship.

* A loving hug brings Grandma and Tanya even closer in a circle. All seems soft and warm in this picture.

* On the left-hand page, the text appears at the top, on the white page. Pinkney has used part of the white page for his illustration and the beige wash as background for the rest. The blue pants are the vertical center and focus here. Jim's orange shirt is brighter than his face, as he eyes his seated grandmother. Beige washes the whole right-hand page. Do you find this treatment more effective than that on the other side? Do they clash on the same page? Tanya twirls to show off her beautiful robe for Grandma, in another very realistic scene.

* Note how Pinkney has used the beige, and the white for the snow, to create the picture and the space for the text. The verticals of father, mother,

Tanya, and the shovel are set against the horizontal boards of the house. Amid all the snow, we focus on Tanya's red jacket.

✳ Mother and Grandma form a close circle now, as Tanya watches from the foreground. She leans in over the table, so she doesn't really seem left out, especially in her red sweater. Note how many details Pinkney puts in here, like stage props, for realism.

✳ Under the text, on the washed beige pages, Pinkney gives us a wonderful picture of family togetherness at Christmas. Grandma is the central focus on the right-hand page, but the tree is the center of attention for the group. We even have stockings on the fireplace.

✳ The family shows concern for Grandma in their faces and postures. Tanya turns her head toward Grandma's empty chair, with the quilt folded and draped over the back.

✳ On the beige two-page spread, the children visiting Grandma are grouped on the left. Grandma, her bed, and her old quilt fill the center of the spread, while a round table and bowl of flowers fill out the right. Try covering the lamp between the children and Grandma to see why Pinkney added that to the picture.

✳ The sketched-in background is unimportant here. The focus is on Tanya at work, the growing quilt, and the helping hands of her mother.

✳ A different point of view in her bedroom puts Grandma toward the back of the picture on this two-page spread. The text has its place on the upper left. We see all of the bed now and the chest at the foot as well. The lines of bedstead, chest, and quilt all lead our eye to Tanya. Children may catch their breath at first when they see what she is so intently doing.

✳ Back in her chair, Grandma looks up from the finished quilt at the obviously delighted Tanya. Why do you think Pinkney painted in that picture on the wall?

✳ The quilt is spread out in all its splendor, joining the family together. Note how Pinkney has placed the figures and the text to compose these pages.

✳ The final vignette is almost square, like the final quilt square shown held in loving hands. The quilt has pulled the family, and the three generations of women, more tightly together.

Many of the books Pinkney has illustrated can also give insights into African-American life. Another artist whose realistic charcoal and pastel illustrations grace important African-American stories is Carole Byard. Her pictures for Phil Mendez's *The Black Snowman* (Scholastic, 1989), with their echoes of the Ashanti and kente, or magic cloth, but set in an American city, are particularly striking and relevant.

Contemporary quilt artist Faith Ringgold has published a picture book based on one of her quilts, which tells the story of a young girl in Harlem. *Tar Beach* (Crown, 1991) has particular relevance because it is full of the squares of the quilt.

Children can learn more about the celebration of the African-American holiday Kwanzaa from A.P. Porter's *Kwanzaa* (Carolrhoda, 1991) with color illustrations by Janice Lee Porter.

ART ACTIVITY

Children may be interested in learning more about quilts and quilting and may want to try making a quilt as a class project. Many fourth grades have done this. If a theme is chosen, the children usually each design a square on that subject. As Tanya did, each must receive or cut a square of the specified size. The design, a simple crayon drawing or a complicated collage of many fabrics and trim, is placed or fastened on the square. Usually the teacher and/or parent volunteers sew the squares together, although the class may do the work if there is a sewing machine available. Instructions on how to place the batting and the lining are available at many fabric stores and in the 745's in the library. Then the whole class needs to have a quilting bee. In the early days of our country, quilting bees were popular social opportunities for otherwise isolated women to meet. They would work together around the quilting frame to finish quilting the layers of a quilt and chat while they worked.

Again, the library has books to show the two ways of quilting. Tanya's grandmother used the easier one, just tacking the layers together front to back at regular intervals.

Tanya's quilt was also an easier design. If they just use different colored and patterned squares, each child could make a small quilted pillow cover or doll quilt. This would be a good opportunity to talk, as Grandma did, about how to place the colors and patterns for a good design.

BOOKS ILLUSTRATED BY PINKNEY

Aardema, Verna. *Rabbit Makes a Monkey of Lion: A Swahili Tale*. New York: Dial, 1989.
Adoff, Arnold. *In for Winter, Out for Spring*. San Diego: Harcourt Brace, 1991.
Carlstrom, Nancy White. *Wild, Wild Sunflower Child Anna*. New York: Macmillan, 1987, Aladdin paper, 1991.
Dragonwagon, Crescent. *Half a Moon and One Whole Star*. New York: Macmillan, 1986.

———. *Home Place*. New York: Macmillan, 1990.

Fields, Julia. *The Green Lion of Zion Street*. New York: McElderry, 1988.

Flournoy, Valerie. *The Patchwork Quilt*. New York: Dial, 1985.

Lester, Julius. *Further Tales of Uncle Remus*. New York: Dial, 1990.

———. *More Tales of Uncle Remus*. New York: Dial, 1988.

———. *Tales of Uncle Remus*. New York: Dial, 1987.

McKissack, Patricia C. *Mirandy and Brother Wind*. New York: Random House, 1988.

Marzollo, Jean. *Pretend You're a Cat*. New York: Dial, 1990.

San Souci, Robert D. *The Talking Eggs: A Folktale from the American South*. New York: Dial, 1989.

Singer, Marilyn. *Turtle in July*. New York: Macmillan, 1989.

The Frog Prince, Or Iron Henry

by Jacob and Wilhelm Grimm,

illustrated by Binette Schroeder

The illustrations of Binette Schroeder, a German painter and portrait photographer, have a quality that we might call "European," as distinct from American or British. Some artists of the picture books from Europe have even been criticized here for making the books "too beautiful," that is, so concerned with painting a series of stunning pictures that they have forgotten the importance of sequencing them to tell a solid story. Schroeder's books certainly have the eye-catching illustrations, but they also succeed in telling a good story. She uses opaque pigment to fill her pages with color, sometimes a single tone, then lights them like stage sets or films. Her characters are realistically modelled to look solid but are placed in sometimes unreal or surreal settings. Some of her books may well seem too sophisticated for children. But in all cases, they are worth examining and comparing with other versions of the stories.

✶ The version used by Schroeder for her *Frog Prince* has the interesting subplot of Iron Henry, which is not in many others. On the jacket, Schroeder uses textured red for the entire background. She inserts a long rectangle, tinged with the red, dropping three-quarters of the way down on the right-hand side. On the lower part of this rectangle the title and author information is printed in black, upper-case letters. Coming out of the red background, leaning in from the left over toward a large well, is the princess, garbed in a gown of the same red. Her hair is the gold of the tall crown that is somehow perched on it. She looks expectantly toward the golden ball held by the frog on the lower right, her hands reaching out toward it. She is very pretty, but more doll-like than human. A dark tree branch with leaves spreads across the top of the picture, up and over from the upper left corner. Rough, pinkish blocks of stone make up the well, its oval top just visible across the bottom of the picture. The water is green, as is the frog on the edge, holding the ball. There is drama and tension between frog and girl in this picture. On the back of the jacket, the tree limb and the well are in the same place against the red background. This time, the pink-tinged rectangle is toward the left, with the ISBN information on the lower part and no princess. There is no frog on the well either, only rings of ripples in the water. We can only speculate on what caused them. The emptiness is dramatically desolate here.

✳ The end papers are the green of the frog and are a real contrast to the red on the jacket and cover.

✳ The green tones continue on the two-page spread. Inserted, green-tinged rectangles contain dedication and copyright on the left-hand page. The same title and author information as on the cover is on the right-hand page in a similar rectangle. Similar overextended, surreal trees overlap each rectangle, with birds in the one on the right. Strange mountains and more surreal trees rise from the landscape across the bottom. A tiny golden coach is being pulled across this strange green countryside by eight white horses.

✳ A symmetrical, deep blue and green-hued, two-page spread is broken by the lighter-tinted rectangle on the right-hand page containing the text and another of those overextended trees on the left-hand page. A row of lollypop-shaped trees is set around the court, on which princesses in dresses of many colors seem to be hitting multicolored balls. Everything is casting a shadow, but is that a sun or a moon in the sky? The king's red robe and golden crown and sceptre are the brightest colors in the picture, but next brightest is the pink and red dress of the princess with the golden hair and impossible crown. She has a ball instead of a racket.

✳ A wedge now holds the text on the left-hand page of this dark green and brown two-page spread. It points our attention to the weird faces on the tree trunks. Otherwise, the trees and roots are realistically painted, but the atmosphere is spooky. A fox watches lower left, as the princess goes off under the trees, tossing her ball in the air; the tree trunks and roots in the foreground seem to surround her.

∗ We have returned to the characters, tree branch, reds, and greens of the cover in this two-page spread, which is set up like a series of frames from a film. A large rectangle is needed for the text on the left. It takes so much space that the princess must peer around it, watching with horrified surprise as her ball splashes into the well. Schroeder cleverly divides the same oval well into three action segments, for the princess, the frog, and the branch. Tears bring the ball back, but the princess has made her fateful promise.

∗ Greens and browns are the tones of this dramatic spread. Stone steps and rocks frame the text on the left-hand side, leading down to the frog, who is helplessly trying to follow the princess. Tossing the ball, she runs off again on the right-hand page, down a wedge-shaped path with columns and shadows like those in nightmares or surreal paintings. Animal heads peer out of the strange greenery on the right. Other oddities include the snail following the frog; the 89 on the stone marker, perhaps for the date of the book; and the unnatural rock formations topped by the trees and stag.

∗ Schroeder paints the dark, gloomy, gray stone wall and steps very realistically. Then she makes a sort of vertical shadow line to divide the left-hand page into three equal parts, and the right-hand page into two parts, one one-third and the other two-thirds wide. The text is barely readable on the far left section. It is interesting to speculate as to why Schroeder chose to obscure the text here. Would another color have worked better without changing the illustration? Although this is one picture, each section serves as a frame for the arduous climb of the frog up the enormous (for him) stone steps. From the top of the steps on the far right, in contrast to the dark stone, golden light fills the doorway. And even if we can't see above her waist, the figure in the golden dress, hands outspread, must be the princess. She obviously never believed the frog would get this far. Behind her, we see shadowy figures, chairs, and wineglasses. And on the lowest step below the door, lit by the light coming through it, is the golden ball. One step up, lying on her back with arm and head falling off the step, is a doll that looks like the princess. Is this significant?

∗ The red tones return across the two pages, broken by vertical dark panels on either side and across the gutter, making each page a separate scene. The text is in one column on the left-hand page, where the king's presence fills so much of the page. It is in two columns on the right, where there is more space. On the left, the king's arm comes diagonally above the frog to the table, where the determined finger points dramatically in front of the princess. Schroeder paints every hair of his whiskers and fur and exaggerates his features for emphasis. The strange dog seems to be wearing a mask, but could he hold a cherry with the mask's teeth? He's another piece of surrealism, as is the strange table that seems to hold only cherries and the absence of anything on what should be walls. And has the king taken his plate away on the right-hand page? The dismayed princess watches the frog eat center stage. We don't know what happened to all the other people seen at the top of the steps.

✳ These pages are again washed in green and seem to portray surreal nightmares. The text rectangle is back on the left. Not another soul is visible, as the golden princess, with a pink ribbon now tucked into her hair, seems to float on air on the left-hand page through endless arches, with the frog's front leg pinched between her fingers. On the right-hand page, two ghostly forms cross a strange bridge. The king's portrait on the wall almost seems sculpted, as the princess approaches stairs that rise in the mist from the dark halls and polished floor.

✳ Schroeder again uses shadow lines to divide a whole scene into action frames. Three are on the left-hand page, one of which blends over to the tilting and dissolving sections on the right-hand page. On the left, the princess, now in pink, seems to recoil in disgust as the frog raises his front legs. In the next frame, she reaches down to grab him. Next, she hurls him at the wall, right across the gutter. Even the text tilts with the thrown frog. He grows larger as he starts to change in the next two frames.

✳ The text tilts the other way at the top of the left-hand page of these green pages. Against a swirling, misty background, Schroeder shows the last three steps of the metamorphosis from frog to prince. Fingers and feet, eyes and teeth—all change in the two views on the left-hand page. On the right-hand page, the princess can now stand with her back to us, gazing down at the prince in frog-stance on the floor, as he looks back up at her.

✳ Schroeder gives us a romantic stage set here, in shades of black and gray, touched all over with blue. The crowns and ball are gold, of course, and the prince is still in green, the princess in pink. But it is the setting that astounds us. A truncated triangular stone seems to sit atop the stone archway on the left-hand page for the text. It is printed in upper-case letters here, perhaps because it is so important. Latticed arches top both pages, coming from stone columns along either side and running along the gutter. Strange, horned animal heads top the columns. One has a flower in its mouth, and the ones in the center facing us have pink-touched tongues. Through the flat-topped arch, we see a row of trees in front of a fence. The fence has curves that are the reverse of the arches. The strange, masked dog turns in front of the archway to look from the golden ball back to us. The fence and trees continue behind the column to the right-hand page, where they stop short of the action. Two crowns, for the prince and princess perhaps, sit on this fence. Under a full moon, bright enough to make shadows, the prince literally leaps out of his shoes to join his princess bride in bed. She smiles and reaches out to him from the blue bed curtains, which are topped with another crown. This scene is certainly more dream than reality.

✳ Now the overall color has brightened to textured gray with a touch of pink. Gray-spotted dogs with red tongues stand on an almost featureless expanse, with only some white pebbles and one tiny flower. The oblong containing the text, back in both upper and lower case, seems to be a slab standing on the ground, throwing a shadow along with the dogs and man. One dog even seems to be coming from behind it. The new character from the subtitle, Iron Henry, stands with the same outstretched hands we have seen on others throughout the book. He is smiling at where we guess the prince must be. On the upper right, we see only white legs and hooves, but the shadow shows us plumed horses. Despite the smile, the empty stage is eery.

✳ The final two-page spread is of almost natural green grass and blue sky touched with pink, although the strange trees and the castle/mountain remain. A young boy at the lower left, with yellow hair and reddish overalls, stares at the first of Henry's broken iron bands, lying in the road in the left foreground. What is the function of the stick he is carrying? The dogs seem to be happily chasing the golden coach up the winding road and over the hill on the right-hand page. Stone-like slabs hold the final text on each page. The tiny figures of prince and princess are barely visible in the coach as they ride off together.

The odd happy ending is only one of the strange elements in this version of the tale. Not only are there many other versions to compare, but there are also several twists and parodies that children really appreciate.

Children ought to have an idea of what we mean by "surreal." Reproductions of the works of René Magritte, Salvador Dali, and de Chirico in books about these artists or on contemporary art can begin to make students aware of what the characteristics of this art are. Then they can see how Schroeder has used it in her paintings.

BOOKS ILLUSTRATED BY SCHROEDER

De Beaumont, Madame Leprince. *Beauty and the Beast* retold from the French by Anne Carter. New York: Potter, 1986.

Flora's Magic House. New York: Holt, 1986.

The Frog Prince, Or Iron Henry by Jacob and Wilhelm Grimm. New York: North-South Books, 1989.

VERSIONS TO COMPARE

Berenzy, Alix. *A Frog Prince*. New York: Holt, 1989.

Isadora, Rachel. *The Princess and the Frog* from the Brothers Grimm. New York: Greenwillow, 1989.

Isele, Elizabeth. *The Frog Princess* illustrated by Michael Hague. New York: Crowell, 1984.

Ormerod, Jan and David Lloyd. *The Frog Prince*. New York: Lothrop, 1990.

Scieszka, Jon. *The Frog Prince, Continued* illustrated by Steve Johnson. New York: Viking, 1991.

Tarkov, Edith H. *The Frog Prince* illustrated by James Marshall. New York: Four Winds, 1974.

Vesey, A. *The Princess and the Frog*. Boston: Atlantic Monthly, 1984.

Mufaro's Beautiful Daughters: An African Tale
by John Steptoe

John Steptoe's untimely death cut off the development of an artist who had continually grown and expanded his skill in many styles of illustration, from *Stevie* begun when he was only 16 and published when he was 19, to the Caldecott Honor book we are examining here. Critics compared *Stevie*'s heavy black outline and intense areas of color to the work of French painter Georges Rouault. Steptoe also had done textured black pencil illustrations, like those for Caldecott Honor book *The Story of Jumping Mouse,* as well as the complicated cross-hatched color we see here in *Mufaro's Beautiful Daughters*. Many of his books offer the positive self-image so necessary to African-American children, while all offer themes and art worthy of examination. Steptoe used real people for models for his human characters in *Mufaro's Beautiful Daughters*. He also did extensive research on the costumes, setting, plants, and animals, so with close scrutiny, readers can learn much more than what is in the story.

✳ The illustration on the cover works as a fine front cover alone. The author/illustrator and subtitle are printed against the blue sky, in black upper-case letters, with decorative touches. But the title is done in elegant hand calligraphy, in keeping with the vanity of the young girl pictured admiring herself in front of the African landscape. Her right arm, on our left, leads our eye to her head and face, while the other hand holds the mirror into which she gazes intently. The mirror is a vertical that frames that side of the picture. The white drapery over her shoulders contrasts with, and emphasizes, her face and skin. Scenery and costume are all correct for the time and place. Even the odd Japanese ornament in her hair would have been used in Zimbabwe, a center of international trade. Steptoe creates this realistic scene of girl and landscape with rich colors and contrasting darks and lights, using transparent paint and fine pen and ink cross-hatched lines. These make the texture and add the depth and shadows of three dimensions. The title refers to more than one beautiful daughter, but we see only one on the front cover. We must open it out to see that Steptoe has also designed his illustration as a total picture from back to front. He has brought sky and landscape across the spine, placing vegetation in the center so that the spine will not interrupt any important subjects.

On the back cover, which also works as a carefully designed picture by itself, we see the other daughter. She is a contrast in many ways: less decorated, working hard rather than admiring herself, in the background rather than the foreground. Yet the formation of birds over her head, shocking pink against the blue sky, points to her importance. The animals also watch her. Notice how Steptoe has created space for the ISBN number as part of the picture.

✳ The color of the textured end papers is one used on the cover.

✳ Steptoe gives us much helpful information and a dedication on the half-title page. Contrast the calligraphy of the title with the simple print of the dedication.

✳ The double-page spread of the title page is rich with the flora and fauna of Africa. Steptoe gives us a sky here quite different from the one on the cover, perhaps for a different time of day, but still pale enough to read the printing of the publication information on one side, and the author and title on the other. The subtitle must be in white here, rather than black like the cover, to show up against the dark blue mountains. Although birds are flying, this is a balanced, quiet composition. Clumps of vegetation, touches of red, and animal heads are all on both sides, with the swooping bird at the center. Careful binding makes the bird's picture whole across the gutter. The sweep of the tailfeathers points us toward the title. The animal's head on the right tilts up to add interest; try to imagine the picture with it horizontal.

✳ We meet the beautiful daughters at their business in a realistic setting. As this spread shows, Steptoe does not usually frame his scenes. They spread out as far on the white page as he chooses to paint them, around, above, below, or next to the text. Here he carefully places trees, rocks, and foliage around the girls, and spices the deep browns with the bright pink birds.

✳ A close-up reveals so much about the character of the girls. The serene beauty of Nyasha on the right contrasts with the angry face and stance of Manyara. Steptoe frames Nyasha with foliage and beautiful pink blooms, while jagged, pale green leaves circle left around Manyara.

✳ Stunning colors of birds and flowers surround Nyasha as she symbolically pours from a jar, showing that she freely gives in her life.

✳ Another scene of the lush African foliage shows us Nyasha, in the strikingly contrasting white robe, bending down to reach kindly toward the snake. Her digging tool lies by her, pointing to the garden.

✳ Perhaps because of the amount of text, or perhaps because that's the picture he wanted here, Steptoe confines the illustration to the right-hand page. Mufaro's arms circle both his daughters. Their different characters are emphasized again by Manyara's self-centered gesture and Nyasha's serenely clasped hands. Do the jars and curves on the right add anything to the circle Mufaro makes?

✳ Steptoe here has Manyara's face and hands emerge startlingly from the left, out of the white page and her white robe. Her angry expression and gesture make clear her reaction to the very real-looking boy whose hand is stretched out under hers. Steptoe has touched the night sky with pinks and purples. Foliage reaches out like black fingers against the sky, echoing the fingers below.

✳ The design of this two-page spread is worth studying. Steptoe has arched green grass over the text on both pages, coming to a point at the gutter. An owl peers into the page on the left. On the far right, Manyara flees off the page, glancing back at the barely visible man with his head under his arm. In a break in the black and green foliage in the top center of the left-hand page appears the head of the old woman. At the top, but more to the right of the right-hand page, in opposition to the woman, the full moon shines in the turbulent sky.

✳ As the wedding party proceeds across the two-page spread, Steptoe has used the procession to partially frame the text. Carefully placed branches and leaves form the rest of the frames. To divide the two pages, he has used a bright red and blue bird perched on one of the branches. It looks as if it is directly in front of us as we watch the procession through the branches. Another bird flies at the upper right, as if leading them, and us, on.

✳ Steptoe again divides the picture that goes across the two pages, leaving similar areas on the left for the text, and on the right for the view of the distant city that is the wedding party's destination. Our point of view is as if we are standing with Mufaro, next to an exotic flower and bird, watching Nyasa, in her striking white robe, and the distant lands far beyond the two purple flowers in front.

✳ Another change of page design and rhythm brings us to the city. Steptoe can show us part of it, extending from the background of the picture on the right-hand page across to top the text on the left. In the foreground, Nyasha meets her distraught sister, hand raised to stop Nyasha, as Nyasha reaches out to her.

✳ Steptoe almost fills the two pages with the stones and decorations of the ancient kingdom. The rich browns contrast with the bright green and touches of pink visible through the bars. Through them also comes the light, illuminating Nyasha. She greets her friend, the snake, bright green as the foliage outside. Note how Steptoe uses the solidity of the rectangles and verticals of the bars to contrast with the curve of the snake, the jar behind him, and the figure of Nyasha.

✳ Our handsome hero appears, framed by columns and stairs, his white robe standing out against the warm brown of his body and the dark colors of the rest of the picture.

✳ This scene of warm embrace, enveloped by draped clothing, carving, and green cloth, fills one page, but does not spill over, although there is ample room. Can you picture another way Steptoe could have designed this spread using the gutter?

✳ Steptoe has gone all out in this wordless "happy ever after." Many details of African life are shown in the village background. Blue mountains, sky, and clouds lie beyond. Shield and drapes break the picture into two parts. The youths, spears, and poles on the left really direct our attention to the sumptuously dressed, obviously happy Nyasha and her devoted consort.

✳ Our final look at the African scene has leaves framing the view of lake, mountains, and sky at dusk. Perhaps the crowned cranes in the foreground symbolize the happy couple, while the other bird, as Manyara, looks away? It is a final tribute to the beauty of Africa.

Students will see certain elements of traditional Western fairy tales, like Cinderella, in this story. They may be inspired to find other African tales as well. There are too many to list here, but favorites involve Anansi the Spider. Just check African folklore in the library.

The 916's and 960's in the library are the places to find information on African history and Africa today. Photographs can show where Steptoe got his ideas for the landscape.

A very informative author and illustrator profile of John Steptoe by Cheryl Abdullah appeared in the September/October 1988 issue of *Library Talk* magazine.

BOOKS WRITTEN AND ILLUSTRATED BY STEPTOE

Baby Says. New York: Lothrop, 1988.
Birthday. New York: Holt, 1972.
Daddy Is a Monster... Sometimes. Philadelphia: Lippincott, 1980.
Jeffrey Bear Cleans Up His Act. New York: Lothrop, 1983.
Marcia. New York: Viking, 1976.
Mufaro's Beautiful Daughters. New York: Lothrop, 1987.
My Special Best Words. New York: Viking, 1974.
Stevie. New York: Harper, 1969, 1986.
The Story of Jumping Mouse. New York: Lothrop, 1984.
Train Ride. New York: Harper, 1971.
Uptown. New York: Harper, 1970.

BOOKS ILLUSTRATED BY STEPTOE

Adoff, Arnold. *All the Colors of the Race.* New York: Lothrop, 1982.
————. *OUTside/IN/side Poems.* New York: Lothrop, 1981.
Clifton, Lucille. *All Us Come Cross the Water.* New York: Holt, 1973.
Greenfield, Eloise. *She Come Bringing Me That Little Baby Girl.* Philadelphia: Lippincott, 1974.
Guy, Rosa. *Mother Crocodile.* New York: Delacorte, 1981.

The Town Mouse and the Country Mouse: An Aesop Fable

by Janet Stevens

Janet Stevens's illustrations are marked by humor. Although she does portray human characters, most of her work depicts animals of all sorts. Some are quite realistically done, while those in fables such as the one we will discuss here may have anthropomorphic qualities. Using intense, more opaque than transparent water colors, with some outlining drawn with markers, chalk, or pastels, she models her forms with shadows to make them solidly three-dimensional. She fills the space allotted to her with activity, frequently breaking her frames. Over the years, her illustrations have had continuing appeal for children.

 ✷ The town mouse and country mouse both appear on the jacket. Although they have many mouse-like characteristics, their gestures and use of paws are very human, and they wear clothes, well, sort of. A pale blue rectangle on the white jacket is the background on which they are placed, but from which they emerge as well. The town mouse sits happily, eyes closed, resting in a scalloped and decorated cup and saucer. She is dressed in a gold ring-necklace, beads, and an earring hat. In contrast to her peaceful repose in the circular cup, her country cousin, in a red-checked shirt, reaches across the lower right toward a rich-looking chocolate outside the rectangle. His eyes and expression show him to be far from comfortable. The cup and saucer, fork tines on the lower left, and the bowl of the spoon coming out of the blue on the lower right all place us, and the mice, on a set table. The decorative, upper-case letters of the title, in the white above the blue rectangle, are the bright green of the decoration on the chocolate. The other information is in black, in the white space below the drawing. On the back of the jacket, a realistic bowl of plain beans and bacon casts a shadow. The cover has a dark blue cloth covering the spine and part of the front and back of the cover. The rest of it is cherry red, with the title incised.
 ✷ The end papers are plain white, as is the background throughout.

✳ The page before the title page shows us, in pale, transparent water colors, the farm scene of the country. In the foreground are barn and cows, while off in the distance, on the horizon top right, are the tall buildings of the city. The pale color and lack of detail here, like the other scenery in the book, contrast with the brighter color, outlines, and details of the major characters. Although there are diagonals in this picture, they are generally in balance, so there is a peaceful feeling here that relates to the peace of the countryside.

✳ It takes two pages for the title, one for each major character. On the left-hand page, the town mouse rests in the cup, as she did on the jacket. This time, there is no background, but there is a pink-topped chocolate in the saucer, a balance to her head and pink ears. In contrast, on the right-hand page, the country mouse stands tall, smiling, broom upright in one hand, carrot trailing greens that, with his tail, lead back to the town mouse. The point of the carrot, however, points us toward the story. The enormous button is a humorous touch.

✳ Above the dedication, Stevens has placed the same bowl of beans and bacon that we saw on the back of the jacket. On the right-hand page, the story begins. This time, the town mouse stands up straight, tail curling, while the country mouse forms a semicircle with his body and tail on the right. Although there is no background, the figures have shadows.

✳ Above a small amount of text, large, rectangular pictures are on facing pages. On the left, the country mouse stands, working his broom diagonally across the diagonal floor boards. Realistic peas spill out toward a carrot and other vegetables. The soup can is pale in contrast. On the right-hand page, the town mouse lazes, amid rich food. She rests on a circular bed, with beads, round candies, an olive, and a cherry. On both pages, the size of the food is in keeping with the size of the mice, adding to the realism.

✳ The picture spills across two pages as the town mouse comes to visit. She is reclining, as usual, but her mouth is open in angry complaint. On the right stands the country mouse, broom in hand, looking questioningly at his cousin. Stevens has the pea pod pointing out left, and the mouse's tail out right, while a nail and twig break through the top frame. Even the boards of the floor are curling up here.

✳ Our point of view is changed completely in this second two-page spread. The mice shrink to a tiny size compared to the cow, who seems to lean down to look us directly in the eye. She is so large that her ear and hoof come out of the edges, while the rest of her goes far above the page. Stevens brushes in just the suggestion of landscape and sky, while the cow's tail whips around with hairs clearly visible. These mice walk on hind legs, with very human body language here.

✳ On this two-page spread, the text moves to the right-hand page for a change. We are back to mouse-size scale, with looming lettuce and tomatoes. Again the human stance of the mice conveys their feelings.

✳ Now the text has moved to the upper left of the two-page spread. Keeping the scale of the mice makes the cat, even asleep, loom frighteningly large. On the left sits the bowl we saw alone on the back jacket and on the dedication page. Here it is integrated into the scene with the mice. The country mouse stands and points; the town mouse leans over and peers dubiously. The circular bowl on one side balances the cat's head on the other.

✳ We return to the text at the bottom of facing pages, with pictures at the top. On the left-hand page, the mice float on a realistic leaf. The town mouse reclines but is not happy. The country mouse is not having much fun either. On the right-hand page, it is the pig's rear end and tail that loom above the mice. The animal seems less real than the cat did. The scattered garbage is real enough, however, as are the human attitudes of the mice.

✳ In the same format, the picture on the left-hand page focuses on the empty, boring, gray space of road. The tree and a bit of landscape form a sort of border, while the mice sit on the patterned blanket on the grass at the bottom, waiting. On the right-hand page, we get a real close-up of the mice, with the road and tree as background. The hands-on-hips pose of the town mouse shows her impatience as much as her expression. The country mouse sits open-mouthed, listening.

✳ Stevens paints the masses of people and the looming buildings in a paler, more transparent pigment than the tiny mice in this change of scale. On the right-hand page, they are so small as to be almost invisible, and yet seem out of scale in another, still pale, change of view.

✳ The scale changes abruptly again across two pages; we come down to mouse level, menaced by the huge feet about to step on us. The mice's claws reach out of the picture, as the feet move on.

✳ The text is tucked in the lower left of the two-page spread here. On mouse level, two large shoes loom on the textured rug on the upper left. Attention is focused on a life-size mousetrap, which the country mouse leans toward, while his city cousin pulls him back by the tail and points away. The square tiles of the floor and the flower pot make the scene seem even more real.

✳ The delectable spread flows across both pages and over the text on the lower left. Above the text, a spoon points toward the country mouse, climbing up the sundae dish. Curved dishes fill the table, with the now coffee-filled cup and saucer we saw on the cover and title page sitting between the mice. Luscious-looking blueberry pie above the cup matches cherry pie below. On the right, the town mouse enjoys a chocolate, while another tips out of the frame behind her. Try not to read this book just before lunch, or the children may become too distracted.

✳ There is humor in the use of the cake wedge as a pillow for the overstuffed country mouse. He leans back, as his cousin bends over him to offer a chocolate. Tasty-looking chocolate chip cookies are in the foreground above some text. More text is on the right-hand page, under the same scene, but with quite different-appearing mice. They are suddenly up straight, alert, looking right.

✳ The repast looks quite different now. Text has moved to the top of the right-hand page, leaving the entire left-hand page for the terrifyingly fierce dogs to overshadow the table, upset the cup, splash out the coffee, and send the country mouse backward, straight into the blueberry pie. We don't see his cousin at all.

✳ The country mouse relaxes at home, bean in hand. Bacon and more beans are in an equally relaxed pile on the floor. Stevens has added no background, so the mouse and his lesson really stand out.

Stevens's mice can be compared with other mice done by Lionni and others. Mice appear in the many Aesop collections.

VERSIONS TO COMPARE

Cauley, Lorinda. *The Town Mouse and the Country Mouse*. New York: Putnam, 1984.

Galdone, Paul. *The Town Mouse and the Country Mouse*. New York: McGraw-Hill, 1971.

Lydecker, Laura. *The Country Mouse and the City Mouse*. New York: Knopf, 1987.

BOOKS ILLUSTRATED BY STEVENS

Andersen, Hans Christian. *It's Perfectly True*. New York: Holiday House, 1988.

Ashabranner, Brent K. *I'm in the Zoo, Too!* New York: Dutton, 1989.

Hazen, Barbara Shook. *Wally, the Worry-Warthog*. New York: Clarion, 1990.

Kimmel, Eric A. *Anansi and the Moss-Covered Rock*. New York: Holiday House, 1988.

———. *Nanny Goat and the Seven Little Kids* retold from the Brothers Grimm. San Diego: Harcourt Brace, 1990.

Kroll, Steven. *The Big Bunny and the Magic Show*. New York: Holiday House, 1986.

Robertus, Polly M. *The Dog Who Had Kittens*. New York: Holiday House, 1991.
Stevens, Janet. *Goldilocks and the Three Bears*. New York: Holiday House, 1986.
————. *How the Manx Cat Lost Its Tail*. San Diego: Harcourt Brace, 1990.
————. *The Three Billy Goats Gruff*. San Diego: Harcourt Brace, 1987.
————. *The Town Mouse and the Country Mouse*. New York: Holiday House, 1987.

Lon Po Po: A Red-Riding Hood Story from China

by Ed Young

The media Ed Young has used for his original art work over the years have ranged from cut paper and pencil drawings to water colors and pastels, as he constantly has tried new media, styles, and means of expression. He usually illustrates the stories of others or traditional tales, but he brings to all his work, whatever the culture represented, his own unique vision. He grew up in China but has lived in the United States for years, so he sees himself as a sort of bridge between the cultures. *Lon Po Po* won the Caldecott Award for 1989. In bringing us this story from China, he was able to draw upon his heritage.

———

∗ Against a textured, pastel chalk, brilliantly orange-red colored background, the archetypical wolf turns his startling white eyes on us as he comes across from the left of the jacket. His black, pastel chalk-drawn body is touched with other colors for modelling and emphasis. Below his head and body, the title has been painted with wide black brushstrokes, like Chinese calligraphy. The subtitle and author information, separated by thin black lines, is printed in letters that have also been done by a calligrapher, who gets credit on the back jacket flap. Opening the jacket out, we see that the wolf's body extends around the spine. There, atop the picture of the body, the necessary information is written in white calligraphic letters like the wolf's eyes. That body continues to the back of the jacket, making one large picture. The left side of the back of the jacket is simply textured background, while on the right, we have the rear of the wolf, with his tail hanging down but pointing toward his head. Young has filled the entire background with touches of other colors on that red, for texture and interest. The dark, black body and the white eyes on the red certainly make an arresting jacket. The cover under it is a bright blue, almost completely covered over by wide, vertical strokes of black pastel chalk similar to the strokes of a wide calligraphy brush.

✳ The same bright blue is used for the end papers.

✳ The title page uses the letters of title and author from the cover, along with the publisher, in black on white. A thin red line frames the page.

✳ As he has done throughout the book, Young divides the two-page spread into frames by using the thin red lines. Sometimes the picture extends across and is broken by these frames, in the manner of Chinese screen paintings. This technique avoids the problem of matching pictures across the gutter. The dedication is one worth discussing with children. They have seen the wolf used as a wicked character enough to understand. Against a portion of the spread colored with orange pastel chalk, a sort of shadow of the wolf on the jacket, made in the same blue pastel color as the end papers, comes across the two pages. Those two eery white circles of eyes are echoed under the ears. But there is an almost human profile on the right, making this more than just the wolf.

✳ A serene landscape spreads across the pages, with one frame on the left and two on the right. Under the gold-touched clouds of early morning, mother waves goodbye on the left, as the sun rises. All the figures are tiny in the expanse of the picture, as they are in Chinese landscape paintings. A hill slopes up to the house where the children wave also. The roof of the house has the curved eaves we see in those Chinese paintings. The tree by it will figure in the story. The third frame shows us the top of the hill. How would the composition change if the hill kept going up on the right, or if it didn't drop off on the left-hand page?

✳ Two frames are on each page here. The first on the left is for the text. The next contains the two smaller children, going up in size to the eldest in the third frame. She holds high a candle, whose light forms another, higher circle like the children's heads. All three frames have for background only purple shadows and that same rich red of the cover. The disguised wolf's head is the highest circular shape in the fourth panel. He is in black and gray, draped with the bright blue of the end papers. His white eye gleams in the candlelight.

✳ The three children's heads are in a vertical row in the first panel on the left, three individual, skeptical faces emerging from the black background. The wolf fills the second frame and the entire framed right-hand page. The frame on the right of the left-hand page shows a close-up of his eyes, nose, and teeth, while the rest of his head continues to the other side, along with the blue drape. He is almost breathing down our necks. The text is white against a black shadow on the upper right.

✳ The wolf's black shadow leaps across the two pages, and out of the top left frame. Next to their own small shadows, the children huddle in a small, triangular group on the right, under the huge shadow. Their clothes add only small touches of color. Again the text is white on the black shadow.

✳ Now Young has used two panels on the left-hand page, and one on the right. In the first, Paotze's head and eyes emerge looking over toward the wolf from under the patterned blue, green, and pale yellow blanket or coverlet. The white text is placed in this section on the blanket. The next frame includes a profile of the wolf looking at the two other children. Only his head to the nose is seen above the blanket, which spreads up and across the pages. The other two children look warily at the wolf from the right-hand page. Only parts of their heads and a braid show against the blanket and the dark of the night.

✳ We can't get much closer to the wolf, as his eyes, nose, and mouth appear on the left-hand page, and the rest goes on over the two frames on the right-hand page. The text is back in black on white in the bottom of the last frame. Notice the gleaming eye, and the multicolored pastel strokes Young has used for the hair on the wolf's face.

✳ To show the glimpse that Shang had of the wolf, Young places just a shadowy outline of his head, nose pointed out of the frame, on the right-hand page. The shape dissolves against a white-touched blue background, which goes across the two frames on the right-hand page, one of which contains the text.

✳ We seem to be on treetop level with the three children on the limb looking down at the wolf far below. The tree is textured bark-brown, set against a blue and green background that suggests the outdoors. The characters are on the left-hand page, while the tree trunk and one limb are on the right-hand page, where the right panel has the text.

✳ We move down to the base of the tree, shadowy in a mist. The left panel has the text here. The tree trunk extends from the right panel on the left-hand side over to the full-page frame on the right, where we can see the wolf emerging from behind the trunk. He looks up with his jaws open, perhaps talking to the children. He does not look happy.

✳ The two frames on the two pages here show different, balanced scenes, taking place at different times, but at the same tree that forms the center. On the left, the wolf swings right out of the frame in his basket as the children pull him up from the limb far above. On the right, we see the children from behind as the wolf hurtles down, head first, the text above him.

* Two more pictures show different events on either side of the tree. We are closer to the wolf in his basket here but do not see the children. The text has become white, to be read against the dark tree trunk. On the right-hand side, we are also closer to the angry, falling wolf, who breaks the frame with his paw. Notice the changing color of the background.

* The wolf's eye, larger than life, glares at us on the left-hand side against the brightening background, as he presumably is falling for the last time. On the upper right of the right-hand frame, small hands let go of the rope that snakes toward us and down through the frame.

* Two panels on the left-hand page contain the text, a textured pale yellow background, and dark shadows that may be the fallen wolf. The trailing gold line may be the rope, but it is hard to say. In the single panel on the right-hand side, three faces peer in a vertical row around the dark tree trunk, eyes wide. Shang's head leans right out of the frame. The red shading along the tree may be symbolic, or may just define the shape.

* The house and tree on the left-hand page are closer than they were in the first picture, here again under the bright morning sky in this final landscape. We can see the actual grasses near us. The text finds space in the sky of the last panel. But for whatever reason, Young has put in no people at all.

* The last red line framed white page has the publication information in simple black print.

Children should be able to find the characteristics that make this story like Red-Riding Hood and those that make it different.

Along with some other Chinese folktales, and China's importance in today's news, this could lead students to a study of China's history, art, and current situation. Chinese history and travel books can be found in the 915's and 950's in the library. There are many books on Chinese art, especially Chinese landscape painting, in public libraries, which can be borrowed to show children the sources from which Young and other picture book artists on Chinese subjects have taken their inspiration.

PICTURE BOOKS WITH CHINESE-INSPIRED ART

Demi. *Chen Ping and His Magic Axe*. New York: Dodd, Mead, 1987.
———. *Dragon Kites and Dragonflies: A Collection of Chinese Nursery Rhymes*. San Diego: Harcourt Brace, 1986.
———. *The Magic Boat*. New York: Holt, 1990.

Monkey and the White Bone Demon by various illustrators. New York: Viking, 1984.

Torre, Betty L. *The Luminous Pearl: A Chinese Folktale* illustrated by Carol Inouye. New York: Orchard, 1990.

BOOKS ILLUSTRATED BY YOUNG

Carlstrom, Nancy White. *Goodbye Geese!* New York: Philomel, 1991.
Hodges, Margaret. *The Voice of the Great Bell.* Boston: Little, Brown, 1989.
Howe, James. *I Wish I Were a Butterfly.* San Diego: Harcourt Brace, 1987.
Leaf, Margaret. *The Eyes of the Dragon.* New York: Lothrop, 1987.
Lewis, Richard. *All of You Was Singing.* New York: Atheneum, 1991.
Martin, Rafe. *Foolish Rabbit's Big Mistake.* New York: Putnam, 1985.
Osofsky, Audrey. *Dreamcatcher.* New York: Orchard, 1992.
Radin, Ruth. *High in the Mountains.* New York: Macmillan, 1989.
Root, Phyllis. *Moon Tiger.* New York: Holt, 1985.
Young, Ed. *Lon Po Po: A Red-Riding Hood Story from China.* New York: Putnam, 1989.
—. *Seven Blind Mice.* New York: Philomel, 1992.

Hansel and Gretel
retold by Rika Lesser,
illustrated by Paul Zelinsky

Although he was trained as a "serious artist," and continues to paint oils of the art gallery variety, Paul Zelinsky's early picture books were done in two different styles. One was serious and realistic, as in *How I Hunted the Little Fellows* by Boris Zhitkov (Putnam, 1979), while the other was humorous and exaggerated, as in *The Maid and the Mouse and the Odd-Shaped House.* But with *Hansel and Gretel* and the subsequent *Rumpelstiltskin* he began to use a style that seems to come from the museum walls, from the paintings of two hundred or more years ago. The people are realistically painted, with nothing left out. Trees have bark, plants have leaves, the sun casts shadows, and the colors are natural. He gives us a romantic land of "once upon a time" that seems to involve children deeply. There are many sighs of appreciation when his books are shown, especially from children who have seen similar paintings in museums. Zelinsky's talent and versatility is apparent in the range of his illustrations.

∗ *Hansel and Gretel* was published with a clear plastic jacket to protect the cover illustration. The spine is cloth covered in a blue that matches the unnatural blue of the sky on the cover. The title characters appear on the left of the illustration, dressed in the Middle European peasant garb of years ago. Gretel is starting up the path that leads to the vital cottage, her walking stick pointing the way. Hansel, however, turns away, looking down. His eyes are cast down; his pose is almost like a statue's. But his staff points up and over as well. They stand on barren rocks. The twisted trees that frame the blue area where the title and author information appear seem barren as well. But there is a contrasting lushness to the vegetation elsewhere in the picture. The candy cottage glows, as if touched by the rays of the sun, despite two more dark and barren trees in front of it. Zelinsky plays dark against light here, symbolizing the elements of the story. He has also balanced areas, rocks against the stump in the foreground, bushes against trees. The stems of the greenery to the right of Gretel's head also point us up toward the cottage. In the framed space, the upper-case letters stand out. The title is bright red, edged in white, perhaps an echo of the peppermint doorway of the cottage and certainly a cheery note under the dead-looking trees. Gretel's socks add another touch of red. The picture on the back cover of the same intense blue uses a lighter blue for an elaborate, old-fashioned frame, within which Hansel and Gretel, in silhouette, hold hands and look toward each other under branches that remind us of those on the cover. This time, Hansel has his foot forward, ready to go.

∗ The end papers, mirror images front and back, portray a peaceful, bucolic landscape under a wide expanse of more naturalistic blue skies. But there is a large cloud in the center that casts a shadow, which may be symbolic, over the area in the center foreground. Where the flaps would be if there were a paper jacket, Zelinsky has drawn us a fancy gold museum-type frame to enclose the front and back information.

∗ The half-title is simple black on white, slightly decorative lettering, like a clearing of the palate and palette of all the color before the story begins.

∗ The title page uses the same lettering as the half-title page for the title, but prints it larger in that same blue as the sky on the cover. Tiny red stars brighten this page.

∗ We are back to simple black on white, ready for the meat of the story.

✳ We meet the major characters in a rectangle above the text, placed on the white page for a border; a format Zelinsky uses frequently. The blue sky and greenery outside the door come from the end papers, but the interior is sparsely furnished. The stance of the father as he empties the few coins into his palm shows his dejection. His wife's impatient posture and annoyed expression contrast with the simple spectator position of the children, holding hands and looking on. The cat also watches. The scene is lit from the doorway, like a Dutch interior by Vermeer.

✳ The text on the left allows a full-page illustration on the right-hand page. The parents' bed in the foreground parallels the children's at the back right. The strong horizontals of beds and the vertical divider between the beds contrast with the angles of worried father, head in hand, and nagging wife, along with the circles of hat, nightcap, and chamber pot. The tones are mainly brown, with the yellow-green blanket around the children perhaps a hopeful note.

✳ Zelinsky chooses here to put the text beneath a double-page spread, so that he can show us Gretel anxiously watching inside the cottage while Hansel gathers the pebbles outside. The muted colors of the scene are lit by the full moon. The circle of the moon is echoed in the wheels of the cart, a tree stump, and another round jug on the right. The angle of Gretel's arm is repeated by the roof and by Hansel's arms and legs. The handles of the cart almost form a triangle with a treetop and Hansel; there is tension in this picture.

✳ A full page is needed here for a dramatic scene. The road rises rather than going horizontally, so father must lean to pull the cart, but he also seems weighted down with worry. Gretel goes along but looks back for her brother. Her red socks and a few leaves are the only notes of cheer here. The wife leans away from her husband, suspiciously looking back at Hansel. Hansel stands straight up and serious, facing away as he reaches out to drop the pebble. The wheel of the cart seems to fill the gap between brother and sister.

✳ Again Zelinsky chooses the two-page spread, perhaps to show us more dramatically how tiny and lost the children seem amid the dark trees and rocks. The vivid orange of the setting sun on the upper left is picked up by the fire Hansel is tending on the lower part of the right-hand page. Gretel's hands show her despair. Note how Zelinsky has placed the mainly vertical tree trunks, and where he puts the rocks, so that the children appear imprisoned and threatened.

✳ A vertical picture on one page shows the children running and reaching up toward the cottage. Even the rock and the bush in front lean that way. The sun seems to brighten the whole top part of the picture. Father leans out of the house to see them, but his wife tells us nothing from her expression or position.

✳ Zelinsky again chooses a single picture on the right-hand page, this time for an unhappy scene. The dark brown, locked door looms over the concerned Hansel and the despairing Gretel. Only the cover or blanket still has a touch of warmth.

✳ In contrast to the first time the children were taken into the woods, this time they come down the path toward us. Gretel and her father both look back toward Hansel, a small figure in the distance here, looking toward the house and even tinier chimney on the upper left. The tree trunks stand tall on either side of Hansel, while the cart angles down toward the figures in the foreground. The wife's actions are vividly clear, as she raises her skirts with one hand to move faster and drags the reluctant Gretel along with the other. The path makes an arc from Hansel to the others.

✳ Zelinsky uses the double-page spread again to dwarf the children amid the trees. The darkness is deeper and almost unrelieved, with just tiny touches of red on birds. The moon seems to light only the rocks and the children on them.

✳ This two-page spread has room to show the children on the left emerging from the dark forest, running in their eager excitement toward the cottage. And what a luscious-looking place it is! We see much more detail on it than we could on the cover. But the hollow tree stump on the lower right may be a hint that all is not flourishing here. Still, there is brightness and blue sky.

✳ We are almost close enough to eat the pancakes off the roof here, as Hansel and Gretel encounter the woman who turns out to be the witch. Their hand positions and Hansel's body show some alarm, but only her long, bony fingers suggest evil as she reaches toward them. The light colors here do not hint at trouble, except for the shadow and dark blue on the right.

✳ The bowl of fruit in the foreground and the red bed curtains on the pineapple poster bed suggest hospitality. But the woman's gesture and Gretel's frightened face, as well as the snake peering over the top of the bed, tell us all is far from well. We can just make out Hansel, caged in the yard.

✳ There are no goodies visible on the house here, only those in the bowl Gretel is bringing, and perhaps in the bowl on the lower right. Gretel stands straight and still. The tree behind her is also still, but its leaves reach toward the thatched roof. The slant of the stone wall and the roof counter that of the roof of the cage and of the witch's arm as she feels the bone Hansel offers. Both he and the witch are hunched, but for different reasons. There are only touches of red in this somber picture.

✳ A fire glowing golden yellow and the red-hot bricks change the mood here. But the angry witch and Gretel's horrified look do not make it seem happy. Zelinsky angles the long board right into the oven. The bowl in the lower right here is echoed in the circle of Gretel's face and the arch of the oven.

✳ A two-page spread allows us to see the drama taking place on the left-hand page, as Gretel almost hurls herself on the oven door to close it on the witch. A tree trunk is at the center along the gutter, with part of the house on either side. A frog sits significantly in the bowl there. Far to the right, Hansel is still locked in his cage. Cookies on the roof add color on the right-hand page to match the color on the left. The circular grindstone on the lower right adds to the design. The green plant growing at the stone may be symbolic.

✳ Zelinsky uses the light from the open door to make a light and dark picture that reminds us of the museum paintings using chiaroscuro, where light and dark contrasts are very pronounced. The bed and bedclothes on the left make a sort of frame, with the sheet leading to Gretel, who is enjoying gathering the treasure. There are colors everywhere in this scene that we did not see here before. On the wall above Gretel hangs a picture of a cake and candy house. It may resemble the one Zelinsky's great-grand-mother painted, which he described for us on the end papers. The side of the tapestry picture is draped parallel to the slant above the doorway through which Hansel walks, looking affectionately back at his sister.

✳ Father's joy as he reaches out to his children is evident. Their happiness is clear on Gretel's face. Even the rock leans toward the children. The sky is blue again.

VERSIONS TO COMPARE

In comparing versions of this story, check particularly how the artists portray the children lost in the forest, what kind of candy cottage they design, and above all, what kind of witch they imagine. Note in particular the strange setting of the version by Anthony Browne. The following are some versions of this story to compare.

Adams, Adrienne. *Hansel and Gretel.* New York: Scribner's, 1975.
Browne, Anthony. *Hansel and Gretel.* New York: Franklin Watts, 1981.
Jeffers, Susan. *Hansel and Gretel.* New York: Dial, 1980.
Lobel, Arnold. *Hansel and Gretel.* New York: Delacorte, 1971.
Marshall, James. *Hansel and Gretel.* New York: Dial, 1990.
Ross, Tony. *Hansel and Gretel.* London: Anderson, 1989.
Zwerger, Lisbeth. *Hansel and Gretel.* New York: Morrow, 1979.

PICTURE BOOKS ILLUSTRATED BY ZELINSKY

Hansel and Gretel retold by Rika Lesser. New York: Dodd, Mead, 1984, Putnam Sandcastle paper, 1989.

The Lion and the Stoat. New York: Greenwillow, 1984.

The Maid and the Mouse and the Odd-Shaped House. New York: Dodd, Mead, 1981.

Rumpelstiltskin. New York: Dutton, 1986.

Segal, Lore. *The Story of Mrs. Lovewright and Purrless Her Cat.* New York: Knopf, 1985.

The Wheels on the Bus. New York: Dutton, 1990.

The Three Little Pigs: An Old Story
by Margot Zemach

Until her recent death, Margot Zemach had, for many years, drawn deftly, then applied her water color paint to depict both animal and human characters in many traditional tales, in her own stories, and in those of others. Her lines are active, not static; her creations are seldom at rest. Her books are filled with joy and good feeling. They have received many honors, including one Caldecott medal.

✳ *The Three Little Pigs* is a recent example of her work. We can tell at once from the appearance of the central characters on the dust jacket that, although dressed, they are truly piggy. Within a black line frame placed on the orange-tan background of the jacket, a brown plank has been placed across the picture. One pig leans over on the left, standing on the board, smiling and smelling some flowers. A second sits on the left side of the plank, one knee up, chewing a purplish turnip from a basket beside him, eyes closed with pleasure. The third pig sits smiling on the banks of the stream, under the plank, feet in the water and mud all over him. Zemach washes in transparent blue behind them for sky, paints in the blue water and most of the brown banks, but leaves a lot of the picture white, including the top where the author and title information appear. Her name is in black, italic-like upper- and lower-case letters, separated from the title by a green line the same color as the pants of one pig and the jacket of another. The title above the line is colored like the turnip within a heavy black outline. The back of the jacket is simply unrelieved orange-tan. If there is a dust jacket, the cover underneath is plain darker green.

✳ The end papers are a darker pinkish purple, almost eggplant color.

✳ The half-title is simply the black-outlined letters of the title from the jacket with no other color.

✳ The title is repeated with the color from the jacket. The author's name is above it here, with a black line for separation. Zemach uses all the rest of the two-page spread to introduce us to the pigs and their mother. There is just enough landscape and background to give us a sense of place. This mother hangs her clothes out to dry with clothespins from a bag hung on the tree. One of her little pigs helps her fold what's dry. This helpful fellow is, incidentally, the smart one of the story. One brother leans back in a chair, feet up, munching an apple, while the other plays in the mud, repeating their roles on the cover and boding ill for their ability to live on their own later. Zemach uses the tree to separate the two lazy pigs from the third pig and their mother. Mother anchors the page by standing straight, clothes pole behind her. She is tied into the picture by the clothesline and the item she is folding with the third pig. Zemach has placed everyone and everything precisely on these pages. She even has three symbolic little birds in the nest atop the tree; their mother is watching in a position similar to that of the mother pig.

✳ Simple black on white copyright information on the left is balanced with the dedication on the right. Zemach adds a basket of apples, perhaps to refer to those that will be part of the story, or perhaps, with the leftover core, to relate to the apple the pig was eating on the previous page. Or perhaps they are part of the dedication. The core adds a humorous touch to this simple basket of apples.

✳ The pigs take their leave on this two-page spread. Zemach gives us just a touch of flowers, grass, and rocks on the left. The focus is on the tearful mother, waving goodbye. The helpful pig is still close to her, gazing affectionately at her as his brothers start across the plank bridge. They wave fondly back, making this a touching scene. The colors used are pale, but still cheerful. The pigs smile, even as their mother cries. There are no borders or lines around the picture; it goes as far as Zemach feels she wants it to. Here and throughout the book, she plans the space for her text in the unpainted parts of her pages.

✳ Although the picture extends across the two pages, we really have two different scenes. On the left under the text, the first pig talks to the man with the straw. The man's back is curved like his haystack and pitchfork, while the ladders and handle form angles against the curves. On the right-hand side, the first pig has put together a sort of house, of many angles, including the leaning door. The flowers all around and the touches of pink make this a lighthearted fairy tale. The tub of mud and other items scattered about in front remind us that this is the sloppy little pig.

✳The two scenes are separated here to fit into the spaces provided. On the left-hand side, the dapper, shrewd-looking wolf leans toward the pig, who doesn't even need to open the door. The pan of mud is still there, but so are the flowers. On the right-hand page, we see the wolf in action. Leaning on his cane, he blows the house right off the page. We are spared the cruel end.

✳ Another two-page spread is really two scenes again. The second pig deals with the stick-seller on the left-hand side. Zemach brushes in more flowers and a tree for landscape. The sticks angle down toward the path that takes us to the stick house under construction. Although the whole house leans, it seems to have been made with a bit more care than the straw house.

✳ The house is actually fairly snug by the time the wolf comes by. Although there are two scenes here, Zemach brings the wolf's tail across the gutter to tie them together. The wolf blows his hat off this time, but away goes the house, and the pig.

✳ Yet another two-page spread with two scenes shows us the negotiations on the left-hand page, with a plank bridge across with a leaning tree; the hard-working brick-laying pig is building his solid house on the right-hand page. Notice he still has taken time to wash his clothes and to put a flower pot in the window. This scene is full of solid horizontals.

✳ By the time the wolf arrives, the pig is securely inside. Again the tail ties the scenes together. The wolf is blowing hard on the right, but only the flowers are moving.

✳ Zemach gives us a sequence of stop-action pictures of the huffing and puffing. Again the plank and tree connect across the gutter. The blowing has dislodged the laundry, but the house stands solidly.

✳ A vignette on the left shows the wolf leaning conspiratorially toward the smiling pig, secure behind his solid window and wall. On the right-hand page, the pig is leaning over to gather the round turnips for the round basket. Notice how Zemach has just dabbed in enough color to make the background trees and landscape believable.

✳ Compare this wolf-pig vignette on the left with the previous one. The wolf has already changed. On the right-hand page, his arms raised like branches, the pig dominates the scene from the top of the tree. Zemach has drawn only part of the limbs, branches, and leaves, and suggested the rest with her paint. There is a clear fence and a hill down which the wolf runs, reaching toward the elusive apple.

✳ In the third wolf-pig vignette, the wolf looks really concerned. And so he should be, for the pig in the rolling barrel on the right has knocked him up into the air. He doesn't look so dapper now. Note how few details Zemach has put in this scene to give us the atmosphere and action.

✳ The wolf has stripped to essentials here; no more Mr. Nice Guy. The two-page spread is a single scene of emotional wolf on one side, wide-eyed pig inside solid house on the other, and tree reaching across to wolf's outstretched paw. The moon and stars make this evening, soup-cooking time.

✳ Four stop-action frames have the wolf hurl himself across the gutter, knocking down the tree, bucket, and some bricks on the way, then hurtle down the chimney, head first.

✳ Sitting at his table, napkin under chin, the happy pig is enjoying his soup. The bowl of apples and the basket of turnips remind us of the previous adventures. Only the tail hanging out of the soup pot and perhaps the bones on the floor recall the wolf.

VERSIONS TO COMPARE

When comparing versions of this story, there will be some where the first two pigs do not get eaten. Differences to look for in the art include exactly how much like pigs and how much like people the pigs are. The differences in how frightening the wolf looks are also interesting, as are the types of houses the artists design for the different pigs. Of the modern and parody versions available, one of the most popular has proved to be *The True Story of the 3 Little Pigs,* told from the wolf's point of view. The following books are interesting to compare:

Bishop, Gavin. *The Three Little Pigs.* New York: Scholastic, 1989.
Hooks, William H. *The Three Little Pigs and the Fox* illustrated by S. D. Schindler. New York: Macmillan, 1989.
Marshall, James. *The Three Little Pigs.* New York: Dial, 1989.
Ross, Tony. *The Three Pigs.* New York: Pantheon, 1983.
Scieszka, Jon. *The True Story of the 3 Pigs by A. Wolf* illustrated by Lane Smith. New York: Viking, 1989.

BOOKS ILLUSTRATED BY ZEMACH

Ginsburg, Mirra. *The Chinese Mirror*. San Diego: Harcourt Brace, 1988.
Meyers, Odette. *The Enchanted Umbrella*. San Diego: Harcourt Brace, 1988.
Phillips, Mildred. *The Sign in Mendel's Window*. New York: Macmillan, 1985.
Staines, Bill. *All God's Critters Go to a Place in the Choir*. New York: Dutton, 1989.
Uchida, Yoshiko. *The Two Foolish Cats*. New York: McElderry, 1987.
Zemach, Margot. *The Three Little Pigs: An Old Story*. New York: Farrar, Straus, 1988.
————. *The Three Wishes: An Old Story*. New York: Farrar, Straus, 1986.

Little Red Cap
by the Brothers Grimm,
illustrated by Lisbeth Zwerger

Austrian illustrator Lisbeth Zwerger has won many awards for her illustration, including the IBBY Lifetime Achievement Award. Her versions of the classic fairy tales, done in ink and color washes using mainly transparent water colors, have large expanses of toned color with few details. She creates an atmosphere that is uniquely hers; her figures are realistic and believable, with costume, anatomy, and gesture all carefully drawn, but with no unnecessary detail. Her compositions are balanced, with main characters frequently in the foreground. Amid the pale tints, she uses touches of intense color for highlights or emphasis.

———————————

✳ On the dust jacket of *Little Red Cap,* we meet the two major characters in a scene repeated inside the book. Amid the usual Zwerger pale, tinted impression of a landscape, Little Red Cap, her cap a bright note of color, walks toward us, looking to the right, away from the wolf, where the wine bottle in her basket is pointing. Her right hand, fingers outstretched, reaches toward the wolf, as her dress and apron swirl that way. And what a different-looking wolf this is! He is quite realistically a wolf, not even wearing any clothes, yet he stands upright, front paws humanly together, with a coy expression that seems far from wolfish. The sketched-in trees in back balance this composition. The picture is within a black line enclosed white frame, on a pinkish beige background. The printed information is in italic upper- and lower-case letters, with the title in purple and the rest in black. The purple matches the girl's bodice. On the back of the jacket in a black outlined oval, we see a portion of the picture inside the book in which Little Red Cap is picking flowers. Note the positioning of the head, balancing the bunch of flowers. These flowers are about as non-detailed as they can be, while still being flowers. The cover inside the jacket repeats the purple of the title letters in the cloth over the spine, with the rest pinkish beige.

✳ The end papers are blush pink.

✳ The title page repeats the lettering from the jacket, and the flower scene from the back of the jacket. The variation in color may be because of the difference in paper.

✳ A large amount of text on the left is opposed to the full-page illustration on the right. This is the general format of the book. The resolute girl stands still while her caring mother ties her apron sash. The room's wall and floor are barely indicated. But the cat leads us into the basket on the table with the cake and wine. The basket is at the front corner, while one back corner points to Red Cap. Note the comforting roundness of the mother and the circles of head and cake. The bright colors are in the girl's dress and cap.

✳ Red Cap advances toward center stage, bright cap and dress clearly visible. Zwerger sketches in tree trunks leaning on the upper right and a hill coming in at an angle from the right. In the right foreground in front of the hill crouches the wolf, paw on hip, waiting.

✳ Here we have the jacket scene repeated. Does it seem more complete when we see the rest of the trees?

✳ This scene includes the one on the back of the jacket. Now the abandoned basket is in the center, with Red Cap's color drawing the eye to her; the wolf slinks off, looking very much like the animal here amid the sketchy tree trunks.

✳ On only a wash background, Zwerger sets a wonderful series of four action frames, like a film, of the wolf dressing up as grandmother. We can almost see him moving here, although there is only a minimum of detail, line, and color.

✳ Zwerger chooses an empty foreground, perhaps for mood, with Red Cap opening the door at the upper right. The fenced-in area and the house offer verticals and angles, but the picture has an empty feeling.

✳ The confrontation takes place amid shades of white and pale gray. The stance of the wolf seems threatening, as poor Red Cap stands there in the doorway. Zwerger puts the gray stripes of the mattress in the lower right and touches of pink in the pillow, but most of the picture aside from the two characters is white.

✳ A rescuer in the shape of a very realistic hunter with dog comes down the hill toward us, ear cocked toward the cottage just visible on the lower right. Zwerger could have had him on level ground but chose this much more difficult pose.

✳ The hunter has taken off his jacket to get down to business. A reddish sewing basket has provided the scissors he has opened and is pointing at the sleeping wolf in the rectangular, reddish-framed bed on the right. Zwerger has the corner of the dresser and the open drawer pointing at the wolf as well. The dog smells one of the flowers left on the floor.

✳ Red Cap is already rescued and is looking anxiously at the wolf as the hunter hauls grandmother out. Zwerger has almost formed an oval or rectangle of the interacting figures.

✳ The hunter opens the wine, and grandmother holds the plates, while Red Cap brings them the cake. Zwerger gives us one wall and a real window with curtain here behind the bench on which the hunter and grandmother sit. But Red Cap comes from a vague area, which Zwerger has simply washed in. Does it matter? This simple, homey scene is Zwerger's "happy ever after."

VERSIONS TO COMPARE

This version is particularly interesting to compare with the Trina Schart Hyman version listed below, which came out about the same time. They contrast in so many ways: characters, scenery, props, costumes, borders, even cats. The age of the main character and the lesson she supposedly learns are other differences to study.

Emberly, Michael. *Ruby*. Boston: Little, Brown, 1990.

Goodall, John. *Little Red Riding Hood*. New York: McElderry, 1988.

Hyman, Trina Schart. *Little Red Riding Hood* from the Grimm Brothers. New York: Holiday House, 1983.

Marshall, James. *Red Riding Hood*. New York: Dial, 1987.

Ross, Tony. *Little Red: A Classic Story Bent Out of Shape*. New York: Doubleday, 1979.

Young, Ed. *Lon Po Po: A Red-Riding Hood Story from China*. New York: Philomel, 1989.

PICTURE BOOKS ILLUSTRATED BY ZWERGER

Andersen, Hans Christian. *The Nightingale*. Natick, MA: Picture Book Studio, 1984.

———. *The Swineherd*. New York: Morrow, 1982.

Brentano, Clemens. *The Legend of Rosepetal*. Natick, MA: Picture Book Studio, 1985.

Grimm Brothers. *Hansel and Gretel*. New York: Morrow, 1979.

———. *Little Red Cap*. New York: Morrow, 1983.

———. *The Seven Ravens*. New York: Morrow, 1981.

Hoffmann, E. T. A. *The Nutcracker*. Natick, MA: Picture Book Studio, 1987.

Janisch, Heinz. *The Merry Pranks of Till Eulenspiegel*. Saxonville, MA: Picture Book Studio, 1990.

Appendix A: Other Cultures in Recent Picture Books

There are so many picture books based on other lands and cultures that we could fill another book analyzing them. The quality of both text and illustration varies enormously. In addition to the questions of authenticity and literary quality of story, one must question the general quality of art and its relationship to the actual art of the culture or people. Even if the illustrations are done by a native, they may be crudely or ineptly fashioned. This could still give a feeling of authenticity to the book, however. The evaluation is never easy.

What we will list here are just some additional recent picture books that are considered fair tastes of other countries or cultures, whether the illustrations are done by genuine natives or by other capable artists who have successfully reflected the art of that culture. All can serve as introductions to the study of these lands and peoples and their art.

Note should be made of the books from Children's Book Press, which specializes in multicultural books with compatible illustrations, although only one of their books is listed here.

BOOKS TO STUDY FOR MULTICULTURAL AWARENESS

Climo, Shirley. *The Egyptian Cinderella* illustrated by Ruth Heller. New York: Crowell, 1989.

Dancing Teepees: Poems of American Indian Youth selected by Virginia Driving Hawk Sneve, with art by Stephen Gammell. New York: Holiday House, 1989.

DeArmond, Dale. *The Seal Oil Lamp: An Adaptation of an Eskimo Folktale* illustrated with wood engravings by the author. Boston: Little, Brown/Sierra Club, 1988.

Ekoomiak, Normee. *Arctic Memories* in English and Inuit. New York: Holt, 1988.

Goble, Paul. *Iktomi and the Berries: A Plains Indian Story*. New York: Orchard, 1989.

Heide, Florence Parry and Judithe Heide Gilliland. *The Day of Ahmed's Secret* illustrated by Ted Lewin. New York: Lothrop, 1990.

Lattimore, Deborah Nourse. *Why There Is No Arguing in Heaven: A Mayan Myth*. New York: Harper, 1989.

Rodanas, Kristina. *The Story of Wali Dad*. New York: Lothrop, 1988.

Rohmer, Harriet et al. *The Invisible Hunters: Los Cazadores Invisibles: A Legend from the Miskito Indians of Nicaragua* illustrated by Joe Sam. San Francisco: Children's Book Press, 1987.

Stanley, Diane. *Fortune*. New York: Morrow, 1990.

Tadjo, Veronique. *Lord of the Dance: An African Retelling*. New York: Lippincott, 1988.

Volkmer, Jane Anne. *Song of the Chirimia: A Guatemalan Folktale*. Minneapolis: Carolrhoda, 1990.

Appendix B: Picture Books for Experienced Evaluators

After a few years of critical examination of the art of picture books, children are ready to handle more complex, less accessible illustrations. They also have developed the maturity necessary to deal with the sophisticated or controversial themes covered in some deceptively easy-looking books that may have a picture book format but are far from the usual "Easy Book." I have found that students from fourth grade up relish the challenge of such books. As a group, they can take a book and tell the librarian or teacher what they see, rather than waiting to be asked questions. They also recall related books and make comparisons and connections with those and with other books by the illustrator they are examining.

By sixth grade, a unit on picture books can have each child choosing an illustrator to investigate and analyze. When these children read to younger buddies, they frequently pick books that they enjoyed when they were younger. Sometimes they seem to appreciate that book more now, while other times they now find it unsatisfying, and they will tell you why.

I will list here just a few books that have evoked serious analysis and deep appreciation in older students.

Briggs, Raymond. *When the Wind Blows: The Story of the Bloggs and the Bomb.* New York: Penguin paper, 1988.

This study of what happens to an elderly British couple when the next war breaks out looks like a comic book. The art is similar to Briggs's *The Snowman,* but the subject matter couldn't be more different. How Briggs uses the comic style to tell his story is one topic of discussion. But the whole topic of nuclear war is another.

Browne, Anthony. *Changes*. New York: Knopf, 1991.

Most students already know and love *Willy the Wimp* (Knopf, 1984) and have been intrigued by *Gorilla* (Knopf, 1985). They know that there is more to Anthony Browne than first meets the eye. So they are willing to take a close look at this very simple book. They discover all sorts of Browne motifs, along with another round of surrealism.

Eco, Umberto. *The Bomb and the General* illustrated by Eugenio Carmi. San Diego: Harcourt Brace, 1989.

The well-known author for adults has written a story about a belligerent general and some atoms who don't want to explode. It is not as simple as it looks. The illustrations are wonderfully inventive collages that should inspire a look through the family sewing box and a classroom full of original art made from bits and pieces. Perhaps a trip to the library for a book on contemporary artists' use of collage would also be useful.

Hastings, Selina. *Sir Gawain and the Loathly Lady* illustrated by Juan Wijngaard. New York: Lothrop, 1985.

Stories from the time of King Arthur seem to have continuing appeal. This is a lesser-known one, so it keeps the suspense. The amount and level of the text limit it to this older group. They certainly can and do appreciate the art. If other picture books we looked at seem to take elements and inspiration from the illuminated manuscripts and Books of Hours of the Middle Ages, Wijngaard seems to have immersed himself in them until he could give us a modern facsimile. The end papers, the borders, the costumes, the settings—all can be examined and admired endlessly. As for the characters, there are great faces, but, of course, the loathly lady is the greatest creation of all. How far the group wants to go into King Arthur, or the later Middle Ages of the pictures, is up to you. If your area has a Medieval Festival-type celebration, plan a visit as a climax. If you can find someone at a craft booth who does calligraphy and illumination, especially with gold leaf, it will really bring that art to life. Gratifyingly, most students of this age approve of Gawain's moral decision to marry the lady.

Innocenti, Roberto. *Rose Blanche*. Mankato, MN: Creative Education, 1985.

Photographic realism is used to set the mood and tell the story of the experiences of a child living near a concentration camp during World War II. Be prepared for heated discussions on what this book is trying to tell us and on whether the illustrations are "too pretty" for this story, or too realistically horrible. See Joseph H. and Chava Schwarcz's book *The Picture Book Comes of Age* (Chicago: ALA, 1991) for a fascinating view of this book.

Macaulay, David. *Black and White*. Boston: Houghton Mifflin, 1990.

This recent Caldecott winner will keep a class arguing for days. Whether the four stories really interrelate, and if so, how, is the big question. But each story, including its art, can also be analyzed to death, and related to other Macaulay books, or not. Nobody could be more delighted with the discussion than David Macaulay himself.

Maruki, Toshi. *Hiroshima No Pika*. New York: Lothrop, 1980.

This personalized account of the bombing of Hiroshima really knocks kids over. The language is simple and unemotional; all the feeling comes through the abstracted, expressionistic paintings, with the colors of an inferno. The subject matter can lead to an examination of the ethics of the decision to drop the bomb, or even of war itself. Study of the art can move to Modigliani-like necks, and German Expressionistic color.

Perrault, Charles. *Puss in Boots* translated by Malcolm Arthur, illustrated by Fred Marcellino. New York: Farrar, Straus, 1990.

This Caldecott Honor Book catches the eye immediately with its cover. Not only is it a more than life-size cat, every whisker delineated, dressed in a ruff and staring straight at you from under a rakishly tilted plumed hat; but also, there is not a word on the cover—no title, nothing—a first in picture book, or perhaps book, history. Inside, the illustrations fascinate children with their realism and truth to period costume and scenery. The design and typography of the book are worthy of close examination and may spark arguments about the choice of picture and text placement. Marcellino's depiction of points of view also raises questions. And, of course, there are all those other cats and pusses to compare, in particular *Puss in Boots* retold by Lincoln Kirstein and illustrated in his own elegant way by Alain Vaës. (Boston: Little, Brown, 1992). Whether you want to discuss the morality of the tale as well is up to you.

Robbins, Ken. *A Flower Grows*. New York: Dial, 1990.

This simple picture story of the growth, blooming, and death of an amaryllis is more than a nature lesson. First of all, the differences between color photographs and Robbins's technique of hand-tinting is not easy to see at first. Students need then to decide why they think Robbins chooses to do this kind of illustration; what kind of effect is he after? Do they think he achieves it? Then it should be off to the library to look at other photographers and their work, black and white or color. Some may want to try their hand at either or both kinds; they had better have a lot of experience before they try to emulate Robbins. And, of course, they need to confront the question of how any photographs are better or worse than other kinds of illustrations, for flowers, for instance.

Sara. *Across Town*. New York: Orchard, 1990.

This book, with a plot and illustrations that could hardly be any simpler, caused one of the longest and most divided discussions of the year. If the students are forced to analyze exactly what Sara is using and exactly what she shows the reader, they realize they are dealing with minimal art. It is the readers who must do the most to create the story, and it is Sara's talent to offer the material from which they can do it so well. Some really don't like it and dismiss it as trivial and silly. Others admire, analyze, and start tearing paper.

Van Allsburg, Chris. *The Mysteries of Harris Burdick*. Boston: Houghton Mifflin, 1984.

Since its publication, this book may have been overused, especially below fourth grade. Make sure your students have not "done" it recently, or it will not hold the necessary excitement. It is probably one of the best spurs to creative writing ever invented. A discussion on the introduction alone can lead to endless speculations on the possibilities of the truth or falsehood of what Van Allsburg wrote there and what he had in mind. Then each picture can be analyzed to see how it relates to its caption and book title. Older students may even want to try Van Allsburg's art style with Conté pencil dust. The most inventive story I saw to come from all this was one that made one complete book, with each picture from a chapter, and it made sense.

Appendix C: Additional Resources for Looking and Learning

Aliki. *How a Book Is Made.* New York: Crowell, 1986.

Bang, Molly. *Picture This: Perception and Composition.* Boston: Little, Brown, 1991.

Evolution of a Graphic Concept: The Stonecutter. Sound Filmstrip. Weston, CT: Weston Woods, 1977.

Gates, Frieda. *How to Write, Illustrate and Design Children's Books.* Monsey, NY: Lloyd-Simone, 1986.

How a Picture Book Is Made: The Making of The Island of the Skog *from Conception to Finished Book.* Sound Filmstrip. Weston, CT: Weston Woods, 1976.

Lewis, Brian. *An Introduction to Illustration.* Secaucus, NJ: Chartwell Books, 1987.

Marantz, Sylvia S. and Kenneth Marantz. *The Art of Children's Picture Books: A Selective Reference Guide.* New York: Garland, 1988.

———. *Artists of the Page: Interviews with Children's Book Illustrators.* Jefferson, NC: McFarland, 1992.

Shulevitz, Uri. *Writing with Pictures: How to Write and Illustrate Children's Books.* New York: Watson-Guptill, 1985.

Swann, Alan. *How to Understand and Use Design and Layout.* Cincinnati, OH: North Light Books, 1987.

Talking with Artists: Conversations with Victoria Chess, Pat Cummings, Leo and Diane Dillon et al. compiled and edited by Pat Cummings. New York: Bradbury, 1992.

Index

by Linda Webster